MANAGING
for the
SHORT TERM

MANAGING
for the
SHORT TERM

The New Rules for
Running a Business
in a Day-to-Day World

CHUCK MARTIN

CURRENCY

DOUBLEDAY

New York   London   Toronto   Sydney   Auckland

A CURRENCY BOOK
Published by Doubleday
a Division of Random House, Inc.
1540 Broadway, New York, New York 10036

Currency and Doubleday are trademarks
of Doubleday, a division of Random House, Inc.

Cataloging-in-Publication Data is on file with the
Library of Congress.

PRINTED IN THE UNITED STATES OF AMERICA

ISBN: 0-385-50435-7

First Edition: June 2002

Book Design by Tina Thompson

Currency Books are available at special discounts for
bulk purchases for sales promotions or premiums.
Special editions, including personalized covers,
excerpts of existing books, and corporate imprints,
can be created in large quantities for special needs. For
more information, write to Special Markets, Currency
Books, 290 Park Avenue, 11th Floor, New York, NY
10017, or email specialmarkets@randomhouse.com.

To Teri

Contents

Chapter 9: Leading for the Short Term   158

Chapter 10: Managing People for the Short Term   184

Chapter 11: Using Information to Navigate Through Decisions   200

Acknowledgments

This book could not have been done without the total cooperation of so many of the 3,000 members of the Net Future Institute, who took time every two weeks for more than a year to participate in real-time surveys. Many of those members also agreed to spend time with us to share their insights and their work habits to make this book as practical and as useful as possible. They are the voices from the front lines of business today, and to them we are most thankful.

We also want to thank all those CEOs, senior executives, and managers who took the precious time from their hectic schedules to candidly discuss their thoughts with us. We are most grateful that almost every person we contacted at every level took so much time not only to express his or her own ideas, but also to help validate the concepts in this book and their translation from theory to practice.

A very special thank you goes to Mary Frakes, an all-star journalist, writer, and editor, whom I have had the great pleasure to work with over the years on numerous projects. Mary was always there on this book, with her great ability to anticipate and always think a step or two ahead, in idea formulation, interviews, writing, editing, research ideas, and even reminding us of those pressing deadlines. I want to thank Mary, my friend, for watching out for our best interest throughout this process.

At the Net Future Institute, a major thank you to Sarah Coito, my trusted assistant, for keeping me on schedule and on track, no matter what city, state, or country I might have been in, and for research, fact-checking, and scheduling many of the interviews for the book. We also want to acknowledge Josh Jarvis, Director of Marketing and Research, for conducting and meticulously tabulating the worldwide research and the numerous Institute studies, as well as for research and fact checking.

At Handshake Dynamics, on whose board I have the privilege to serve, we want to acknowledge CEO Laurence Bunin, who helped us with concept validation and actively participated in numerous in-depth discussions about many ideas expressed in these pages, as well as for reviewing the manuscript; and strategy consultants Sebastian Vos and Cliff Rotenberg for brainstorming sessions, especially around the concept of agency theory.

We want to thank Shaz Khan at Deloitte & Touche, for sharing and comparing his great research with ours over the course of many conversations, and Harry Somerdyk, for thoughtfully reading an early manuscript and working with us on the concept of "street truth." And thank you to all those people who helped in various ways to open doors, clear paths, or just discuss ideas, such as Sam Albert and Rich Engelage.

Thanks to the many agents of the Leigh Speakers Bureau, for arranging for me to lecture in front of some of the best organizations and the brightest minds throughout the United States and the world in our continuing journey and sharing of knowledge.

Thank you to Doubleday Editor Roger Scholl, who worked with me from the conception of the idea for this book all the way to its completion, adding sound direction, guidance, and perspective, as well as very fine editing, all along the way. And thanks to Wes Neff, my literary agent at the Leigh Bureau, for putting Roger and me together and for continual support.

While researching this book, we found that many executives and managers have a solid grounding on what matters, both profession-ally and personally, and that they strive to keep their work in a proper context within their lives. It became clear that many rewards do not come from either short or long time periods, but from special moments within those periods.

I want to especially thank my family for such great support all the way through the creation of this book, which took many days, nights, weekends, and holidays. To my two sons, Ryan, 13, and Chase, 10, who are growing up fast in a faster world, thank you for slowing down and waiting for me while I finished. And my biggest thank you goes to my lifelong partner and wife of 16 years, Therese Granger Martin, to whom I dedicate this book. Thank you, Teri, for the encouragement, guidance, unyielding support, and especially for creating more positive and special moments than I could possibly count.

I
What Is Managing for the Short Term?

1

The New World
of the Short Term

Work today is like a perpetual motion machine set on fast forward. A souring economy globally, a U.S. recession, and massive business fallout from the terrorist attacks of September 11 are driving businesses and individuals in those businesses to rethink how they move their organizations and themselves forward.

The challenges of this rapidly changing business environment mean that there is more work to do than there are people to do it. The workload and pace can seem overwhelming—that is, if anyone ever has time to stop and think about them.

Managers are facing constant change, in a time when there has never been more to do and less time in which to do it. Workers at all levels, from the rank and file to senior executives, are coming in early, leaving late, and often working at home at night and on weekends.

Bombarded by requests from above and below in the management structure, managers end their days feeling that they didn't get anything done but are completely drained by the effort of putting out fires. Strategies and vision are discussed at off-site meetings, only to take a back seat once everyone returns to the office and the realities of day-to-day life or the latest crisis. Executives and managers dash from meeting to meeting, often coming out with a longer to-do list than the one they went in with.

Middle managers have to deliver on higher expectations for performance in a shorter time frame, using a workforce that makes higher demands of its own on the organization. As a result, managers are finding themselves rolling up their sleeves and, in many cases, performing some of the work they are simultaneously supposed to be managing others to do.

But middle managers aren't alone in facing tougher expectations. Senior executives are facing more demanding situations outside the company, from shareholders and the capital markets to customers. Executives are being pushed by those external forces to deliver more and more in less and less time.

These pressures have been building over several years. They were first felt when the emergence of the Internet created the concept of "Internet time." When the networking of the world began to change business, both start-ups and their larger competitors had a sense that nothing could happen quickly enough. The little guys' mantra was "Get big fast," while more established competitors were haunted in many cases by the specter of the proverbial "seven guys in a garage" inventing something that would destroy their business. But the need to meet greater expectations in a shorter time with fewer resources really began to be felt in the bones of the business world as a whole with the recession that began in early 2001, when unemployment figures began to head higher. In the months that followed:

- Between March and December 2001, 1.2 million Americans lost their jobs.[1]

- For the first time since 1990, more than half of major U.S. companies—58 percent—reported layoffs during the 12 months prior to June 30, 2001.[2]

- The wave of layoffs did not simply affect a person here and a person there. In November 2001, there were 2,699 mass layoffs of 50 people or more, compared to the 1,697 layoffs of the previous November. Those November 2001 layoffs represented 293,074 jobs, compared to the previous November's 216,514.[3]

Workers, managers, and senior executives alike watched as their colleagues found themselves hunting for jobs, and worked even harder to try to avoid getting the next pink slip and being sent out the door. Complicating matters was the disappearance of nearly $5 trillion in market capitalization between March 2000 and October 2001, led by the massive bursting of the Internet bubble.[4] The stocks that figure represented had helped fuel expansion for many companies; when it vanished, companies were forced to rely once again on corporate earnings and profits to fuel any growth. As a result, that growth, whether by acquisition or increased sales, became much harder to achieve, until it finally turned negative and the United States slipped into recession.

The upheaval and its impact on both individuals and companies have reached seismic proportions, and touch virtually every area of every company. The recession alone did not create these pressures. However, it has increased the need for a means to help companies and individuals continue to make progress toward their goals when it sometimes seems that everything is conspiring to prevent it.

Lest these statistics suggest that workplace pressures will disappear with the country's emergence from recession, consider one more finding by the American Management Association: Only 25 percent of those major companies reported cutting jobs because of decreased demand for their products and/or services. A majority of the layoffs were attributed to structural changes or productivity gains. This indicates that at least some of those jobs may not return with economic recovery. And the pressures are not simply a function of a decimated workforce; as we will see, many are created by fundamental changes in the way business is conducted.

Workload isn't the only challenge. Managers and employees throughout the organization are driven not only by the sheer volume of work but also by directives from corporate that seem incomplete or, worse, inconsistent and difficult to comprehend. Senior executives try their best to communicate the corporate vision and strategy throughout managerial ranks and the organization. However, many managers are not receiving or totally grasping those messages.

In too many cases, those confusing or misunderstood messages are causing a major disconnect inside organizations between executive and middle management. When that happens, managers end up acting in what they believe is the best interest of their organization, regardless of whether or not it supports the corporate vision.

A NEW APPROACH

A new approach is needed to help organizations get more in sync with themselves so they can optimize their potential in these pressing times. Almost as important, this new approach needs to help managers and workers within the organization feel good about what they do, by allowing them to clearly understand the value of their day-to-day individual contributions to the overall purpose of the organization.

Welcome to the world of Managing for the Short Term.

> While strategy will continue to determine the vision and direction of an organization, managing for the short term can empower organizations and managers to execute that strategy more precisely and effectively.

Managing for the short term is a new approach to work. It is an operational philosophy for executives and managers at all levels, a mandate to work more closely aligned with one another around corporate strategies, and make progress within much shorter time frames. Given the realities of the business world today, doing so is no longer an option; it's a requirement. While strategy will continue to determine the vision and direction of an organization, managing for the short term can empower organizations and managers to execute that strategy more precisely and effectively. In addition, information from managers who understand their roles in furthering the organization's goals can affect the planning process in a more real-time way, allowing strategy and direction to be fine-tuned more quickly when necessary.

To be clear, managing for the short term is not short-term management. Short-term management implies that one is managing with no greater goal beyond just getting through the next period of time. Managing for the short term involves purpose. Truly managing well for the short term means being so connected with the organization, so in sync with its goals and objectives, that a manager knows which short-term actions are appropriate and will best improve the organization's overall performance given its long-term strategy.

Managing for the short term is not simply about moving faster. It is about moving smarter. It is about effective implementation and operation within the context of mission and vision. Strategy is implemented through a series of small steps and rapid, short-term decisions within that long-term view. Managing for the short term forces managers to become more effective at achieving the measurable results required by today's climate in both the public and private sectors of the business world.

Managing for the short term is about moving efficiently, about organizing processes around small, manageable tasks that allow plenty of opportunity for quick reaction to change. It is about coping with the realities of a more mobile workforce and temporary strategic alliances among business partners. It's also about deriving breakthrough strategies from immediate tactics, results, and information, rather than the other way around.

Managing for the short term comprises three major principles:

1. To manage for the short term, everything in business life has to be quantified. This quantification has to be driven down to the personal level, so that each executive or manager understands precisely what he or she can do to either contribute to or impede the organization's ultimate goals and objectives. This should lead to an interrelated company-wide understanding of individual, group, departmental, and divisional contributions.

2. Managing for the short term requires managers at all levels to focus on moving the organization forward in incremental steps in shorter time frames. As they accumulate, these smaller steps should provide incremental benefit to both the organization and the individual taking them. Any required large-scale projects should be broken into smaller pieces with shorter time frames that deliver results-as-you-go.

3. Managing for the short term requires a more focused internal leadership, with highly interactive, internal communication to and among managers at all levels. It requires executives to listen more, and to ensure that the strategy has been received and embraced by those below. After understanding and embracing the organization's objectives, the manager is responsible for keep-

ing the executive ranks informed about market events. The right information has to flow in both directions to get to the right people at the right time.

Managing for the short term is about:

- Closing the gap between where a company wants to go and where the managers and employees can, or plan to, take it

- Leading by communicating and establishing new relationships among all levels of management

- Using information in new ways to navigate through decisions at all levels

- A two-way view: Senior executives need to understand the pressures under which their subordinates operate, including customer expectations, while middle- and lower-level managers need to understand the external pressures behind corporate dictates that they may not immediately grasp or support

- Creating new habits and behaviors at all levels and focusing work on what really matters

- Being holistically in sync with an organization's strategy, not counter to it

- Making day-to-day progress, not just getting through the day

- A fact of life and an advantage

To have the most impact, the concept of managing for the short term will need to be implemented throughout an organization. However, even small steps can move that organization toward its goals. As each individual learns new skills that will change how he or she works, those efforts can benefit not only the individual but also the organization as a whole.

It Just *Is*

An important part of managing for the short term is the idea that managers might actually be able to feel good about doing so. A work environment in which workers don't see the difference their contributions make, or don't feel that the organization recognizes the importance of what they do, is not an environment that's likely to operate at optimum efficiency. Acting and reacting in short-term increments does not always jibe with what people like to see as their ultimate mission and role within an organization. Even though someone may be moving an organization forward a bit at a time, that individual may have a difficult time feeling good about how his or her work time is spent unless there's that big win or monster project so often traditionally associated with the big raise or promotion. In an era when the scope of projects is being broken into smaller, more manageable pieces and companies must be able to change gears quickly, that focus on the "big bang" is likely to produce frustration.

Part of the problem is that being highly proactive has traditionally been considered a plus; being highly reactive has not. "Thinking long-term" gives the illusion of being able to control circumstances, regardless of whether that illusion has any basis in reality. Reacting to actual circumstances, by contrast, can create a feeling of powerlessness, of being pushed by forces beyond one's control. No wonder being reactive is perceived as such a negative!

However, managing for the short term is not simply reactive management. It is not just responding to the next event or marketplace disruption that comes along. It involves both proactive and reactive management at all levels and at the appropriate time for each. It involves managers understanding the needs and interests of the executive team and sending the right word up at the right time. It involves executives reaching down in a highly interactive manner to involve managers in the decision-making process and to benefit from their operational knowledge. And it involves the most effective use of the information exchanged during those efforts.

In a world that can change quickly, inflexibility is more dangerous than ever. No one likes to admit that there are situations that go beyond our ability to control them, but that possibility always exists, and is often made manifest at unexpected times. The September 11 terrorist attacks on the World Trade Center and the Pentagon destroyed whatever illusions anyone might have had about their limitless control over circumstances. When both business and personal frames of reference can change dramatically overnight, organizations and individuals are better served by being prepared to fine-tune strategy on an ongoing basis, so that managers who must manage for the short term are able to be not just reactive but proactive as well.

Many of the factors that define the world of work today—the pressure to produce quick results, the networking of everything and everyone, the need for documentation and quantification, the need to accumulate incremental successes instead of waiting for "the big win," the need for better communication between strategy and operations—are not necessarily positive or negative in themselves. Whether we like it or not, the fact is that this is how things are.

These are the forces that are driving the need to manage for the short term, and wise managers and executives both recognize that need and adapt to it. As we will demonstrate repeatedly, whether that need is considered good or bad, it just *is*.

WHAT IS SHORT TERM?

The concept of managing for the short term is not an abstraction. It is based on the very real experiences of managers and executives around the world. Part of the primary research for this book is based on studies done by the Net Future Institute, of which I am Chairman and CEO. For the past two years, the Institute has conducted surveys of its 3,000 business executive members in more than 50 countries. The Institute has members from more than 1,500 companies of various industries and sizes, including more than half of the Fortune 100.

We have been surveying these senior-level executives every 14 days on a variety of subjects over a two-year period. These surveys reflect a broad spectrum of their concerns. Topics range from organizational subjects, such as employee retention and short- versus long-term incentives, to more personal issues, such as approaches to meetings and e-mail.

This research provides a snapshot of management thinking on key issues of corporate behavior, governance, and culture. This snapshot includes both quantitative and qualitative data, offering a wide-angle perspective on executives' and managers' views, concerns, suggestions, and solutions. Throughout the book, you will see many verbatim comments, labeled "Voices from the Front Lines," from these executives and managers to give you a sense of what others like yourself are feeling about work issues these days.

In addition, we personally interviewed more than 100 senior executives and managers in the course of our research, and we share their direct experiences in the following pages. In some cases, we noted distinct differences between senior executives—defined as those with the title of CEO, Chairman, President, Principal, Partner, CIO, CMO, COO, General Manager, Executive Vice President, or Senior Vice President—and managers—defined as those with the titles of Vice President, Assistant Vice President, Director, Manager, or Supervisor. In other cases, the two segments were more alike than different. In all cases, we were looking for the experience of real executives and managers on the front lines of business today.

Often, interviewees would start by saying, "But my industry is different. . . ." However, what we found rather consistently is that though industries are different in terms of product or service, the management lessons are consistent and quite similar across industries.

It has become clear that we live in dramatically changing times, with shorter and shorter time frames for success, no matter which financial or performance metrics are used. Many executives already are developing new thinking and practices for managing for the short term. This book attempts to synthesize some of those practices and present them in a way that enables senior executives and managers to use them day by day.

Managing for the short term is not just about getting through the day. A Net Future Institute survey of its members found that short term for most managers means the current quarter, followed by the current year[5] (see Figure 1.1). There was virtually no difference among senior executives and managers; "a quarter" was the definition of "short term" for the majority at all levels.

Contrast the way these executives and managers define "short term" with the "short-term" behavior of companies discussed in a 1985 *Harvard Business Review* article on the strategic planning process:

"Most companies select goals that are too short-term. It is almost impossible for a company to create a truly sustainable competitive

FIGURE 1.1

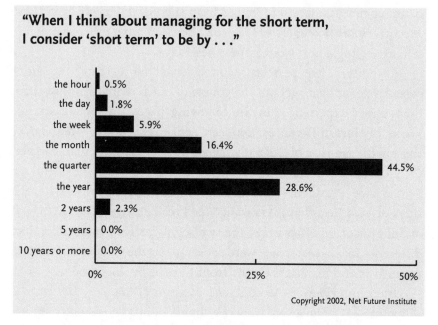

"When I think about managing for the short term, I consider 'short term' to be by . . ."

the hour	0.5%
the day	1.8%
the week	5.9%
the month	16.4%
the quarter	44.5%
the year	28.6%
2 years	2.3%
5 years	0.0%
10 years or more	0.0%

0%   25%   50%

advantage—one that is highly difficult for its competitors to copy—in just five to 10 years (the time frame that most companies use). Goals that can be achieved within five years are usually either too easy or based on buying and selling something."[6]

The article's author points out that a strategic planning process focused on 5- to 10-year goals is not long-term enough to accomplish strategic goals such as competitive advantage. The article also argues that a strategic planning process focused on 5- to 10-year goals isn't flexible enough to enable companies to take advantage of immediate opportunities, and isn't necessarily appropriate in fast-moving environments—a premise with which we completely agree.

It is interesting to note the difference between the 1985 view of 5 to 10 years as a "short-term" time frame for achieving strategic goals, and the view of "short term" expressed by our managers and executives. It would seem that the pressure that companies faced in 1985—the need to accomplish goals in a shorter-than-optimal time frame—is even more intense now. As we will see later in the book, many executives and managers now would consider a 5- to 10-year time frame a luxury, even for long-term goals.

VOICES FROM THE FRONT LINES

What Is Short Term?[7]

"Short term I consider current-quarter decisions. Sometimes even decisions impacting the next 12 months could be considered short, depending on when the fiscal year ends. Mid-term decisions are items that have impact in the second to eighth quarter looking forward—especially if their impact is not in the current fiscal year. Long term are decisions that have significant impact beyond two years."

"I would consider 'short-term' management to be from this month through one year, while 'long term' is from two to five years. My experience is that there is too much concern over the short term, with disregard for the long term, which is really what provides the longevity that successful companies need."

"Short term would be two years or less; long term would mean three years or longer. I think most businesses tend to primarily focus on the short term with very little consideration for the long term."

"Short term is almost zero—make decision now!"

Managers' perspective on "long term" now is actually closer to that 1985 definition of "short term." There was no difference between senior executives and managers when asked about what "long-term" management meant to them. Two years was most frequently cited by all levels of management as being long term, followed by five years.[8] (See Figure 1.2.)

In some cases, the work defines the meaning of "long term." In areas such as facilities planning or construction, a long-term project that involves land and equipment purchase, building permits, and construction may involve several years. In an industry with rapidly changing technology, it could mean a year.

Because of these differences, the precise definition of "short term" or "long term" isn't the key lesson the average manager should draw from the concept of managing for the short term. What is critical is the manager's own comfort level with having to manage with a shorter time frame in mind than he or she may be accustomed to.

FIGURE 1.2

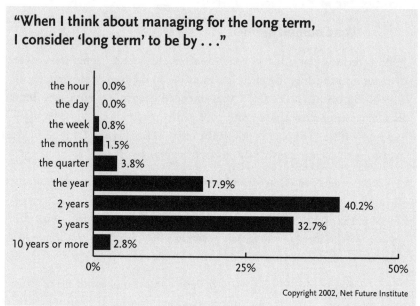

"When I think about managing for the long term, I consider 'long term' to be by . . ."

THE PRESSURES TO MANAGE FOR THE SHORT TERM

The disconnect between managers and their companies is increasing at precisely the same time that the margin for error in a company is shrinking. The forces that contribute to that shrinkage include:

- The demands placed on a reduced workforce

- Well-informed investors demanding a quick return on investment

- Information-armed stakeholders

- A global business environment that offers greater competition

- The increased importance of technology and the pace of techno-logical change

- An empowered workforce and new demographics that mean increased competition for the most valued employees

- A more sophisticated and informed customer base

VOICES FROM THE FRONT LINES

The Changed Definition of Long Term[9]

"With the top-down pressure to produce by-the-quarter results, the term 'long term' changes significantly. (Last year it was a year out.) It is all about making sure that the team contributes positive results in the new quarterly model."

"I am a sales VP, so I see *life* in 90-day increments! My joke is that strategic planning for me is where I am going to have dinner tonight!"

"For planning purposes, I try to work on a vision that is three to five years out. I define concrete steps in quarterly intervals for the next 12 months and a general goal for two years out. The plan itself needs to be reevaluated at least annually, and twice yearly is better."

"A lot depends upon the project, though time frames are definitely collapsing in all we do. What has disappeared is considering long-term planning as something with a three-plus-year time frame."

"In Turkey's very chaotic economic environment, 'short-term' and 'long-term' terms needed to be refined every day."

THE DEMANDS PLACED ON A REDUCED WORKFORCE

At the beginning of the new century, reductions in the workforce left American workers and managers doing more with less. Layoffs, reorganizations, global outsourcing of jobs, mergers, and acquisitions all have meant that the people companies retain have had to pick up the slack for their departed colleagues. In most cases, that has meant longer workdays, as people must handle tasks with which they may be unfamiliar, do tasks they used to delegate to others, and generally do it all more quickly. As we shall see, the workday of many managers has boiled down to doing whatever is most urgent rather than whatever is most important.

Even when the economy begins to emerge from a recessionary mode, the demands placed on the workforce may be slow to change.

For example, companies may be reluctant to staff up to their former levels. Executives may hesitate to give up the gains in productivity figures created by cutting payroll, fearing that increasing the work-force may slow or eliminate any improvement in the bottom line. And the impact on a workforce that has been suffering from work over-load does not go away overnight; for one thing, additional pressures to manage for the short term will not disappear regardless of the state of the economy.

Information-Armed Shareholders

Today shareholders have unprecedented access to a wealth of infor-mation about a company's products, competitors' products, and every conceivable market movement—all of which is available on a minute-by-minute basis. Wall Street's internal stopwatch is ticking loudly in every top executive's ears, and companies must demon-strate success quarter by quarter and month by month, not just year by year. A slower economy has even prompted cries on Wall Street for companies to once again focus on paying dividends rather than concentrating solely on growth—a far cry from a few years ago, when for many companies the concept of paying dividends to share-holders was either an afterthought or a joke.

The growth of cable and satellite TV channels—CNBC, BBC, CNNfn, and Bloomberg TV, to name only a few—and the Internet also has led to a dramatic increase in the demand for not only deliv-ery of moment-by-moment information but also in many cases personal appearances by company spokesmen. "CNBC syndrome" means that executives increasingly are having to appear to explain the company's performance—not just once a year in front of stock-holders, where questioning can be controlled to some extent, but periodically on TV in front of the entire world before professional interrogators.

It is not only the volume and detail of information available to shareholders that have resulted in increased scrutiny of corporate per-formance; it is also the tools to compare that performance. Technolo-gy that facilitates screening and ranking of stocks on a quantitative basis is available to institutional shareholders, such as managers of pension funds or mutual funds, and to individual shareholders as well. Sophisticated screening tools can compare a given company to its competitors on a quantitative basis without the need to wade through annual reports. Though by no means the most important reason why companies are increasingly focused on quantitative measurement, as we'll discuss later, such tools have certainly enhanced shareholders' ability to compare corporate metrics.

VOICES FROM THE FRONT LINES

The Impact of Wall Street[10]

"I find that publicly traded companies are really in a tough place. They are trading off enormous short-term pressure for monthly results against the strategic investments that will create value over the longer term. While analysts are recognizing the ROI in technology, they are not as good at assessing the ROI on people. For example, shrinking the training budget in the hope that technology and stock options will fill the gap is a false economy."

"Wall Street measures organizational performances on a quarterly basis. Consequently, business leaders are forced to focus on short-term targets and deliverables, as they cannot afford, or are not rewarded for, long-term infrastructure investments."

"Most managers act in response to the way that they are measured. Over the past eight years, we have become conditioned to manage 'reactively' to external forces such as the stock market, and this has taken focus from thinking and acting proactively and strategically. The stock market has become the 'political poll' of business."

"In my industry it seems that smaller, closely held companies look much further down the road than the larger, publicly traded companies."

"In essence, the workplace compensation environment is now mimicking the corporate balance that publicly traded companies must create: short-term results with bona-fide long-term strategic plans."

"I believe that, for many firms, executive leadership teams and the board of directors make decisions based on short-term gains for the shareholders and not what is best for the company/stakeholders long-term."

Coupled with this greater level of information is a greater awareness of all things financial, prompted in large part by demographics. Retirement plans have given individuals unprecedented participation in the stock market, which in turn has led to heightened interest in the world of business generally. Baby boomers, traditionally a do-it-yourself crowd, are coming into their peak earning and investing years, and they're keeping an eye on their money in ways undreamed of by their parents, who were content to let their broker tell them when to buy and sell—if they even owned stock at all.

Information-Armed Stakeholders

As technology has linked companies and their business partners—suppliers, distributors, and in some cases even competitors—it has created a new web of structural pressures. Information about the company's performance is more widely available than ever, enabling people whose livelihoods are affected by a company in any way to keep closer tabs on what's going on. In many cases, that information is necessary to provide the kind of customer feedback that should drive the company, as we will discuss later. However, it also puts additional pressure on the leaders of what I have previously called "open-book corporations"[11]—companies that open up internal information to the outside world. The flip side of providing business partners and employees with the information they need to be more effective in their business roles is that they also can use that information to measure the company's performance—and that of its leaders.

Internal networks also have meant that employees are better informed about what is going on inside the corporation. Companies encourage their workers to share knowledge to maximize its benefits. However, that greater level of exchange among employees means that it is easier for workers throughout the company to know more about what is going on elsewhere in the organization.

Employees also are obviously a key part of the pressure on corporate leaders to produce consistently strong bottom-line results. Many companies that match their employees' contributions to their 401(k) retirement plans award that matching money in the form of stock in the company itself. With retirements riding on the value of the company's stock, employees have additional incentive to be concerned not only about their jobs but also about the company's ability to be profitable and attract the investor demand that keeps the company's stock price high and their retirement plan balances going up. After all, they are not just employees but investors. The key is for those employees to understand precisely how they can help increase the stock value, as we'll explore later.

The Global Business Environment

The importance of global branding and operations facilitated by the Internet cannot be overestimated. Instant communication to any developed area of the world has combined with companies' continuing need for bottom-line growth to accelerate the shrinking of the world. Consider these facts:

- U.S. exports quadrupled between 1980 and 2000, from $344 billion to more than $1.4 trillion.[12]

- Foreign investment in U.S. companies in 2000 was nearly $321 billion, compared to just over $15 billion in 1992.[13]

- Approximately 646,000 employees worked for U.S. companies that were either established or acquired by companies overseas during 2000.[14]

- In 2000, phone and data traffic on international switchboards was more than 100 billion minutes for the first time.[15]

- Flows of funds and equities across U.S. borders are 54 times higher now than in 1970.[16]

- Top corporate executives who consider their companies successful on a global level spend 40 percent of their time on global issues. That compares to 25 percent of the time of executives overall.[17]

In this increasingly interdependent world, change felt by companies in one part of the world jumps national boundaries more easily than it used to. When one financial market gets the flu, others around the globe often sneeze, too. In 2001, the Japanese markets were the first to feel the immediate impact of the terrorist attacks at the World Trade Center and Pentagon, slumping even while U.S. markets were closed. Other examples include the Mexican devaluation of the peso in 1994–1995, the Asian financial crisis of 1997, and the Russian currency crisis of 1998, all of which affected markets beyond those countries' borders.

Competition, too, is more global in the networked world. With the dawn of e-marketplaces and the networking of supply chains around the world, it has become easier for buyers to increase price pressure on suppliers. And while the Internet has opened up a new world of consumers, the ability to sell globally has brought new demands. Language, culture, transportation, and manufacturing—all become more complex when selling globally.

The geopolitical situation has not made conducting business any easier, either. The more companies become global, the more they must worry about how the local political climate affects their employees and facilities overseas—not to mention being concerned about the impact in the United States of political unrest and terrorism around the world. Unstable political situations and fluctuating foreign currencies also can affect global companies' ability to sell their products outside the United States. That in turn can affect their stock prices. One such incident occurred in February 2001 with Procter & Gamble, the largest U.S. maker of household products, following the devaluation of the Turkish lira.

When Turkey devalued its currency by roughly one-third, Procter & Gamble told analysts the move would knock two to three cents off the company's profit for that quarter, a 1 percent drop.[18] Turkey is the company's twelfth-largest market, and its $400 million in sales represents just 1 percent of P&G's $40 billion total sales. Nevertheless, the market responded by driving down P&G's stock price by 6 percent in one day. Whether the currency problem was the sole factor in the company's shortfall is not the point. The point is that the market reacted immediately to the company's announcement that global pressures caused the problem.

The Pace of Technological Change

It took AT&T 75 years to build an $8 billion business providing long-distance telephone service. But at the dawn of the new century, a cloud began to rise over the horizon: voice-over IP. With the emergence of the Internet and its ability to handle voice traffic as well as data more cheaply than traditional networks, revenues from long distance began to shrink dramatically, not only for AT&T but for its competitors as well. What took 75 years to create was decimated practically overnight. "That's a juggernaut that cannot be fought. People have heart attacks on that," says AT&T data network account executive Gerry Stahl.[19]

Even if existing products are not being made obsolete by new technology, businesses have every incentive to constantly introduce new products. As the business environment has become more global and competition ever more intense, one way that companies try to make sure they make their numbers is to introduce new products they believe can help capture market share and increase revenue. Time to market has become crucial. The sooner a company can introduce its new products, the more time it has to sell them when they are most valuable and can command the highest price, before a competitor can mobilize and introduce something to compete with it.

However, the rapid pace of change has meant more and more "stuff" that needs to get done. If a company introduces seven new products instead of five, the number of employees who must deal with them doesn't necessarily increase proportionally.

Also, the pace of technological change affects the amount of learning that everyone in a company has to do. In many cases, the life cycle of a product has gotten shorter as innovations by competitors have come increasingly quickly. But as more products are introduced into the marketplace, the pressure on workers to cope with additional offerings increases. Sales reps and customer service centers must get up to speed on more products while staying current on existing products. And it's not only that workers are being overwhelmed with more and more information. In many cases, the problem is also the increased complexity of finding the right information in an efficient way, wherever it exists in the corporation.

Technological evolution affects not just technology companies but all companies. For example, the updating of a communications system at an auto manufacturer means workers have to learn how to use it.

A Demographically Empowered Workforce

When the baby boomers entered the workforce in the '60s and '70s, their enormous numbers meant that businesses had at their disposal a well-educated army of people who were in competition with one another for the jobs available. However, the baby bust that followed the boom, which applies to workers born between 1964 and 1979, left companies scrambling for the next wave of entry-level employees in the 1980s and 1990s. The wave of change brought about by the Internet intensified the problem, requiring new skill sets most often found in the younger workers who were in short supply. Despite the ebb and flow of economic conditions that influence employment statistics, demographics and technology have meant that workers are generally more empowered than ever before.

Coupled with that is the increasing sophistication of the jobs that exist. Many routine tasks that required low-level skills are being automated, reducing the need for armies of unskilled workers. As this process continues, the jobs that remain within a company tend to be those that require the higher-level skills possessed by the people that companies really want to keep or hire.

Both of these trends mean that despite fluctuating employment statistics, workers are generally more empowered than ever before to control their careers. Moving from one company to another is now considered normal. Moreover, in some cases, employees who stay with one company for years are even suspected of not having the drive and ambition necessary to thrive in today's competitive business environment. In an age when skill sets change rapidly, employers are constantly looking for people who can infuse the company with new and maybe unfamiliar—but better—ideas and practices.

A More Sophisticated and Informed Customer Base

Just as investors have more information with which to compare company performance, so too do ordinary consumers. The Internet has made it easier to compare such points as price, products, and customer service. It also has facilitated exchanges among consumers about a company's products, performance, and corporate actions. That information has increased the speed with which a company must at least recognize changes in the external environment. Decisions must be made quickly, even if the decision is not to react. And they must be reversed just as swiftly if they are proved wrong.

> Managing for the short term enables companies, their executives, and their managers to minimize the number and scale of those failures, while enhancing opportunities for demonstrable successes.

All of these forces put pressure on organizations to deliver rapid results consistently. To do so, setting a strategic direction is simply not enough. That strategic direction-setting must be followed by moves that get everyone in the company on the same page to enhance the company's efficiency and effectiveness. If they are not, moving at the pace of business today can take a company a long way down the wrong path toward major losses, both in resources and direction, before anything can be done to reverse the motion.

Managing for the short term enables companies, their executives, and their managers to minimize the number and scale of those failures, while enhancing opportunities for demonstrable successes that can acquire the support and resources—internal and external—so essential for long-term success.

A New Alignment Needed

In order to manage effectively for the short term, executives, managers, and entire organizations must be better aligned to meet the market's demand for speed. Companies are being held to much tighter time frames to produce the results the market wants, yet organizations as a whole are not set up to move quickly enough to satisfy those demands.

Both senior executives and managers recognize the need to move faster. While the chief executive is held to delivering consistent short-term results within the longer-term corporate strategy, managers often find themselves simply executing what was mandated at the last annual meeting of employees and managers—a mandate that may have outlived its usefulness shortly after it was developed or announced.

Even worse, managers sometimes find themselves working without a clear understanding of how they can best support a company's strategy and direction, and are forced to make it up as they go, believing they are acting in the best interest of the organization.

The manager of the future needs the flexibility to modify, adapt, and even contradict some of those mandates in the best interest of the shareholders, based on information that was not available during the planning stage. It is this new, real-time market information that will provide companies with competitive advantage, as managers recycle this new knowledge back into the planning process at corporate.

Even though organizations are moving too slowly, many organizational decisions already are being made on a short-term basis. Net Future Institute research shows that 61 percent of executive members believe that organizations most often make decisions on a short-term basis.[20] However, only 28 percent of managers say they personally make decisions on a short-term basis. When it comes to making decisions with the same time frame in mind, organizations and managers are out of sync with each other.

This is why chief executives, who are being required to deliver on a dime, are having difficulty getting their troops to move as fast as Wall Street requires—and why companies and their executives are being penalized for that difficulty. This also helps explain the slow movement of organizations; managers simply are not fully equipped to manage for the short term in the context of a longer-term strategy. And even more important, long-term strategy is not closely and interactively linked with the necessary short-term management decisions.

With tighter time frames and increased focus on achieving immediate business results, managers require a new management approach and set of skills. They need a new way of working and thinking so that individual activities are coordinated with the pressing needs of their chief executives. They need both the tactical skills that enable managers to manage their time and tasks more effectively and the skills that can affect strategy, such as understanding what information is needed when and by whom.

Managing for the short term is that new approach. It requires arming managers for the real workplace of today and helping them understand that, far from being helpless, they can adapt successfully to the demands that that new workplace makes on them.

Managing for the short term benefits both the organization and the individual manager. By linking strategy to incremental action, it benefits the organization by enabling it to move more efficiently in the direction of a strategy that reflects reality. And it benefits the individual by helping him be more effective, which can improve morale and help make those long days feel more worthwhile.

2

The Manager and the Business Blur

It's no secret that most managers are overworked. Managers at all levels are coming in early and leaving late. They are managing through layoffs while trying to keep their employees motivated. They are feeling the pressures of shorter time frames in which more must be accomplished. Much of this overload can be attributed to two factors: information and immediacy.

Technology has provided the means to be in constant contact, no matter where someone is. That means that everyone receives more information more quickly, and typically it carries with it the expectation of an immediate response. The information flow is nonstop, whether you want it to be or not. Managers are constantly interrupted by top executives who need an updated report, by subordinates who require a bit of quick direction, by numerous and various personnel issues, or by changes in the marketplace.

This feeling of daily pressure affects everyone, regardless of industry, business, or location. There are just too many things to do. Every manager has to be an expert juggler today, keeping as many balls in the air as possible, dealing only with those getting closest to the ground.

Today's business environment is very unforgiving. Managers and workers are facing an insurmountable number of tasks and objectives on a quarterly, monthly, weekly, daily, or even hourly basis. Just as it is helpful for managers to recognize the pressures behind directives from the CEO's office, senior executives must understand the day-to-day pressures under which their managers operate. These pressures and distractions often create obstacles to managers moving as rapidly as the market demands in trying to deliver on long-term strategy.

THE DAILY PRESSURES: MANAGING IN THE FAST LANE

The difficulty is not so much that interruptions necessarily require a deviation from a manager's thought or activity process; most can handle that. It's that the deviations never stop, at least during what used to be known as "normal office hours." As a result, many managers have had to shift their work hours to take advantage of times when they can be most productive.

The Metro Orlando Economic Development Commission focuses on creating jobs and attracting capital to Orlando and surrounding counties in the central Florida area. During a five-year period, the commission assisted hundreds of companies with more than $6 billion in capital investments.

Paty Wright, Senior Director of Corporate Business Development at the EDC, articulates the plight of many managers:[1]

> We are continually being inundated with voluminous e-mails, on a 24-hour basis. Sometimes, there are an extraordinary number of inquiries that have to be answered in a very short time. There are very compelling arguments about the speed of information being requested; it must be accurate and it must be fast. Experts who handle massive amounts of confidential information are having to find new ways to be faster in this age of speed. We're running so fast, you might almost say at Mach speed. We are in an age where information is king, but speed is the supreme ruler. If you don't have speed, you're not in the game. We also see many frustrations. As professionals, we have high expectations of the caliber of work we're capable of producing. Now with speed, endless e-mail and meetings, we continuously have to find new ways to reinvent our-

selves so that we can compete in this time-sensitive environment. There is little time for a celebration or a pat on the back. With new projects, new information, and new clients, we're always running.

Part of the plight of managers is that the never-ending demands on their time can come from multiple sources simultaneously.

"As a manager, you can be pulled in so many different directions, so it's imperative that you keep your job in focus," says Greg Carroll, manager for Aetna Inc., the health care benefits organization.[2] Carroll reports directly to a group head, in his case a function head of the Southeast Region. However, he also has dotted-line responsibility to the national team and the director of integration.

Like many managers, Carroll comes in to work facing a barrage of e-mail and voice mail, and six to eight meetings a week, both staff meetings and functional meetings. He has 25 direct reports, and delegates heavily to his team. He tries to accomplish at least 75 percent of what he sets out to do in a given day. Carroll spends much of his time interacting with his management team, but makes clear that they must do their own jobs.

He views the role of executive management as being heavily communications-oriented. "An executive manager needs to know each of his direct reports. He doesn't have to know how to do each manager's job, but he needs to know what is consuming the manager's time. An executive needs to set clear expectations."

Another manager in health care is Liz Carbon, Pharmacy Director for Distribution at Premier, Inc., a health care alliance collectively owned by more than 200 independent not-for-profit hospitals. And like Carroll and many other middle managers, she finds herself with more and more to do and less and less time to do it.[3] Says Carbon:

> I find myself coming in at 7 A.M. and staying until 6 P.M. and feel like I'm not getting everything done that I planned at the beginning of the day. I don't know where the time is going. There's an overabundance of work in business these days, so we work through lunch and bring things home. I hate leaving things undone, but I find myself leaving with a bit of a load for the next day. I've been in business for 16 years and can't remember a time of ever being this stressed. I like what I do, but everybody in work these days is

overwhelmed. Yesterday I was working on seven projects all at the same time. Managers need to understand what they were hired for and what are the expectations.

Part of the reason that Paty Wright, Greg Carroll, Liz Carbon, and many of you are being pulled in so many directions is that work today is more complex and often involves the coordination of many different parts of the organization. Consensus takes more effort than individual action. The other reason is that technology has made contact—and therefore interruptions—so easy. Managers are more accessible to more people because of technology, including cell phones, car phones, laptop computers, pagers, handheld devices, and e-mail, which is available wherever there is a phone (or wireless technology). As a result, managers feel that their days and weeks are speeding blurs, as they try to find meaning in what they do.

THE PRESSURES OF NETWORKING

The world is interconnected as never before. In 1999 alone, 90 million Internet devices were added to the online community, for a total of more than 260 million, and the number of users worldwide is expected to more than double by 2003 to 600 million.[4] The power, given the right connections, to reach anyone at any time shapes not only the business world's abilities but also its expectations. A world in which global "virtual meetings" are nothing unusual is a dramatic change from the day when companies thought they could build an entire business on the ability to deliver a faxed message *on the same day*.

During the old days of mainframe computing, when massive computers were housed within big glass cages, the processing of information was centrally located. If an executive wanted information, he sent down a request to the head of Management Information Systems (MIS), as it was called in those days. Eventually the desired information would be cultivated, assembled, sorted, packaged, and delivered. The concept of real-time information being used to drive business processes was foreign. The only people in an organization who really needed to know anything about technology were the MIS management and staff, because it was essentially an internal service and support function.

Then, in the mid-1980s, along came the explosive growth of personal computers and individual computing. Department heads within profit centers began purchasing their own desktop computers. True technological empowerment began, as individual managers throughout organizations loaded Lotus 1-2-3 and created their own spreadsheets, giving them more immediate information and thus more control over the business.

In the '90s, these computers were linked together, first within departments, then department to department, then throughout the enterprise, and finally company to company. In the mid-'90s, the commercial Internet came along, providing new ways for companies to interact first with their customers and ultimately with everyone in the value chain, including suppliers, manufacturers, distributors, vendors, employees, and even shareholders. In addition to introducing new ways of connecting individuals, the Internet boom of the late '90s also introduced new ways to conduct business, with new (if unprofitable) business models. Many of the dot-com companies fell by the wayside in 2000 and 2001, but they nevertheless left in their wake a changed world of business, as established companies adopted the technologies and some of the business habits the dot-coms had innovated.

This growth of interconnectedness created enormous opportunities for those who capitalized on it. As would be expected, many technology companies led the way in innovative uses of technology. Hewlett-Packard and IBM linked their employees around the globe, creating self-service benefits to management and instant, real-time company information; Dell and Oracle moved much of their business to the Internet for buying, selling, and receiving products.

But other industries quickly caught up in feeling the impact of networking technology; it now permeates every aspect of management, allowing more communication both down and up the line. In the food sector, Sysco, the $19 billion food-service distributor, began providing its business customers with electronic inventory management systems. In financial services, American Express and Fidelity Investments allowed customers to personalize and customize their individual views of those companies' Web sites. Bank of Montreal and Wells Fargo introduced online mortgage applications, and Bradesco, based in São Paulo, Brazil, redefined banking in South America by offering banking via the Internet using cellular phones, with e-mail and general Web access.

The Internet, as the mother of all networks, has created the potential—and in many cases the expectation—that everything and everyone will be constantly connected. The integration of interactive, handheld devices with telephone and Internet-based networks has led to businesses functioning on the unspoken assumption that both managers and information are available all the time in some fashion. It also has created the assumption that everyone, at least at the managerial level, has a basic familiarity with the tools of technology, such as computers and e-mail.

To managers, this is good news for business in general; they view this total connectivity as a benefit. Almost 100 percent of respondents to a Net Future Institute survey said that the "networking of everything" has made business either better or much better[5] (see Figure 2.1).

Managers clearly recognize the positive side of technology, or more significantly, the use of technology to connect people and events and improve business. As noted above, however, there is a downside. Connectivity has led to a constant stream of interruptions. For someone who can't or doesn't want to simply walk into a colleague's office, there

FIGURE 2.1

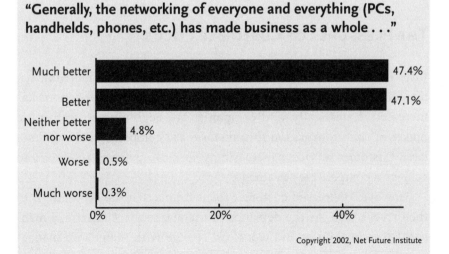

"Generally, the networking of everyone and everything (PCs, handhelds, phones, etc.) has made business as a whole . . ."

Much better	47.4%
Better	47.1%
Neither better nor worse	4.8%
Worse	0.5%
Much worse	0.3%

Copyright 2002, Net Future Institute

VOICES FROM THE FRONT LINES

Time Spent on E-mail[6]

"I spend one to two hours working on e-mails. That does not include time preparing materials ultimately sent via e-mail. Including this would make the total exceed four hours."

"I conduct the majority of my business via e-mail, both internal and external. E-mail is my other job—adding four hours a day."

"Too much of my time is spent responding to e-mails when the phone would be faster and more efficacious."

"In our company, e-mail has taken over our lives. I receive over 200 internally generated e-mails per day, many with 30- to 45-page attachments on them, and over half have messages that are a page long. We feel we can copy everything to anyone who may have a remote interest, and our expectation is that people will read everything. I spend on the average 20 hours per weekend just wading through the stuff that I didn't have time to read during the week."

---

is telephone, car phone, cell phone, fax, pager, instant electronic messaging, and, perhaps the most ubiquitous example of information overload, e-mail. And it has created pressure on individuals to learn, use, and stay up-to-date on technology to be maximally productive.

THE PRESSURES OF CUSTOMER FOCUS

Interconnectedness also has enabled companies to focus more on customers' needs. The volume of information about customer actions has increased dramatically, and companies are beginning to realize the power of that information to transform the company, as we will see later. Customer service is increasingly seen as a priority and a way to achieve a competitive advantage.

However, increased customer focus means that the customer is in the driver's seat. As the demands of the marketplace change, a manager's responsibilities and workload change with them. And managing change is one of the biggest challenges facing managers today.

THE PRESSURES OF MANAGING PEOPLE

The tasks of managing people have become more complex. An empowered workforce has greater mobility, and the task of retaining valued employees becomes more complicated. The quantification of business life has meant increasing discipline in evaluating workers—discipline that can be time-consuming for managers. Also, new emphasis on workplace issues such as diversity, sexual harassment, and workers' desire and need to achieve a better work/life balance has increased managers' responsibilities—and the time needed to deal with them.

THE PRESSURES OF PROCESS

Any era of great change in the business world is usually accompanied by changes in company organizational structures. When companies merge or acquire another company, or when they reorganize themselves, that action in turn means new priorities, retraining, adapting to new roles, new networks of communications, and new reporting responsibilities. It means an increased need to communicate just what the heck is going on. In many organizations, especially the biggest, it means attaining consensus. And consensus is time-consuming, particularly when departments or projects are highly interdependent and not all profit centers are considered equal.

THE PRESSURES OF SPEED

The need for speed is felt across the board. However, the lower in the organization, the more likely a manager is to feel that his organization does not move quickly enough to cope with the pace of business. Our research shows that more than two-thirds of managers feel their organizations move too slowly[9] (see Figure 2.2).

> People are dealing with more tasks, chores, goals, and even desires than can be fit within a given period of time.

FIGURE 2.2

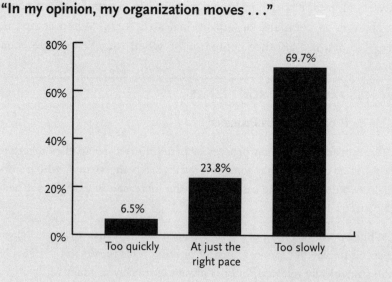

"In my opinion, my organization moves . . ."

This stems in part from middle managers not having as broad a perspective as senior executives. However, it also means that middle managers, who tend to be closer to operations and customers than their superiors, see the impact of executive decisions more directly than do the executives who make those decisions. And middle managers, particularly those in sales and customer service, often hear from customers most directly when a company takes a wrong turn.

THE MODERN LAW OF INUNDATION

All of these pressures have taken their toll on managers. There are few who can honestly say at the end of every day that they accomplished every goal they had set at the beginning of that day. People are dealing with more tasks, chores, goals, and even desires than can be fit within a given period of time.

Managers are searching for strategies to deal with this inundation. Many find themselves working nights, weekends, and vacations to tackle the most strategic issues because they are forced to deal with "all the other stuff" during the regular workday. So many managers and workers—no matter what profession, rank, or industry—find themselves moving things to do to the next day. This is because of what I call Martin's Law of Inundation, which says:

- You cannot really perform the number of tasks you have within the time frame allotted.

- The number of tasks you are required to perform within a given time frame will continue to increase.

- The increase in the number of tasks always will occur *before* you have a method of completing all the current tasks.

- If you dramatically increase the number of tasks you perform within a given period of time, the number of tasks handed to you will be increased exponentially before all the first tasks are completed.

Let's examine each component of Martin's Law of Inundation:

- You cannot really perform the number of tasks you have within the time frame allotted.

There are too many changes happening too quickly today to permit managers to accomplish all the tasks necessary in the traditional eight-hour day—or even in a 12- or 18-hour day (we assume you need a few hours for sleep). Juggling strategic and

---

VOICES FROM THE FRONT LINES

What a Manager's Day Is Like[10]

"With the pressures to perform quarter to quarter, I find myself and my management team focusing more and more of our time on short-term, tactical, margin-generating activities (to-do's)."

"While my list of both strategic and tactical things to do is extensive, I do place the items in priority, so that all of the critical issues are addressed. My workday does not end until the critical items are addressed. Some days I get beyond the three to six critical issues. All voice mails and e-mail are responded to within 48 hours, most within four hours."

"The percentage of items I complete that I plan to work on generally relates to how late I'm willing to stay. Unfortunately, 'surprises' always pop up and I generally get interrupted quite a bit, so it really depends on how important those other items are and how much extra time I'm willing to put in to work on them."

"Task management is a relatively personal art. I've found that technology is useful, but does not make an unorganized person into one who is organized. The sense of accomplishment which comes from managing tasks to their conclusion or their agreed-upon termination is often the sole satisfaction derived from effectively managing tasks . . . assuming, of course, that one has a financial foundation or secure position from which to work."

"Time-management issues and interruptions interfere with my ability to accomplish as much in my workday as I would like."

"Managing departments today requires managers to be far more active than was the case 20 years ago. The list of tasks that fall into my day-to-day activities may or may not fall into what I might consider normal for the role. But staffing levels due to downsizing now create to-do lists of 'must do,' 'should do,' 'need to do,' and 'can hopefully wait.' The tasks required are constantly changing."

tactical demands means that many managers find themselves sorting those demands by the quality of the time and attention they demand. Tactical issues often take up the traditional workday, while strategic issues get attention at times when fewer distractions are likely to occur—before or after normal work hours.

- The number of tasks you are required to perform within a given time frame will continue to increase.

    With the intense focus on the bottom line that we saw in the last chapter, companies are constantly under pressure to increase employee productivity. Sometimes technology can come to the rescue here, but getting more production out of the same individual generally means that there is by definition an upward pressure on the number or complexity of tasks assigned to any individual. Revenue per employee is a key measure of productivity, and unless companies can find ways to increase revenue per employee without piling on more work, individual workloads will continue to increase. And even if a company increases revenue per employee, there's always next year for investors to ask, "What have you done for me lately?"

- The increase in the number of tasks always will occur *before* you have a method of completing all the current tasks.

    This leads to a sort of "survival of the fittest" in terms of task management. There is a constant struggle between the new tasks coming in and the existing tasks that await completion. Often there is no possibility of replacing the old tasks with the new, which simply go on top of an ever-increasing pile. What gets attention may depend on things that have nothing to do with the task itself. In fact, important things may be postponed precisely because they're deemed so important that they require a lot of time and attention. Unfortunately, that time may never arrive because of intervening issues that may be perceived as less important and therefore easier to tackle.

- If you dramatically increase the number of tasks you perform within a given period of time, the number of tasks handed to you will be increased exponentially before all the first tasks are completed.

    This principle is based on what is sometimes known as "Army

justice": If you're really good at something, they'll throw you back in there to get shot at again. It is the task-management equivalent of compounding interest: work added to work not yet completed.

THE IMPACT ON THE INDIVIDUAL

Managers overwhelmingly view widespread connectivity—the networking of everything and everyone—as having a positive impact on life at work, at least from the standpoint of enabling them to produce more[11] (see Figure 2.3). However, as productivity has risen, so has stress, particularly in their personal lives. Managers are able to accomplish more, both personally and professionally, but there is little room for "downtime."

These managers feel in general that the networking of everything increases productivity, both corporately and personally. However, that productivity comes at a cost.

When it comes to personal life, the increase in productivity takes a back seat to the amount of stress caused. More than half of Net Future Institute survey respondents said the networking of everyone

FIGURE 2.3

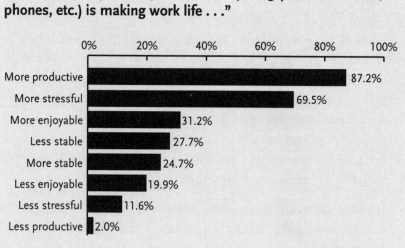

"The networking of everyone and everything (PCs, handhelds, phones, etc.) is making work life . . ."

	%
More productive	87.2%
More stressful	69.5%
More enjoyable	31.2%
Less stable	27.7%
More stable	24.7%
Less enjoyable	19.9%
Less stressful	11.6%
Less productive	2.0%

and everything is making their personal lives more stressful[12] (see Figure 2.4). Interestingly, many (40 percent) also saw this networking as making their lives more enjoyable, while 30 percent said it makes their lives less enjoyable. Managers also have mixed views as to the impact of this networking on the stability of their personal lives, with 26 percent saying it made their lives less stable and 26 percent saying it made their lives more stable.

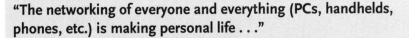

Being in communication all the time is the most wonderful and awful thing.

The pace of technological change is unlikely to slow soon. The pressure to increase productivity also is likely to increase managers' efforts to try to squeeze more into every 24 hours. Given the constant pressure from the top to become more efficient and therefore more profitable, managers will survive only by thinking differently about how they spend those 24 hours. In short, they must not only manage for the short term but also accept that that is the way the world now works.

"Being in communication all the time is the most wonderful and awful thing," says Joe Puglisi, CIO of EMCOR Group, one of the

FIGURE 2.4

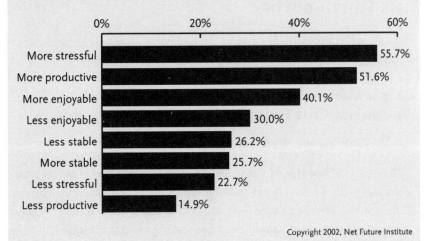

"The networking of everyone and everything (PCs, handhelds, phones, etc.) is making personal life . . ."

More stressful	55.7%
More productive	51.6%
More enjoyable	40.1%
Less enjoyable	30.0%
Less stable	26.2%
More stable	25.7%
Less stressful	22.7%
Less productive	14.9%

Copyright 2002, Net Future Institute

world's largest specialty construction firms, with 22,000 employees in 50 subsidiaries and annual sales of $3.5 billion.[13] "It's a universal problem," Puglisi says about being connected all the time. "You are infinitely more accessible than ever before. I spend 18 hours a day in communication. I answer my own phone when I'm here, but I spend more time troubleshooting than designing where we might go."

Puglisi is responsible for setting technological standards for the 50 companies as well as "selling" new technologies internally. "My job is in part marketing; if I can't sell you on the project, we don't do it," he says. This is one area where the networking of everything has allowed executives, such as Puglisi, to communicate with more of his fellow managers and executives more quickly than ever before. "The EMCOR companies are my customers, so if my services were not in demand, I'd be a budget-cut candidate. We try to provide value. Everything we do is reactive; there is no project-in-a-box. We just try to deliver things incrementally."

This connected-all-the-time reality has more and more managers coming in earlier to get some work done before the daily onslaught. For example, Puglisi goes to work by 7 A.M., while most others arrive between 8:30 and 9 A.M. This used to be a productive time for him, until his early-bird habits became known. "Everyone on my staff has caught on, even in the other time zones, that I'm an early bird, so as soon as I get in I get instant messages, even from the West Coast," Puglisi says.

Time-Shifting Work

The Law of Inundation is causing managers at all levels to shift when they perform work that they consider to be productive.

Voices from the Front Lines

Battling the Workload[14]

"The basic philosophy in my company is to completely overwhelm directors with work. Things inevitably fall off your plate, but usually they are the lower-priority, less important ones. Occasionally, something is not done that should have been, and you're in trouble."

Many executives find their most productive time to be early morning or late night. In one survey, the vast majority of executives and managers cited the time before 9 A.M. as one of their most productive times of the day[15] (see Figure 2.5). Much of the day or week is spent dealing with issues that were not seen at the beginning of that day or week. Those might include a pressing personnel issue, a new move by a competitor, or a newly announced change in management. However, this early-in approach is what managers are doing when managing for the short term.

Where do executives and managers feel they are most productive? Most (65 percent) of respondents to one survey say at the office[16] (see Figure 2.6). Given their response to the question about when they are most productive—generally before 9 A.M. and after 5 P.M.—it seems clear that hours spent in the office are expanding.

It's not just the volume of work that causes managers to time-shift duties. As we have seen, it also may be the interruption of unforeseen issues: Corporate may have just asked for quarterly numbers earlier than expected because the parent company needs them earlier, or your computer may go haywire.

And as business becomes more global, it is "expected" that anyone is reachable almost at any time. For example, European companies with large U.S. operations cause American-based managers to start their workdays earlier to coordinate with corporate.

FIGURE 2.5

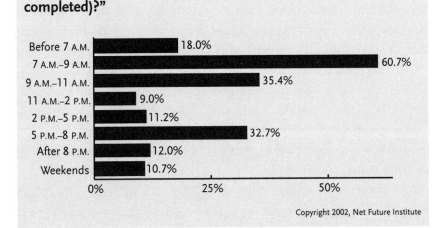

"When do you feel you are most productive (in terms of work completed)?"

Before 7 A.M.	18.0%
7 A.M.–9 A.M.	60.7%
9 A.M.–11 A.M.	35.4%
11 A.M.–2 P.M.	9.0%
2 P.M.–5 P.M.	11.2%
5 P.M.–8 P.M.	32.7%
After 8 P.M.	12.0%
Weekends	10.7%

0%   25%   50%

FIGURE 2.6

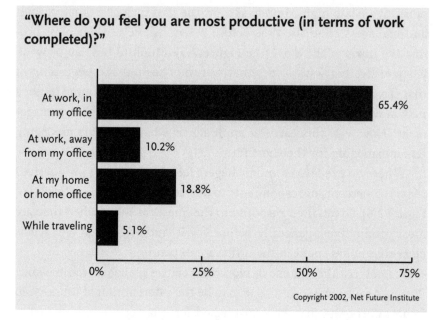

"Where do you feel you are most productive (in terms of work completed)?"

- At work, in my office — 65.4%
- At work, away from my office — 10.2%
- At my home or home office — 18.8%
- While traveling — 5.1%

0%   25%   50%   75%

Many managers eventually find themselves doing something that they have no choice about doing but just wish they didn't have to. "In the course of the normal workday, I primarily do things that seem trivial," says Nancy Weil, Senior Vice President, Marketing, at a subsidiary of a $3 billion financial services corporation.[17] "Your day gets away dealing with low-level things with hard deadlines."

Among her duties, Weil is involved in trade-show planning as well as advertising. "In the larger strategic view, our specific location in a particular trade show doesn't matter all that much, but it has to be decided. So what I find is, you prioritize things with deadlines on them and you do the strategic stuff later, 6:30 P.M. to whatever.

"In an ideal world, you would do just what matters strategically. Unfortunately, in today's stripped-down company, managers also have trivial but deadline-driven stuff," says Weil. "I'm not sure how you're going to bring it back around. With today's technology, you're available 24 hours a day, at two in the morning. It used to be that nobody called you at home."

However, the environment is causing Nancy Weil and many others to take smarter steps, because everything is driven by the next quarter.

> **Voices from the Front Lines**
>
> ### When Does Work Get Done?[18]
>
> "I try to get to the office at about 7:30 or 8 A.M., especially if I need to complete something important without interruptions. We have an open-door policy at work and, while this makes for a good culture, I often get interrupted, which impacts my productivity. If I leave my quiet time until the end of the day, my concentration levels are lower, plus I get distracted by the day's events."
>
> "I get most of 'my' work done before and after the main part of the day. During the main part of the day (9 to 5) I am largely engaged in meetings (mix of planned and informal) or trying to clear obstacles for others."
>
> "Early mornings before most staff arrive at work is my time to prepare for the day, to send key messages and to read those detailed documents where I need to be fresh and focused. Lengthy trips are also great for catching up on your 'read later' stack."
>
> "I find that I am most productive in later hours of the day, given that fewer people are interrupting me with phone calls and meetings that take place during regular office hours. When I work later in the day, fewer interruptions occur."
>
> "I find early mornings in the office are the most productive period. It's quiet, few people are around, the phone is not ringing, and I have a fresh mind. As the day goes on, no matter what I have scheduled, the day tends to get away dealing with new issues and 'emergencies.'"

It's Not About the Money

It's true that managers are paid to deal with all of these problems; after all, that's why they call it "work." But when it comes to what drives executives and managers, it's not just their pay package. At the top of the list of what matters to them is autonomy and challenge, followed by environment and opportunities[19] (see Figure 2.7). The more time managers must spend dealing with things that don't provide that autonomy and challenge, the less motivated they are likely to be.

The good news is that executives and managers do tend to feel they are working on things that they view as being either tactically or strategically relevant[20] (see Figure 2.8), However, fewer feel

FIGURE 2.7

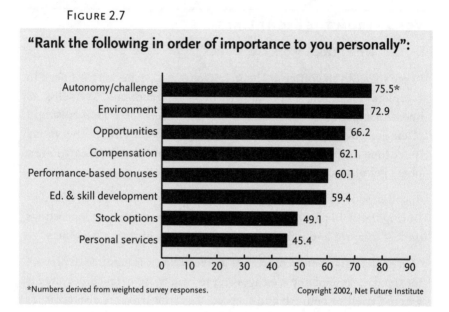

FIGURE 2.7

"Rank the following in order of importance to you personally":

Autonomy/challenge	75.5*
Environment	72.9
Opportunities	66.2
Compensation	62.1
Performance-based bonuses	60.1
Ed. & skill development	59.4
Stock options	49.1
Personal services	45.4

*Numbers derived from weighted survey responses.   Copyright 2002, Net Future Institute

that others in their company recognize that relevance. This raises two interesting questions, which we will explore in subsequent chapters. First, how well are companies communicating how the work of these executives and managers advances the corporate goals? And, second, is the relevance of their work not being recognized because the managers are working on things that they perceive as relevant but that may be misaligned with the organization's overall goals?

FIGURE 2.8

"I spend most of my time at work on things that . . ."

- I deem tactically and/or strategically relevant: 77.0%
- Other people in my company deem tactically and/or strategically relevant: 52.4%
- Other people in my company could/should be doing: 30.6%
- We should hire someone else to do: 14.6%
- I deem NOT tactically and/or strategically relevant: 16.5%
- Other people in my company deem NOT tactically and/or strategically relevant: 8.6%

Copyright 2002, Net Future Institute

THE VIEW FROM THE CORNER OFFICE

Managers are not alone in feeling pressure. The chief executive traditionally has been at the top of the corporate pyramid. He is the one perceived by many to have the best view, the golden-parachute clause, and the largest compensation package. But life at the top isn't as easy or as glamorous as it might seem to those below. To some extent, the pressures on managers are an indirect result of the pressures on the company as a whole and its senior executives.

The top of the pyramid is a more unstable perch than ever. To keep from being toppled, management teams are having to produce results in shorter and shorter time frames. With the accelerated pace of change in the business environment, businesses are reshaping themselves, reorganizing, merging—all to try to better compete in a brutal marketplace. And those changes spell peril. Reorganizations, mergers, and cutbacks represent slightly less than three-quarters of all executive transitions.[21]

STRIKE ONE, YOU'RE OUT

Executives brought in to turn around a company's performance are being given less time to make concrete improvements; even CEOs already in place are under pressure to move the company forward quickly or move out. CEOs these days are likely to have a much shorter tenure.

- Almost 50 percent of chief executives in one study of CEO transitions had held their jobs for less than three years.[22]

- In that same study, two out of three companies ranging in size from 660 to 900,000 employees installed a new CEO between 1995 and 2000.[23]

- Nearly 80 percent of CEOs in 1990 had been replaced within the decade. One in four of those companies went through three or more CEOs according to the same study.[24]

- In the year 2000, 42 CEOs of the 200 biggest companies in the United States left their jobs, compared to 22 the year before.[25]

- In the first six months of 2001, almost as many CEOs of Fortune 1000 firms were hired (53) as had been hired the entire previous year (69).[26]

- From January through September 2001, 722 CEOs vacated their positions. At the close of 2000, 1,106 CEOs had left their positions during the year.[27]

And this doesn't even begin to trace the ripple effect on senior executives and managers, who often change jobs or leave the company once the boss does.

The torrid pace of CEO turnover abated somewhat in 2001 with the worsening of economic conditions. However, John Challenger, CEO of the international outplacement firm Challenger, Gray & Christmas, says the pressure on CEOs is still strong.[28]

"Right now if you look at CEO turnover compared to a decade ago, there's no comparison. They're in a much more precarious position today than they were then. This seems to be a temporary slowdown. I think it's because earlier in the year [2001], CEOs were being more heavily scapegoated for economic conditions that people are now more willing to ascribe to the recession."

Anyone comparing the slowdown in 2001 to the previous year must recall that the year 2000 saw record numbers of CEO departures as dot-coms began to struggle. "There was a period from about August 2000 to February 2001 where they were averaging over 100 [CEO departures] every month," Challenger says. "That was perhaps inflated because the dot-com founders were being pushed out. We saw immense turnover then, but it's still very heavy."

Also, some boards of directors may fear the consequences of changing management when times are tough. Says Challenger, "Companies may feel they have more leeway during a stronger period to let a CEO go because the company is moving in the right direction. In a recession it's more risky. There's always chaos after a CEO leaves. You have to find the next one; they have to create new alliances, get the lay of the land. People who were tied to the old guard leave. All of that makes for problems that must be resolved. There's always a period when a company doesn't make much progress.

"In terms of longer-term trends [in CEO turnover], there's certainly no change. They are certainly far more vulnerable than a decade ago."

OUT OF TIME

"CEOs and company management used to have a little breathing space," says Harry Somerdyk, Managing Director of the publishing practice of Spencer Stuart, the Chicago-based executive search consultants.[29] "Early on, communicating wasn't as instantaneous as it is today. Shareholders were always captive and only got the information management wanted to share."

Now, of course, instantaneous communication and data transmission provide shareholders with information from a variety of sources. That fact has changed the nature of the CEO's job.

"The successful CEOs need to have at their fingertips a multitude of information at all times," says Somerdyk, who recruits and counsels many CEOs of large companies. "They used to rely on staff and department heads, but now they need much more detailed information than traditionally."

Part of what is driving that need for more up-to-date information is the short-term focus mentioned earlier; top executives must produce demonstrable results quickly. "This doesn't take away from forward-looking planning, but there is much more data and much more time needs to be devoted to shorter-term elements," says Somerdyk. It is no longer enough to simply set corporate strategy. That strategy must not only be made clear to everyone in the organization; it must also be constantly guided by information from the troops, who are in closest contact with the marketplace.

The shorter-term focus that drives the need for more detailed information means that the information must flow well both ways, not just from the top down. For companies to be able to keep a company's long-term vision in sync with the real world, a dramatic increase in communication between senior executives and general management needs to occur. That in turn will drive new skill sets for the successful manager of the future, which will be discussed later.

Not only does the short-term environment demand the gathering of information; it also affects the timing and usage of it. "CEOs need to put that information in context," says Somerdyk. For example, how are earnings per share going to be impacted by economics in each region when a market changes?

Information delivered to a senior executive will have to take into consideration the context of the enterprise as a whole; moreover, it will have to be delivered in a timely fashion, even if no immediate action is required. It needs to convey not only what changes have occurred but also why and how conditions vary from what was expected.

"That's where talent will play a big role in companies more and more. The CEO will have to rely more on upper, middle, and senior management to do more. As information-driven data increases and time remains constant, CEOs will have to rely more on his or her managers. The better managers will have the CEO context in mind, and that's the pool from which the next CEOs will be drawn," says Somerdyk.

For chief executives, knowledge-enabled shareholders are simply a fact of life. Their existence, however, does require a new skill set for senior executives and managers, skills that they may not have dealt with before. The information needs of shareholders change what chief executives expect to be available to them at any time, which in turn affects how managers have to prepare in the short term.

"Our CEO wants the capability to pull up actual expenditures in certain areas. He wants to know where is that spending, what does it look like, using online, real-time information that's no more than 24 hours old so he and other executives and managers can make more proactive decisions," says B. George Saloom, President of Zions Data Services Company, a subsidiary of Zions Bancorporation, which has more than 400 banking branches throughout the western United States.[30]

Technological capability is constantly altering the speed at which information is available to an organization, as well as the expectations of executives who want to tap into real-time information streams and leverage the information internally. For example, at Zions Bancorporation, the real-time monitoring of spending affects the company's planning time frame. "It's almost a continuous planning cycle; a lot of our planning is done in a short time frame. It definitely affects the technology side," Saloom says. "I don't know too many areas it wouldn't affect. If it doesn't affect them, they may not be as relevant to the process. Maybe they need to be looked at as to what their purpose of life is. The concept of reevaluating purpose and procedure needs to be more dynamic."

This change in how quickly information is delivered and integrated throughout an organization also can be tapped as a powerful strategic weapon. "We're looking at a product-development cycle that's going to be a lot shorter. The problem is that we have to be careful to remember what we've come to do. Are we developing products that are what the customer desires? Sometimes if people aren't developing products, they don't feel they're doing their job, but if you create things customers don't need, sometimes you're just confusing them," says Saloom.

The pressures of information-armed shareholders have made senior executives much like the customers they serve. They need the right information at the right time, delivered in a way they can use.

"Being a CEO these days is like playing chess," says Moe El-Gamal, President and CEO of Global Systems, Inc., a North Carolina–based Internet service provider.[31] "The CEO has to balance the short term with the long term. You keep your eyes on the road, but you have to watch the signs on the side of the road as well."

These signs can range from market changes and shifts in the competition to internal managerial changes. With 62 employees, Global Systems has the ability to morph with market conditions more easily than can a company with 50,000 or 100,000 employees. However, the principles of managing the troops for the short term are basically the same. Says Moe El-Gamal:

> We gather the people once a month and explain how it is. We have demand and supply and try to have them understand the business in as simple terms as possible. I ask them to ask for different ways to increase revenue or reduce cost and give them bonuses for it.

Being a CEO is different today, because now there are three areas to watch. In the past, you watched only one variable: supply and demand. Today, you watch marketing itself, or supply and demand. But the second thing you must watch as a CEO now is technology, so you can determine where the technology can take you and what to invest in. The third thing a CEO must watch today is the external environment, including stock volatility and the political situation. Things change daily today.

I delegate and we have to all work as a team. Everyone is empowering their teams as well. Everyone today has to be a strategist. You have to have execution and implementation strategy as well, and allow people to implement in their own way. Before, having information made you very powerful. Now it makes you powerful if you share it.

In the past, people were told how to do it and not allowed to think a lot. They used to motivate them in different ways. Today, people need much more involvement. In our software department, for example, we have no rules on when someone has to work, just what they have to deliver.

TECHNOLOGY IN THE EXECUTIVE SUITE

The importance of technology has now been recognized in the executive suite, albeit reluctantly in some cases. Gone forever are the days of technology executives presenting technical slide after slide to a roomful of top executives who stare blankly while waiting to hear the ultimate cost they would have to sign off on. Senior executives who used to hear technology phrases such as "terabytes of data," "MIPS (millions of instructions per second)" and "cost per workstation" are now more likely to be hearing CIOs talk about enhanced employee productivity, better customer retention, and measured returns.

However, there is now even more pressure to understand precisely what technology might enable a company to accomplish, within what time frames, and at what cost. Though not all CEOs and CIOs are working in partnership, the best CIOs in the better companies generally are members of the executive committee and help steer the company's vision.

State government is no exception. Most states now have a CIO, though there were only a few in the early '90s. John Thomas Flynn was one of the first state CIOs in the United States when then governor of Massachusetts William Weld appointed him to the office in 1994. Flynn later became CIO of the state of California, overseeing a staff of 8,000 technology workers with an IT budget of $2 billion. The state had 280,000 employees and total revenue just behind that of GM, Exxon, and Ford.

"The CEO needs to give more recognition to the role of technology, which is more the exception than the rule today," says Flynn.[32] "The CEO needs to understand the role of IT in fulfilling their mission. In state governments today, the CIO still doesn't report to the governor, except in a few cases."

Flynn ultimately traded his chief information officer role for the life of the chief executive officer, as head of TechEd Strategies, a California-based consulting organization under the Community College Foundation, an organization dedicated to advancing education.

Even though he is one of the most tech-savvy senior executives an organization could have, Flynn still finds himself facing the same external pressure faced by all top executives: the pressure to deliver. However, he has realized that senior executives today can be more successful by focusing on shorter-term increments that all support a company's overall strategy.

"For CEOs to be successful today they must manage for the short term," says Flynn. "You've got to show success, and you have to show incremental success."

Success in this area is not only about understanding the technology and what it can do today. It's also about looking forward to see where technology might provide a future strategic competitive advantage. And given the rate at which technology changes, this is a monumental challenge regardless of one's level in the corporation.

THE PRESSURE TO COMMUNICATE

Communicating with the workforce will play an important role in an organization's ability to cope with the pressures outlined above. As

global competition and increasingly savvy consumers cause businesses to pick up their pace to succeed, executive managers will constantly have to refresh and articulate their company's vision and
direction to keep everyone pointed in the same direction and motivated by positive reinforcements of success.

Ensuring that workers can achieve those successes and help the
company reach its business goals requires clarity about everyone's
role in achieving them. Executives clearly recognize the importance
of providing that clarity. The good news from the executive suite is
that 73 percent of executive managers feel that they are communicating to their subordinates the roles of those subordinates' projects or
tasks in the context of the organization's long-term strategy and
direction either well or very well[33] (see Figure 2.9).

However, managers who responded to the same survey felt very
differently. Fewer than 35 percent felt their executive management
had done well at communicating how their specific projects and tasks
advanced the company's overall goals[34] (see Figure 2.10).

This difference in perception is dramatic. The percentage of executives who feel they've done a good job of communicating is almost the
exact opposite of the percentage of managers who feel the same way.

As we will see in the next chapter, this creates a disconnect. That

FIGURE 2.9

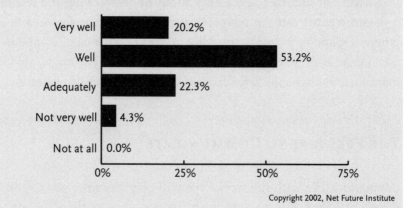

"How well do you communicate to your subordinates the roles of
their daily, weekly, monthly, and quarterly projects and tasks in the
context of your organization's long-term strategy and direction?"

Very well — 20.2%
Well — 53.2%
Adequately — 22.3%
Not very well — 4.3%
Not at all — 0.0%

Copyright 2002, Net Future Institute

FIGURE 2.10

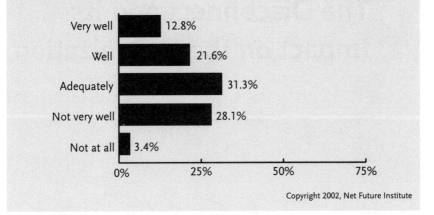

"How well does the executive management communicate to you the roles of your daily, weekly, monthly, and quarterly projects and tasks in the context of your organization's long-term strategy and direction?"

Very well	12.8%
Well	21.6%
Adequately	31.3%
Not very well	28.1%
Not at all	3.4%

can lead not only to inefficiency but to frustration—frustration for the executive who is responsible for overall corporate performance, and frustration for the managers who need to feel that what they're doing is relevant but who may not be sure if the rest of the company agrees.

Even if managers feel that what they are working on is relevant, that sense of relevance may not be well integrated with the overall needs and goals of the corporation at a macro level. If managers feel their work is relevant—even in the absence of good communication from the top—they may out of necessity simply be defining what's relevant on their own, without regard to whether those actions in fact move the company in the direction that its strategy is supposed to take it.

3

The Disconnect and Its Impact on the Organization

Companies now bear the burden of greater expectations and shorter time frames in which to meet them. At the same time, managers, who are responsible for actually moving the organization toward those goals, are being inundated and pressured from all sides. Top executives are responsible for looking toward the horizon, while managers are lucky if they can see over the pile of immediate tasks on their desks.

The fast-forward pace of business life is a factor for everyone at every level. But there is too often a gap within organizations in how well managers' day-to-day activities are perceived—by managers *and* by senior executives—to further the corporate goals. When companies are moving at a dizzying pace, managers who make decisions that are not in tune with the organization's overall needs and goals can take the company a long way down the wrong path before the disconnect is even noticed, much less corrected. And yet simply ponderously lumbering toward a long-range vision without demonstrable successes along the way can spell the demise of not only the long-term strategy but also the chief executive and the executive team who came up with it.

Complicating the problem is the fact that managers and executives have somewhat different constituencies.

CORPORATE TRUTH VS. STREET TRUTH

Top executives tend to deal with the macro issues: Where will the company get the money it needs to pay its bills, to grow, and to reward investors for their investment? In many cases, the chief executive's bosses are outside the company: the board of directors and the investors.

Managers' bosses are inside the company, and have a somewhat narrower focus than does the chief executive. Though managers also deal with the outside world, they do so in a different way. Managers generally are closer on a day-to-day basis to customers and their short-term demands, needs, and expectations—which may not be the same as the demands, needs, and longer-term expectations of the corporate strategy.

This gap can be the ultimate undoing of a leader's strategy. There is inherent potential conflict between the strategy and "will" of an organization's leaders and the motivations and drivers of the individuals who are charged with actually making things happen within that organization.

It is the difference between what I call "corporate truth" and "street truth."

The *corporate truth* is what the chief executive or corporate leadership announces to the world, Wall Street, or even the company's own employees what the business is going to do. This often is based on self-perceived capabilities of the chief executive, who may think, "This is the best course for the company and I believe I can pull this off." Typically, a consulting firm might have been involved in helping define the market situation and perhaps even the company direction, adding external credibility and context to that market situation. The corporate truth usually is based on the direction, vision, and strategy of the company. It is often a "from-the-top-down" pronouncement.

The *street truth* is the reality of the company's workforce, which hears the message and determines—individually and collectively, consciously or unconsciously—how much of that pronouncement actually will be realized. It is the truth of the middle manager who, upon hearing or reading the corporate pronouncement, has thoughts that range from "That's a brilliant idea; our company really can do this," to "What on earth is he thinking? Our customers don't want us to do that." The street truth is more closely aligned with the day-to-day realities of the people who do the work, whether manager or employee.

The Managers' Conflict Between Short and Long Term

The distance between corporate truth and street truth is coupled with the balancing act that senior executives and managers must perform with the long and the short term. Many want to live in the "long-term world" but find themselves dealing with the realities of current business. It is clear that many are torn between the strategy of the long term and the realities of the short term. Here are some comments from executives and managers who responded to a survey on management decisions:[1]

> "Personally: my preference is to decide given a long-term focus. Culturally, I am cornered often into a short-term mind-set."

> "I'd like to think I make decisions for the long term, but in reality I do a lot of 'fire fighting' day to day that involves a lot of short- to medium-term decisions. Also, some long-term decisions turn out to be shortsighted due to the rapid advances in technology that render long-term plans obsolete a lot sooner."

> "Technology is driving change at a much more rapid pace. Five-year plans are out of date quickly. We work from a three-year plan, and it must be updated regularly. Without publicly traded stock, we are afforded the cover to work on annual plans without being forced to make short decisions to placate shareholders or the market. Longer-term decisioning is found more often at senior levels."

> "I pride myself on long-term strategy, but it seems that over the last year, more and more decisions respond to short-term realities. It is time to step back and check out the whole chess game again!"

> "Most small businesses and nonprofit organizations have no choice but to focus on the short term in the current economy. That being said, most do not focus on the long term even when times are good.

My experience suggests they are not different in that regard from most of the larger firms, even Fortune 100 companies that I have worked with over the years."

"The present situation of my company obliges me to make short-term, tactical decisions in order to achieve company success. If the situation was another one, I would focus on mid- or long-term strategic decisions."

THE PRICE OF THE PERCEPTION GAP

College professors have been discussing and teaching a variation of this issue since the early 1970s, when Harvard Business School professor Michael C. Jensen began writing about "agency theory," or the relationship between various people or entities that are attempting to accomplish a given goal.

"Agency theory postulates that because people are, in the end, self-interested, they will have conflicts of interest over at least some issues any time they attempt to engage in cooperative endeavors," Jensen wrote.[2] "When I teach agency theory, I do not find students surprised at the existence of conflicts; they live in the middle of them constantly, and those conflicts which are not experienced personally can be shared in the daily torrent of offerings from the world's media. Because of the universality of the conflict, the danger is that we may take it for granted rather than fail to see it at all." He continues:

> I find that students and business people are excited by the central proposition of agency theory, and that central proposition is not that people are self-interested, or that conflicts exist. The central proposition of agency theory is that rational, self-interested people always have incentives to reduce or control conflicts of interest so as to reduce the losses these conflicts engender. They can share the gains. Moreover, the theory provides a general structure to point the way to a variety of classes of solutions to these problems.

Agency theory states that in an agency relationship there is a contract under which one or more persons, who can be considered the principal, engages another person, who can be considered the agent,[3] to help further the principal's goals. States Jensen:

"The principal can limit divergences from his interest by establishing appropriate incentives for the agent and by incurring monitoring costs designed to limit the aberrant activities of the agent." The reality for all executives and managers is that this "cost" is a real thing, both financially and in effectiveness of the organization.

The costs involved in this relationship—in enlisting someone else to help achieve something—are measurable, Jensen says. They include the cost to the principal of monitoring the relationship—expenses such as budget restrictions, auditing, incentive compensation systems, and operating rules, which help ensure that the agent is approaching the delegated activity in ways that the principal desires. Another cost is bonding expenditures by the agent, which could be contractual guarantees to have finances audited by an accounting firm.

Another way to look at the issue is that because any organization involves delegation, agency cost could be considered the actual "cost" of running an organization. The basic issues involve two variables:

1. Where the authority to make a decision resides, or decision rights

2. Where the best information is located to enable something to actually happen

> **The fast pace of today's business environment, coupled with the constant stream of new information, only increases the potential for the right information to be either unavailable or in the wrong place when it is most needed.**

Herein lies the disconnect: The information needed to make a decision is not always available at the time and location that it is needed. In a corporation, managers may not have enough information about how their work relates to and advances the overall corporate strategy and vision; executive leadership may not have the right information at the right time to understand customer expectations or rapid shifts in the market. And the fast pace of today's business environment, coupled with the constant stream of new information, only increases the potential for the right information to be either unavailable or in the wrong place when it is most needed, causing misalignment of corporate truth and street truth.

Managers and senior executives generally want to be empowered; as we saw in the last chapter, autonomy and challenge were listed by Net Future Institute members as the most important factors in job satisfaction. And every company experiences some disconnect between corporate truth and street truth. However, as more corporate leaders delegate and empower more managers to make more decisions, the risk that those decisions will be disconnected from the corporate vision increases. That in turn can widen the gap between corporate truth and street truth.

"As you go down the chain, knowledge of the organization's objectives goes down, and this can create tension," says Laurence Bunin, CEO of Handshake Dynamics, a New York–based strategic consulting firm that focuses on gaps between strategy and execution.[4] Says Bunin:

> Companies are amazed to find out how poorly the organization's vision and objectives are being received by the middle managers and staff. Sometimes, they refuse to accept the reality of the communications effectiveness, citing the large effort and cost they expended on corporate communications programs and team meetings aimed at communicating the vision.
>
> What we see in a lot of companies is that executive leaders are able to set and articulate a clear vision and strategic direction, but they are increasingly frustrated when managers and staff are not able to implement the vision effectively. This is even more surprising when executives feel that their managers and staff are strong at execution.
>
> What's missing is the ability to translate the vision into tactics. Companies often have leaders that have a strong sense of vision and can set direction, and they have strong managers and staff that can execute tactics. But to be strategically meaningful, the tactics have to be well orchestrated. This requires coordination and planning.
>
> The challenge is finding the time to do the strategic planning necessary to translate a vision into well-orchestrated tactics. This key management skill is becoming a lost art. As a result, executive managers become frustrated that their vision isn't becoming reality, even when they communicate the vision clearly.

The question becomes "How do you delegate effectively while minimizing the costs associated with that delegation?" Narrowing the gap between what an executive pronounces and what a manager executes requires managing for the short term in three important ways. An organization must:

1. Dramatically increase managers' knowledge and understanding of a company's direction. The short-term decisions that dominate managers' lives must be clearly linked to the overall corporate vision— or at least not work against it. To delegate without increasing the distance between corporate truth and street truth, companies must enable managers to make decisions that are consistent with the corporate strategy, even without an executive staring over their shoulders. And those managers must understand how their short-term actions are not merely expedient but actually link them to the corporate vision and further it. The resulting autonomy and opportunity for advancement satisfies the self-interest of the manager.

2. Expect and deliver measurable results. Those short-term moves linked to strategy must individually and collectively produce clearly demonstrable results that validate the vision and enable a CEO to demonstrate that the overall corporate direction is viable. Those results satisfy the self-interest of the CEO.

3. Flow market information back. The corporate strategy must incorporate flexibility and a constant flow of information as a priority, so that strategy is constantly in touch with new information and changing market conditions. This helps keep strategy and short-term actions connected, each with its own role but supporting and reinforcing each other. This is the enabler of the first two directives.

Executives As the New Facilitators

Many senior executives spend considerable time and resources on the delivery of information to their organization's investors. The investor relationship has been fine-tuned over the years. When managing for the short term, more attention has to be paid to internal forces, such as attaining internal "buy-in" from all the managers and their troops. This involves more than getting managers to nod their heads; it means having them understand precisely where they fit and what they actually can contribute.

VOICES FROM THE FRONT LINES

Balancing Tactical and Strategic Decisions[5]

"The decision-making process is usually tied with the objectives required. If objectives are short term, the decision will be based on short term. If objectives are long term (less and less the case), the decision will be mid-term."

"To be an effective leader requires the aptitude to manage/balance the short-, medium-, and long-term aspects of the organization's goals. One can't be ignored for the sake of another."

"Although decisions are made on a short-term basis, they are still inside the guidelines of a long-term vision/purpose. Technology changes, mergers and acquisitions, new industries, and other events require that you make decisions for the short term without losing the vision."

When managing for the short term, an organization's leader will function as a broker between the external and the internal forces, a facilitator of both expectations and execution. That bridging will need to occur constantly, using the kind of incentives that motivate both investors and managers to move in the same direction. This will help close the gap between corporate truth and street truth.

Another reason for the disconnect within an organization is that the long-term interests of the organization do not always coincide with the long-term interests of the individuals in that organization. A company might be aggressively expanding in one area while the manager of that expansion is focused more on getting promoted or moved to a different department as a personal career advancement. An executive has to be constantly aware of his managers' mind-sets.

Managing for the short term is complex; executives must not only articulate the corporate strategy to management but also take a strong leadership position within the organization to ensure that the strategy is properly understood and executed.

"Companies with dynamic leaders minimize cost," says Bunin. "This is different from command-and-control. It really is about setting vision and direction so that middle managers can extrapolate what to do without being told what to do."

This means that organizations should focus on recruiting and personally training top general management with the acumen and skills to build and manage appropriate strategic plans in an uncertain and changing environment. The vision and direction of an organization must be clearly articulated; more important, it must be clearly understood. In addition, top executives must clearly define their role and those of the next-level general management.

"A key skill set critical to success when managing for the short term is the ability to build strategic plans in this environment," says Bunin. "CEOs have a tough enough job acting as intermediary between the investment community and their internal organization. Once the CEO sets and articulates a clear vision and strategic objectives, it is up to the next line of command, typically the COO or unit general managers, to pick up the ball and build strong strategic plans. These top managers need to have the managerial wherewithal to manage the uncertainty, risk, and change in the vision and direction coming from the CEO, and marry it with the operational realities of the business."

While the chief executive is the facilitator between the investment community and the top internal managers, the top internal managers are charged with facilitating between the chief executive and middle management. In this case, however, top internal managers have an added burden. They must not only convey the company strategy accurately but also make it relevant for their individual divisions or areas of responsibility. The middle managers who work for them must know what it means for themselves and their employees, both in terms of what is expected and of what individual incentives there are to deliver on those expectations.

Managing for the short term requires a bridging of the gap between executives and managers. It is about closing the gap between corporate truth and street truth, which can be massive in any organization, regardless of size. It is about getting the organization's response to the demands of the short term in alignment with its overall long-term strategy.

4

Managing for the Short Term vs. Planning for the Long Term

In a series of seminars I recently conducted for small groups of Fortune 1000 senior executives, we discussed long-term strategy compared to the idea of managing for the short term. I had barely mentioned the topic of long versus short term before a lengthy debate among the participants took on a life of its own. Many of the executives lamented that they were forced to be more short-term-focused than they would prefer. They said they found themselves always reacting to events, which they felt kept them from fulfilling long-term strategy.

After the seminar, one of the participants, a vice president of a Fortune 100 firm, approached me and said: "I don't understand why so many people think short term is a negative. I think it's a positive!" This manager understood that managing for the short term can be successful when it is within the context of an organization's vision and strategy. This linkage between the short and the long term is essential; unfortunately, it is the piece that is missing in many organizations and that can lead managers to overlook the positives of the short term.

The concept of managing for the short term has traditionally suffered from a stigma when contrasted to the notion of being a long-term visionary thinker. Short term was considered bad, while long term was considered good. While long term connotes something lasting, well thought out, and perhaps even capable of leaving a legacy, short term brings to mind shallow, reactive, and even shoot-from-the-hip thinking. When everybody already is working as fast as they can and believes that short-term thinking means only reacting to the crisis of the day, it's understandable that a manager might question the idea of focusing on the short term.

However, the reality is that managers today have to be more oriented toward the short term to be better synchronized with their organization's needs. In addition, this orientation allows an organization to be better in tune with the changing needs of customers and their desire for quick gratification.

Once a manager gets over the negative perception that anything short term is inherently bad, short-term execution and long-term vision can begin to be aligned. It is this alignment that can achieve both short- and long-term results, even though the immediate focus is on the short term.

Beyond being demanded by the current business environment, managing for the short term also can have distinct advantages for the manager who understands how to use such methods to support the company's overall strategy:

1. Because it focuses on quantifiable information, managing for the short term is based not on guesswork but on reality. It is, by definition, market-influenced, as customer contacts and interactions actually can cause management to adjust if the organization is set up to do so.

2. By providing incremental forward motion, it offers the opportunity to correct errors quickly before they become disasters.

3. By producing documented immediate results, it offers opportunities to garner support needed to implement projects on an ongoing basis.

4. By focusing on information flow, it provides companies with a fresh influx of ideas, constant updates, and the ability to stay abreast of and capitalize on change.

THE TWO KINDS OF PLANNING

Any company's strategy must be accompanied by planning for how to achieve it. However, managing for the short term means that the planning process must be an evolutionary one rather than produce a fixed-in-stone mandate. And it must recognize that to move forward given the short-term demands of the business environment, organizations must achieve in incremental, short-term steps. Think of it as eating several cookies during the day as opposed to having a big piece of cake after dinner. There is equal enjoyment in both cookies and cake; they're just different. They're also not mutually exclusive.

When a company suffers from the kind of disconnect between corporate needs and corporate behavior that we discussed earlier, it's difficult for any amount of well-thought-out strategy to overcome the confusion that results. Aligning the corporation requires that all soldiers be headed in the same direction and be able to turn on a dime when necessary. Strategy now requires that forward motion proceed by frequent quick steps, which allow greater latitude in how the ultimate direction is reached, instead of giant strides.

Traditional planning has been calendar-based. A corporate mission is developed, usually at the top; it outlines where the company wants to be. The word is handed down, and off everyone goes—often back to be distracted by the day-to-day events that can make the original strategy seem distant or even irrelevant very quickly.

Of necessity, strategic planning has to become more event-driven—not just by major events, which happen relatively infrequently, but by the cumulative impact of smaller events. That is not to say that strategy changes with every whim of the marketplace. It does mean that the planning process is connected to and takes into account the impact of incremental changes in both the externals and internals affecting the company.

Let's look at these differences more closely:

- Planning by events versus planning by the calendar. Event-driven planning is not a once-a-year chore; it occurs more frequently, and is based on what is happening in the marketplace.

Calendar-Driven Planning	Event-Driven Planning
Based on time	Based on events
Produces a document	Produces a sequential process
Is declared	Is interactive and iterative
Focuses on goal	Focuses on process
Creates obstacles to change once strategy is set	Creates environment for constant change
Creates strategy implementers	Creates manager-strategists

- Sequence versus document. Calendar-driven planning develops and promulgates a strategy and then lies dormant until an executive decides a new strategy needs to be devised and promoted. With event-driven planning, strategy is constantly updated—not necessarily changed, but reexamined in light of new information.

- Interactive versus declared. Event-driven planning is based on listening to a constant flow of information from the people and numbers that most closely reflect what's going on in the marketplace. With calendar-based planning, strategy is handed down from the top and likely involves input from or interaction with external consultants.

- Process versus goal. Event-driven planning focuses not only on where a company wants to be but also on the steps involved along the way.

- Creating an environment that embraces change versus creating obstacles to change. Event-driven planning recognizes that the strategy may need to change in incremental ways as its impact is realized day to day; calendar-based planning sets the strategy and lets others deal with its impact.

- Manager-strategists versus strategy implementers. Event-driven planning relies on managers to be able not only to act in alignment with strategic goals but also to recognize opportunities that can influence strategy and supply the information needed to convince others.

Event-driven planning is facilitated by regular communication among key strategy-makers. At Redix International, Inc., a software-development company with offices in Freehold, New Jersey, and Walnut Creek, California, President and CEO Randall King meets weekly with his key managers; those meetings constitute the company's planning process. "We have a long-term plan for items we want to incorporate into the software,"[1] says King. That development plan gets modified perhaps three to four times a year, but not based on any particular schedule. Rather, the shifts in direction occur based on discussions during the weekly meetings about what demands from clients reveal about where the marketplace is heading.

"Every once in a while, something kind of comes out of the blue. If it's a single thing, we're not going to be distracted. Occasionally we'll get several requests for the same thing, or something becomes more important than we had anticipated. Especially in our business, which is market-driven, if you're not looking at where the market's heading and not willing to give it what it wants, you're not going to be in business for a long time," says King.

And when the development plan shifts, the company's chief technical officer not only redirects programming efforts but makes sure to explain to the software developers why the change is necessary and how it affects the company's metrics for success. "It helps them do a better job. If they understand what the market wants, then they can do a better job and suggest other ways in which they might be able to accomplish the same thing," says King. That ability to integrate responses to market demands with clear communication about how changes in the plan relate to the company's overall strategy is a classic example of event-driven planning.

ORGANIZATIONAL PACE VS. INDIVIDUAL PACE

There's a conflict between the perceived time frames in which managers work and the time frames in which organizations work. Across the board, senior executives and middle managers believe that organizations make decisions primarily for the short term. In one survey, only 5 percent of respondents said they believe that, most often, organizations are making management decisions on a long-term basis[2] (see Figure 4.1). Generally, they tend to see this as a negative.

By contrast, these same executives and managers see themselves personally as making management decisions on a medium-term basis[3] (see Figure 4.2). This is also true across the board, for both executives and managers.

Comparing the two responses, it is clear that executives and managers feel their organizations operate more for the short term than they do personally. The obvious question this raises is how in sync managers are with the pace of their own organizations. At a time when companies must deliver quarter by quarter, a primary focus beyond that time frame can be problematic.

In thinking about the implications of these results for the organization as a whole, it is important to keep several things in mind. First, if managers see themselves as managing for a longer time frame than the rest of their organization does, they run the risk of not being able to meet others' expectations, including those of executive management and shareholders. Also, when managers are focused on a time frame different from that of their organization, this can lead to the kind of disconnect discussed earlier, which means the organization is not running at optimum level. It is neither the organization's nor the manager's fault, but it does need to be rectified.

FIGURE 4.1

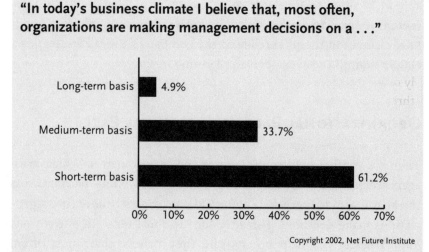

"In today's business climate I believe that, most often, organizations are making management decisions on a . . ."

Long-term basis   4.9%

Medium-term basis   33.7%

Short-term basis   61.2%

0%   10%   20%   30%   40%   50%   60%   70%

FIGURE 4.2

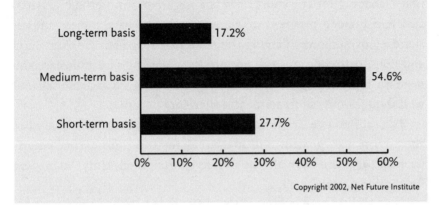

"In today's business climate I feel that, most often, I make management decisions on a . . ."

VOICES FROM THE FRONT LINES

Planning for the Long Term[4]

"My whole area dictates that one look at multiyear projections and tasking. In fact, it often projects for lifetimes, or at least into the next generation. To consider anything less than long term in years is short-sighted. However, short-term goals and objectives are also still at least one to two years at a minimum."

"Most Japanese-based consumer electronics companies have long-term plans (something that they are famous for). But what is just as important is what is called the 'mid-term' plan. Neither short term (quarterly or yearly), nor long term (five to 30 years), mid-term plans deal with three-year intervals. These plans are recalibrated every year for the coming three years."

"Long-term [information services] planning was more lip service than reality until about two years ago. The day-to-day 'tactical' issues continue to dominate, but longer-range 'strategic' planning is beginning. Looking out past the current year is happening, but looking out more than two years is a real leap of faith given technology and infrastructure changes."

And when managers across the board perceive a difference in focus between themselves and their organizations, it can become a self-fulfilling prophecy. Even if an organization is managed well for the short term, managers who don't perceive that it is, or who believe that managing for the short term is a negative, can become dissatisfied and impede progress. If managers do not have a clear understanding of the forces driving the need to manage for the short term and how their decisions roll up into the company's overall plan, any need for rapid change is more likely to be perceived as arbitrary, not well thought out, short term, and therefore negative.

This difference in perception is another distinction between short-term management and managing for the short term. "Short-term management" can also be seen as shortsighted; truly "managing for the short term" isn't.

Let's look at an example of the difference between the two. Let's say a company has been planning to put a new product into production. Even though it would be expensive, there is a lot of consumer demand for it, and it could serve as a replacement for another product for which demand is falling off. However, a new senior management team comes in and decides to adopt a strategy of being the low-cost provider in that market. In addition, retooling the equipment to produce the product would prevent the division from making its numbers.

A manager who is practicing short-term management might scrap the new product, even though he feels it could be an important one for the company over the long term. He mutters to himself about why executive management would abandon something with so much potential for the company.

If that manager were managing for the short term, he might still scrap the product, at least for the moment. However, he would also explore outsourcing production and ways to change the production process so that it could be manufactured more cheaply. He would constantly monitor sales of the aging product and make sure executive management had up-to-date information about those sales. And he would make sure that his division makes its numbers, so that he has the credibility if he chooses to lobby for the product later.

Whether or not they recognize or acknowledge it, managers are increasingly forced by daily and quarterly events to focus on the short term. They just don't necessarily feel good about it. For many managers, it is a source of frustration. No matter the viewpoint, there is widespread agreement that short is getting shorter, and that long term is really not that far off.

The negative connotation of "short term" is a major obstacle to successfully and masterfully managing for the short term. For an organization to be optimally successful, that must change. The balance between strategy and managing for the short term should not be seen as a zero-sum game; the two go hand in hand. Less rigidity in the strategic planning process enables managers to cross the bridge between time-based and event-based planning when market changes require them to do so.

Because they may be better positioned to see short-term moves as pieces of a larger puzzle, senior executives sometimes have an advantage over managers in seeing short-term moves in the context of long-term strategy. Executives tend to see the environmental forces driving the need to make short-term plans—the shareholders, the global environment, the capital markets, as outlined earlier. By contrast, lower-level managers may see only what looks like an arbitrary directive from the top, and follow their own plans for succeeding in the business, which may be based on their contact with customers or their personal desires.

Even when executives already, in fact, manage for the short term, they may not feel they are doing so because they see their longer-term rationale behind those decisions. Meanwhile, lower-level managers may not feel they manage for the short term because they believe that it is something to be done only out of necessity. The challenge is to increase everyone's comfort level with managing for the short term by providing the strategic context for it.

One organization that understands this required linkage between the time-based strategic direction planning process and event-based planning is Standard & Poor's, a leading provider of credit, assessment, and analysis. As a division of McGraw-Hill, one of the world's largest publishers of textbooks and business-related information, Standard & Poor's is best known for creating the famous portfolio index known as the S&P 500.

Vickie Tillman is one of three executive vice presidents of Standard & Poor's; she leads its Credit Market Services, the department that provides domestic and global credit analysis and ratings, risk analysis, and other credit services to the global financial community. Tillman understands the challenge of reconciling events and time-based planning with overall strategy.

"It's an ongoing problem. I've never put together a plan where something didn't happen in the interim," she says.[5] "Some events are within your control, and some are not."

Tillman is consistent with the majority of other executives and managers in how she sees the short and long term. "A long-term plan is two years at most," she says. And like many executives who manage for the short term, she is focused on mission and where the organization is headed, while realizing there will be events along the way that might be distracting.

"You need to have an understanding of your external environment, and your organization has to be flexible enough to manage the changes. You also must have the organization understand the priorities you're putting out there. We said that over the next couple of years we are going to have to do One, Two, and Three. We set up the priorities and rally the institution around them. It's all about setting up priorities that you believe in and sticking to them," Tillman says. She keeps the priorities on a chart board behind her desk, with opportunities by region, by product, and with a to-do list revolving around execution. This approach helps an executive keep focus on what truly matters, which is part of the challenge.

The other part of the challenge is being able to change direction and even back out of a path already started. This is difficult for most organizations once executives, managers, and employees have "skin" in the game. Typically, an individual or group of executives or managers proposes a specific course of action, product line, or company direction. For what seem like the right reasons at the time, there is agreement to move forward with that plan or in that direction. Then a market change or some external event occurs that would have resulted in a different decision had it happened before the decision was made.

The problem is that someone has started moving down a particular path, and someone has assumed "ownership" of that direction.

Responsibilities and authorities have been assumed; budget and staff have been allocated. After all the work that went into "winning" the approval, it is difficult to go back and say, "Things have changed, so let's change what we all agreed to do just a short time ago."

This was one of the refreshing aspects of the early Internet start-ups, which changed—sometimes radically—as the market evolved and shifted. The ability to change rapidly was considered a positive in most of those companies. Granted, they were entering new territory, where gaining early market share could determine leadership positions and experience offered few lessons in how to proceed. One of the lessons these companies taught the business world is the value of having the flexibility to change with market changes, and the ability to integrate those rapid changes with the planning process.

This degree of flexibility means that an organization needs to be able to manage the inevitable inefficiency as projects and the resources already devoted to them are abandoned or reassigned. That is part of the price required for being more efficient in pursuit of the overall strategy. This type of flexibility is not impossible for large, established companies—look at Microsoft's about-face in the 1990s once it decided that the Internet would indeed become important—but they must work much harder to turn on a dime than does a smaller company.

> **The hardest thing to do is to stop something you've already started.**

To effectively manage for the short term, it is necessary to keep checking to make sure that everything that is happening should still be happening. Standard & Poor's has even instituted a process to make sure that it doesn't continue down roads that should be closed off, which sometimes requires hard decisions. Says Tillman:

> Sometimes, things get crossed off because you can't do it. Every so often, we review what not to continue. The hardest thing to do is to stop something you've already started. Every few months we gather and say "What do we put on the 'stop' list?" It's so hard to stop things. I'm in the people business in an enterprise of analysts and thought leaders. I have to remind myself that it is the combined intellect that has come up with something and there is a lot of pride around that.

We have an annual plan, but the agendas of our meetings are around the unified objectives of the executive management team. You have to have joint objectives. Sixty-five to 70 percent should be looking forward strategically and not getting caught in the day-to-day tackling. The big issue is "Is the business aligned?" The senior management has to drill down the message of the strategic vision and what the priorities are. If something happens and we have to put off something, or change something because of events, we have to communicate that all the way down.

You have to constantly clarify roles and responsibilities, and you have to be flexible. We're teaching people to be able to change, which is the most difficult challenge we have. You have to set the example.

It is this mix of vision and planning in combination with day-to-day flexibility that allows an organization to manage for the short term while being aligned with strategy. Event-based planning is critical to check for activities that were approved based on assumptions that may now be outdated, and to reveal projects that should be added to the "stop list." In difficult economic times, this becomes easier; budgets can be slashed across the board and new projects halted across the board. However, you cannot stop all projects, or the organization will have no growth.

"If you wait for the moons to be aligned perfectly, it doesn't occur," says Tillman. "You can't assume a huge event is going to happen, but you have to plan for a certain amount of risk. You must be diverse in product, be able to look at the business and shift resources and priorities into another channel, as needed."

> Unless a strategy or long-term plan is executed in a way that provides both incremental, measurable success and the ability to adjust to changing conditions, it will not survive the pressures and realities of the short term.

S & P has an advantage in that its product line is diversified in markets throughout the world, so that if one market changes in a way that impairs bottom-line results, another market might be simultaneously changing for the positive, thus maintaining balance.

With constant checks to make sure everything being done is still relevant to the overall direction of the organization, the planning process becomes both short and long term. Unless a strategy or long-term plan is executed in a way that provides both incremental, measurable success and the ability to adjust to changing conditions, it will not survive the pressures and realities of the short term and the organization will never be aligned.

Strategic planning may be most successful when accompanied by scenario planning—asking the traditional "what if?" "It means looking at your business and deciding if the trees really grow to the sky or not," says Michael Franks, Director of Strategic Planning for O'Sullivan Furniture; with $394 million in annual revenues, the Missouri-based company is the second-largest manufacturer of ready-to-assemble furniture in the United States.[6] "Most people who have to forecast do so based on what's happened historically. If you do so, you're assuming all trends are linear, and very few things in business are. If you don't have any tool other than history, you're at the mercy of things that have no precedent." Having examined what you might do if all plans go south means that if they do, the company has alternative paths roughly traced instead of having to bushwhack its way through completely untrodden forest.

To perform that examination, Franks says, "You have to really understand the assumptions that underlie your original plan."

The fact is that without the short term, there is no long term. The company overall is forced to deliver quarter by quarter, without much breathing space. However, unless they are tied to an overarching vision that all managers understand, those results will not be relevant to the long-term direction.

STRATEGY: A JUMPING-OFF POINT

One example of a company that aligns its vision and strategy with its ability to manage for the short term is MasterCard International. "Being flexible and being able to respond to problems and opportunities is important," says MasterCard International President and CEO Robert W. Selander. "While we may have set objectives, new things come about and you need to have a reprioritization. You have to walk away from budgeted items sometimes," he says.[7]

MasterCard set a new strategy in 1997, which is still in place. "But you add to it, rather than redo it," says Selander, who reorganized the company so that it could take advantage of new developments, such as e-business and projects that require nurturing. Selander modified the processes for reaching the organization's goals, while keeping them linked to the strategic objectives. "We're recycling through our objectives more than once a year," he says. "An individual will come in and say, 'I was working on this but things changed,' so we adapt. If you have a strategy you believe in, you can motivate your people. If you're successful at one thing, you do more of that."

Another example of a company that links its vision and strategy while managing for the short term is Unilever Cosmetics International. The company, owner of Pond's, pursued a long-range plan for many years. However, in the mid-nineties, there was a shift in anti-aging technology, which caused a shift in the category of products serving that market.

"Pond's had been around for 150 years, so anti-aging made a lot of sense for us," says Mike Indursky, Senior Vice President, Strategic Planning and Marketing, Unilever Cosmetics International.[8] "It brought us up to date, making us modern and very relevant. Our brand was already standing for trust, so we did a market study on where consumer heads were and how it might segment with the new anti-aging focus."

Unilever analyzed the data and conducted multiple segmentation analysis, then plotted the market trends, identifying how the markets would grow and not grow in the future. To keep its long-term strategy and vision synchronized with its short-term actions, it not only conducts periodic market reviews but also regularly reviews segments geographically.

"If we spot an attractive country, our plan has to be able to change," says Indursky. "We're good at reacting. The long-range plan has to be something you can throw things at, and it gives you a discipline. If a country goes bad, what are the reasons you said you wanted to be there in the first place? Without that, it doesn't work. It's okay to vary from the plan, but the decisions must be based on the facts."

The difficulty in reconciling the long-term plan with the realities of the short term cannot be overestimated. Often, there is a disconnect because of the measurement metrics. Organizations must more tightly link long-term plans to day-to-day realities. They also must align the metrics to motivate managers at every level, which sometimes means real-time corporate support for the individual manager faced with unexpected market changes.

"The person running the country owns the P & L, so that's where you need the corporate discipline. You need a process that doesn't allow someone to do as he wishes," says Indursky.

"The onus has to fall back on the governing body. The manager needs to show why deviation from the plan is the right thing to do. There should be numbers against it, and it should be for the greater good of the organization."

ATTITUDE ADJUSTMENT TIME

Clearly, working with two types of planning requires a certain amount of attitude adjustment. Managers and executives alike need to understand that saying they manage for the short term is no longer a negative but a necessity—and can be an effective way to function.

The idea that a series of reactions to events actually can be good for a business, rather than bad, is not intuitive. Many managers feel that they work all day just "putting out fires" and that they "don't get any actual work done."[9] In fact, "putting out the fires" can be a major benefit to the organization. It may not move the individual manager forward in his or her mind, but it may move the organization as a whole forward. It's easy to forget that even if it doesn't feel productive personally, a doused fire that allows a subordinate to become productive again or helps colleagues tackle their work can benefit the organization as much as a task that helps the individual achieve his or her personal targets and goals.

No one questions the need for firefighters to respond quickly to events when they occur. Corporate firefighters are doing the same thing, and they can be the most valuable people in the company. The trick is to tackle the fires that are the most threatening to the company's immediate needs. Firefighters often battle blazes by digging a trench or setting afire a swatch of forest to prevent a fire from spreading; the line is called a firewall (just as the software that helps shield a company's computers from the outside world is called "the corporate firewall"). It may be helpful to think of the daily firefighting done within corporations as digging the firewall that will keep the fire from bringing down the entire forest. In some cases, "putting out a fire" may be the one thing that most benefits the company.

However, to expect employees and managers to think and act in this way, companies must compensate them for doing so; otherwise, self-interest alone will dominate any concern about strategy or the corporate benefit. Self-interest has to be aligned with corporate strategy, and compensation is one way to do that.

Managers become frustrated because they often feel that the short-term demands placed on them are a negative, and that the "short-term stuff" isn't as important as "long-term stuff." They fail to recognize that in today's business environment, managing for the short term is a reality with which everyone is having to come to terms.

The issue is not going to go away. "I spend time trying to figure out what skill sets our students are going to need in the future," says Tyler C. Tingley, Principal and Chief Executive Officer of Phillips Exeter Academy,[10] one of the oldest and most respected private secondary schools in the United States. Graduates of the school, just an hour outside Boston, with its sprawling campus comprising 118 buildings widely dispersed over 471 acres, enrolled in 94 colleges and universities in 2001.

Tingley, who has run the academy for five years, finds himself facing the same short- and long-term issues for which the school is

---

VOICES FROM THE FRONT LINES

Mixed Feelings[11]

"With the changing lifestyles and work styles that have become the fad, it is difficult to formulate and maintain a management style. At this time, I am not sure if this is positive or negative."

"Short-term thinking (or no thinking at all) is the biggest threat to our organization. Were I responding for (some) other managers I would say short term is by the minute and long term is by the day. Breaking out of this cycle is immensely difficult, as it is driven by intangibles, such as culture and style, from the top down."

preparing its students—issues that will sound familiar to every executive and manager. Says Tingley:

> In school organizations, when it comes to short term and long term, there are two major problems. There are fewer people who have the time to do the long-term-driven things, so a lot is crisis-driven. The second issue is of multiple constituencies. There are parents, students, the community, academics, and trustees. I go through the calendar a year in advance and block out periods of time to focus on long-term programs and planning. I guard that time zealously. The short-term stuff just happens. I have to prioritize it a lot and delegate, and I have learned to give myself time to do serious thinking.

It is this "serious thinking" time that cannot fall by the wayside when managing for the short term. This is a critical difference between short-term management and managing for the short term. Managing for the short term, though driven by markets and even crises, still requires an overarching vision of purpose and an understanding of where you and the organization are headed. Remaining highly adaptable to situations while focused on overall direction, both personally and organizationally, can provide balance to the individual executive and manager. It is this balance that allows managers to feel good about managing against what appear to be shorter- and shorter-term goals and objectives, while delivering on tougher and tougher expectations.

THE CFO AS SHERIFF

An often-cited impediment to change is the finance department; in one survey of both executives and managers, finance was named the single biggest departmental obstacle to change (see Figure 4.3).[12] Responsible for monitoring the comings and goings of the company's money, the chief financial officer is often seen as the one who won't fund a new project that the proponent is certain will help the organization become more productive, more efficient, or more profitable. When that money isn't forthcoming, the CFO frequently is the one who takes the blame.

However, blaming the CFO for an organization's shortcomings is like going after the sheriff for enforcing the law. Like the sheriff,

FIGURE 4.3

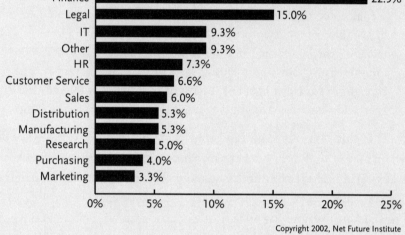

"Which of the following departments presents the greatest impediment to change?"

Department	Percentage
Finance	22.9%
Legal	15.0%
IT	9.3%
Other	9.3%
HR	7.3%
Customer Service	6.6%
Sales	6.0%
Distribution	5.3%
Manufacturing	5.3%
Research	5.0%
Purchasing	4.0%
Marketing	3.3%

Copyright 2002, Net Future Institute

finance is merely applying numbers to the corporate strategy; the "law" he's enforcing is the company's budget. Like the chief executive, he has a broad view of how an individual department or initiative supports (or doesn't support) the overall corporate goals, and he must often be the "bad cop" to the senior executive's "good cop" (sometimes he must even be the "bad cop" to the CEO himself).

The CFO also is often one of the prime voices calling for the quantification of everything. The finance department works with numbers, and any benefit that can't be quantified doesn't exist on the spreadsheets by which it lives.

To effectively manage for the short term, any executive who wants his operation to produce demonstrable results quarter by quarter must look at the information flow within the corporation, how individual managers are enabled to use that information, the integration of corporate strategy and day-to-day "street truth," and how all of these factors can be used to improve the organization's numbers.

For example, a consumer electronics company's strategy might be to enter a new market overseas and compete on features rather than price. Executives would need to be sure that product developers are aware of the strategy so they focus on providing state-of-the-art design. They would ensure that the results of initial market research were available not only to marketers but to designers as well, and that managers in the new market were empowered to plan marketing strategy based on those results. And they would examine the test-marketing results for clues to new products that might prove profitable.

All of these processes must also feed into how the corporate strategy is developed and executed. If they are aligned, the budget the CFO has to enforce will be a truer reflection of what the company wants to achieve.

II

MANAGING THE ORGANIZATION FOR THE SHORT TERM

5

It's All About the Numbers

THE QUANTIFICATION OF BUSINESS LIFE

Traditionally, making the numbers has been defined primarily in terms of revenue: keeping a project within budget, making a sales quota, or meeting revenue forecasts. However, today making the numbers has a much broader meaning, and is even more important for both individuals and organizations.

Human relations, capacity planning, performance—in a host of areas, numerical models and standards are replacing anecdotal evidence, intuition, and guesswork. On an individual level, this means getting a performance review that puts an employee within a certain numerical rank; that number can spell the difference between staying employed and being laid off when times get tough. On a corporate level, it means applying a dollar figure to the lifetime value of a customer, creating mathematical models to gauge the probability of customer actions, prioritizing projects based on numerical grades, or hitting revenue targets not just in an absolute sense but in exactly the way that Wall Street expects.

To "make the numbers," companies must first establish them. To manage for the short term, everything that can be quantified must be quantified, and activities must be measured in "units." In today's fast-paced business environment, with tighter and tighter margins and time frames, having numerical processes in categories across the board enables managers to measure performance and recognize problems quickly. Making the numbers then becomes the foundation for both short- and long-term success.

There are rewards—some overt, some unstated—for making the numbers. At the departmental level, funding for new business development or growth is likely to be more easily obtained by a department that is making its numbers. At the personal level, the manager who consistently makes the numbers is the one who moves up or receives additional responsibility. Those who make the numbers in extremely difficult times might even receive extra attention and reward.

With this almost fanatical focus on making the numbers, much attention is paid to surviving another day, week, month, and quarter. In many cases, less attention is paid to how a company grows long-term and what it ultimately stands for. This is especially true in tough economic times, when every expenditure is scrutinized, every new hire is questioned, and only plans with measurable, short-term results are approved.

Several factors are driving this move toward the quantification of business life:

- The pressure on the bottom line. To reduce costs, supply chains are becoming tighter, so that products must be more closely monitored in real time to reduce the amount of inventory, prevent backlogs of supplies, and meet changing customer needs.

- The dominance of the database. The emergence of sophisticated database storage and retrieval technology enables companies to capture and manipulate an enormous amount of data. That ability leads to increased measuring capabilities in many areas. And because technology tends to work with specifics rather than abstractions, those measurements usually involve numbers. For example, it's much easier for software to generate a numerical average of responses to a multiple-choice question than to give a general sense of respondents' additional written comments.

- The need to compare. Quantification helps ensure that apples are compared to apples and oranges to oranges. It allows the productivity of one operation to be measured in real time against the productivity of another operation, so executives and managers can drill down to management and employee performance. With real-time comparisons of employees performing similar functions, it's easier to track individual worker productivity, no matter where in the world the worker is located.

- Technological advances in analyzing customer behavior. Technology allows more sophisticated examination of customer interactions. In addition to forecasting future customer behavior, technology also allows customer satisfaction to be factored into compensation plans.

- Legal constraints. A litigious society has put increased pressure on human resources departments to document that personnel decisions are made equitably and protect employee rights. As a result, companies have increasingly resorted to incorporating some sort of numerical ratings in making hiring and firing decisions.

- Wall Street and shareholders' demands for hard data.

LEARNING TO LIVE BY THE QUARTER, MONTH, WEEK, DAY

To understand this focus on the numbers, it helps to examine closely the corporate subcultures that have always had to live by the numbers. For example, sales departments are particularly well suited for managing for the short term. The types of challenges this environment presents are nothing new for salespeople, who have always been measured and compensated by the numbers. They live and die by how many sales calls they make, by how many orders they write, and particularly by how many dollars come in at the end of the month.

Sales is perhaps the ultimate area where numbers count. Sales is, by definition, managed for the short term; generally, a sale is not a sale until the money comes in the door. Sales results speak for themselves: A rep either does or doesn't make quota. And if the answer is "doesn't" for very long, the rep is gone. Even in companies where "relationship selling" is the norm, sales reps are still focused on short-term results. If the relationship doesn't mean an immediate sale, chances are the rep's call log has to reflect that the customer at least has been contacted to determine if his or her needs are being met. And the rep is simultaneously thinking not just about that one customer but also about other customers who do need something that month.

Sales reps know that if one product isn't selling, the rep for a pharmaceutical company can't simply go back to his supervisor and say, "Well, physicians just aren't prescribing this drug anymore, so let's reduce the sales quota." If one product isn't selling, you promote another. You find different customers. You figure out a different way to promote it. In short, you focus on doing what works.

The focus on the numbers doesn't let up just because a company may be under pressure; if anything, difficult times intensify that emphasis on quantification. AT&T has been facing challenges in a shrinking long-distance market, and stiff competition in its expansion areas. The challenge of making the numbers falls especially heavily on the sales force.

AT&T sales executives frequently—sometimes even daily—get an e-mail memo from an executive vice president that says, "What did you do to increase shareholder value today?" The memo doesn't say, "What did your division do?" or "What did you do yesterday?" The three most important words in that phrase are "you," "increase," and "today." AT&T also sends similar notes focusing on sales revenue.

Such memos underscore the fact that a short-term focus on the numbers also is tied to the longer-term strategy of increasing shareholder value and departmental revenue.

THE DEATH OF THE LOW-HANGING FRUIT

Anyone in sales understands the phrase "low-hanging fruit" when they are told to go after it. It refers to the relatively easy sales of a product or service to the most obvious targets. The low-hanging fruit might be the largest customers, the newest, the biggest spenders, or those who buy the latest or most profitable of that company's products. Low-hanging fruit is more abundant in great economic times, when increased consumer spending drives creation and manufacturing of an increasing number of products and services and more businesses buy more.

The reality is that just about every sale still has to be made, and at any given moment, some of the obvious candidates aren't buying. This could be because of internal reorganization, shifts in company strategy or direction, or even a change in short-term tactics. In an economic downturn, it becomes even more difficult to make what might be an easy sale in boom times.

Of course, the concept of low-hanging fruit means different things at different levels of the organization. To senior management, it might strictly be a view of numbers. Executives might say, "We know we can sell 10 percent of our goal within the first week" if that is what the company generally has garnered when launching a new product or service. This is based on past experience and track record. Sales management might pass the sales goals along to individual salespeople.

Moving within management levels to the ultimate salesperson— the one who actually has to go visit the customer and close the deal— the low-hanging fruit may not seem so low.

"Most of the fruit is not definitively low-hanging," says longtime sales executive Art Cohen, Senior Vice President of Advertising of ACTV, Inc., a New York–based company that creates and markets technology for addressable and interactive advertising and is backed by Liberty Media and Motorola.[1] "It's not that clearcut anymore. Companies change more rapidly today and their competition changes, so what used to be defined as low-hanging fruit may now no longer be, and other companies may emerge in their place, especially in a difficult economy. It's all really a numbers game."

In good times, with the economy and business humming on all cylinders, it might take 20 phone calls to get five meetings that result in two sales. In tougher times, the numbers might change to, say, 40 phone calls to get five meetings that result in one sale. It simply takes more work to make a sale or close a deal. The concept of low-hanging fruit is fraught with peril, because in a down market, the idea can provide false expectations that never can be realized in anticipated time frames. However, when managing for the short term, every aspect of business, whether it be sales figures, products produced, or market need, must be precisely quantified.

"It's definitely about the numbers," says Joseph Hovancak, Sales Center Vice President at AT&T.[2] Hovancak is responsible for 120 employees covering four states, with a team that is responsible for selling a host of communications products and services to medium and large business customers. Part of his responsibility involves not only making his numbers for corporate, but also ensuring that his entire team makes its numbers—in the hundreds of millions of dollars—as well. Says Hovancak:

> We sell voice, data, Internet hosting, equipment, and managed services. A quota is allocated for each service and it is expected that these quotas be achieved. For the shareholders, it is about growing revenue, so it is important to manage optimizations (pricing down our existing revenue base) to minimize losses (maintaining our customer base) and to make the budget. It is also important to make the productivity numbers for each service and ensure participation by every account executive. For example, one salesperson might be at 150 percent of quota but another at 20 percent. Our goal is to create a culture where people grow, and everyone makes their numbers.
>
> At the beginning of every day, I roll up my sleeves, review my plan, and take action. I am prepared to do whatever it takes to assist my teams; that's what it takes today. If you want to make the numbers, you need to lead by example. A strong and supportive leadership team is one of the keys to success. It's very simple: If more team members are achieving their goals, we have better numbers. We utilize contests to build momentum, create teamwork, and have fun. Each week one team competes against another. We have trips and cash bonuses to ensure that everyone is participating.
>
> It's about the team seeing, hearing, and feeling what's going on. Results are posted everywhere. Celebration calls are scheduled to recognize significant achievements. When there's a big win, every player who contributed is recognized and details about the win are shared. If someone is working hard but they're not making the numbers, a mentor will be assigned to help the team member achieve their goals. The key is to determine if it is a "skill" or a "will" issue.
>
> To make your numbers, you have to have a plan. It's about knowing the objectives, knowing your customers, having a plan,

and executing the plan. The way to look at it is that between 8 A.M. and 5 P.M., that's show time. If it doesn't generate revenue, then don't do it. No sale is easy. You have to work for every sale, but every sale is possible. At the end of the day a person should love their job, they should listen to their customers, and of course, make their numbers.

LETTING THE NUMBERS DO THE WORK

Numbers can be a strategic weapon in the hands of the manager who can quantify a proposal's benefit or lack thereof. By demonstrating a particular project's financial impact, a manager can let the numbers do the work of persuading management of his or her point of view.

That ability can be key to advancing an executive's career to the uppermost levels of the corporation. Among Fortune 700 CEOs, one-third held positions in either finance (22 percent) or sales (11 percent) at some point in their careers.[3] A deep understanding of a company's customers and how they provide its revenue streams becomes particularly important in light of the fact that CEOs overwhelmingly tend to come from within a company's ranks. A study of 476 private and public companies from 25 countries and 50 industries showed that only about 15 percent of CEOs come from outside the corporation.[4]

Nowhere is the heightened importance of the numbers seen more clearly than in technology departments, which are often responsible, directly or indirectly, for an increasingly important part of any company's expenditures. Even when technology spending itself is down, the technology-based processes that IT is responsible for initiating or maintaining have a significant impact on the company's ongoing expenses, which in turn affects its profitability.

With the ongoing integration of the Internet into every company's business strategy, chief information officers are increasingly moving beyond the numbers of technology to the numbers of the business itself. It has been some time since the role of the CIO was simply to keep the machines that support other areas of the company running. As a strategic competitive weapon, information technology now creates vital links between a company and its customers, business partners, and the outside world in general. And managers are finding that the most effective way to persuade others of the impact of technology is to let the business numbers make their case for them.

Fred Marshall, Chief Technology Officer for Berendsen Fluid Power, one of North America's largest distributors of hydraulic and pneumatic equipment, was faced with a common managerial dilemma. The company was interested in using a sophisticated data-networking technology that Marshall felt was ahead of its time and could be a problem. His answer: Use the numbers to make his case:[5]

> We adopted them for one of our internal networks. The [technology] provided no benefit to the systems of our customers, though there was tremendous benefit to our internal customers.
>
> We created a help desk system. The intent was not so much to solve the internal problems, though it certainly helped do that. The value is in the management reporting. It allowed me and the company to see which piece of equipment was causing the greatest amount of trouble. We keep statistics on how many calls each technician handles, how long it takes to close a ticket. Looking at those statistics, it became clear that if we adopted this technology for all our networks, instead of needing about three technicians per 100 employees, we would need about eight per 100 employees.
>
> I went to the CEO and told him I needed more space in the building, because I would need to have 65 technicians just to serve our 800 employees. I showed him the statistics, the reports that documented that. It was a combination of that (the reports) and looking at the lack of any real benefit to our external customers.

Berendsen also has a system that applies "the numbers" to the often-tricky process of prioritizing service calls performed by the company's technicians. Conversations between technicians and distraught users were becoming, well, "animated." The company needed to find a way to ensure that technicians were working on the most important problems instead of those sent in by people with good connections, or those that were quick fixes and could boost the technician's own work statistics.

> The system prioritizes what's most important for them to work on. If they're walking down the hall to do something and their pager goes off and sends them to do something else, it has a priority that's

higher than whatever it was they were going to do. We have priorities from 1 to 10. The system sets the priority based on a user's answers to a set of yes/no questions that the help desk person asks when they call in with a problem—things like "Can you perform your primary function? Is the problem affecting others in your group?" Depending on their answers, the system assigns a priority.

We've been told that IT employees say, "My job is so well-defined that I know I get to do every day what I need to do." They know that what they're working on for the company is really what the company needs.

The monitoring systems Berendsen has set up also have other benefits in quantifying what's going on. The systems also can profile employee behavior:

> Every department and manager has productivity statistics on every employee: the number of calls taken, the time on the phone. We had one employee who quit yesterday, but we knew three weeks ago she was going to leave. We had noticed the number of calls she was handling had gone down, the duration of the calls, the number of cell phone calls. She wanted to stay off the phone because she was looking for another job.

MEASURING THE INTANGIBLES

Sales departments have the advantage of using numbers that are fairly straightforward: number of units sold, dollars of revenue, profit per unit sold. But as the world shifts to a more information-based economy, an increasingly large proportion of the value of any company lies in intangible assets. The issue of quantifying nonfinancial assets and performance is beginning to attract global attention.

The Global Reporting Initiative, funded in part by the United Nations, has issued guidelines it hopes will help elevate corporate reporting on social and environmental performance to the same level of accountability and measurability as financial reporting. Guidelines for measuring and reporting performance in such areas as energy usage, biodiversity, and human rights have been tested by multinational corporations from 10 countries, including such well-known names as Panasonic, Halliburton, Ford Motor Company, General Motors, Procter & Gamble, and Nike. The goal is to give companies a way to report information that can be compared in the same way that revenues, earnings, and operating expenses are compared now.

Other companies focus on such things as measuring innovation, good relations with business partners, employee satisfaction, and leadership. Skandia Insurance Company Ltd., the $16 billion Swedish insurance and financial services firm, was one of the pioneers of what is called "nonfinancial disclosure," covering intangibles such as those mentioned above.

In 2001, the company revised its process to focus on the information that is most useful to its stakeholders, says Jan Hoffmeister, Vice President of Intellectual Capital Management for Skandia.[6] Also, given the heightened awareness of the need to compare intangibles accurately, the company wants to ensure that it is in alignment with other initiatives such as the Global Reporting Initiative. Says Hoffmeister:

> Every company is competing for resources and for attention. We all have to tell the outside world—potential investors, customers, employees, regulators—what we are and what we stand for so they will want to invest in us or join the company or buy our products. The global attention being paid to nonfinancial disclosure has a lot to do with the new economy, where nonfinancial assets are driving the future creation of value. We have to be good at managing that, and we have to be good at telling people how these value drivers look, and what is their potential for driving value in the future.
>
> Skandia is a huge financial services company, and many of the people who have money invested with us in variable annuities, mutual funds, etc. are investing primarily for their retirement. To the extent that we can through our actions motivate other companies to disclose high-quality nonfinancial information, it would help the people who invest on behalf of our customers and reduce the risk of the investments, increasing ROI for our customers and thereby increasing Skandia's revenues.

Hoffmeister says the company is developing a conceptual framework for how to organize the information so users can make sense of it. "The data has to be capable of being understood by the reader. In the old days we learned how to read a balance statement; we have not been taught how to look at nonfinancial information."

That means the company is refining the principles on which the information that is used to measure nonfinancial assets is chosen: principles such as relevance, accuracy, usefulness, timeliness, and consistency. "If the reporting company is reporting on these value drivers, the user has to be able to form an opinion about how they will impact future value creation," says Hoffmeister. "You have to be able to predict the impact, the consequences of that data. For example, if we measure how loyal our customers are, you should be able to look at how that might affect future cash flow." At Skandia, that means narrowing the number of measurements and focusing them more closely on the ways in which investors and employees need to use the information. A later wave of information gathering about how the data is used will involve other stakeholders, such as customers and business partners.

Skandia's example demonstrates that the quantification of business life doesn't just mean financial numbers. It means translating subjective information into data that can be compared and analyzed on an objective basis.

GOING BEYOND MAKING THE NUMBERS

When turning every decision and action into numerical equations or metrics, it is important to keep sight of why you and your organization are there in the first place. This is sometimes difficult when the work pace is frantic and market pressures mount. That is the lesson of Southwestern/Great American, Inc. Founded in 1855, it is the oldest direct sales company in the United States.

Southwestern/Great American, Inc., comprises several divisions, one of which sells books and other products door to door. The Nashville-based business fields an independent contractor sales force of nearly 3,000 students each summer to market family-oriented, educational products. Great American Opportunities provides consumable products and professional consultants to direct school and other nonprofit fund-raising programs, while Heritage House, Inc., is a mail-order business selling collectibles and books. Family Heritage Life Insurance Company specializes in cancer and intensive care insurance and Southwestern Professional Services and Business Resource is a recruitment company. Other divisions include Southwestern Company UK and Favorite Recipes Press.

The employee-owned and -controlled company has found that being numbers-driven doesn't mean eliminating core company values. Rather, the company feels that having values can support the company in achieving its financial goals.

"Making the numbers only, unfortunately, can make the focus wrong, and it's having too much influence on shares and market perceptions," says Bob Sircy, Vice President and Corporate Controller of Southwestern/Great American.[7]

"It's really about the greed in all of us. We all want our stock to go up, and the short term is more exciting. You can see the results today. However, the most astute investors realize that wealth in the long term is seeing that a company grows."

Southwestern walks a fine line between making numbers and retaining corporate culture. There are quantifications and individual metrics for each company, several of which Sircy serves as Chief Financial Officer. Because one of the companies is a direct-selling organization, metrics include how many doors are "knocked on," how many times the salesperson gets in the door, and how many sales are made. The same type of metrics are used for the other companies.

"We convert sales to units," says Sircy. In addition to obvious unit measurements, such as books, the company even breaks down goals into four-hour segments each day for each student salesperson. This allows Southwestern to gauge results practically in real time. The company installed an SAP system to automate its tracking to allow sales managers to see details of their specific sales forces on a regular basis, rather than have to wait for reports.

Although it focuses on numbers on a daily and even hourly basis, Southwestern takes a more holistic view of its businesses. As do many companies, it creates an annual profit plan and revises it midyear. Employee compensation is linked to the plan, ensuring company-wide focus on objectives.

"We focus on hitting the plan because all bonuses are tied to it," says Sircy. "It's cultural. When we do a good job, everyone knows they share. The hardest part is to teach people that knowing where they stand can improve their performance. People need to know the score. You also need a clear view of the metrics, and people don't always want that.

"Some folks are naturally gifted, but most of us need targets to shoot for. We tell employees, 'If we hit our profit plan, here's what the profit sharing will be.' Unfortunately, investors look at short-term results.

"We try to make the business personal. Sales managers give us information and then we say, 'Based on what you said, here's how much money you're going to make.' We also constantly remind them why they're working for us."

Southwestern realizes that in an economic downturn, values and employee relationships matter even more.

"Salespeople judge themselves on their personal results. In a downturn, they have to rethink how they do business. We remind them of the value of their stock and how they are part of something bigger. Our senior managers are very value-driven. Our philosophy is that we build our people and people build our companies. We also teach people that if you have a problem you go up, and if you have good things you go down," so that managers understand that executive management is there to help, while good news from managers should be shared with the workforce.

"Philosophies are critical," says Sircy. "A company has to stand for something. While numbers are important, the mission is as important. Companies underestimate the importance of a reputation. That affects people all the way through a company. We know, of course, that real value comes from underlying earnings.

"If you don't constantly remind folks of values, they will focus only on numbers. As managers, we have to constantly remind employees of our values and the mission of the company," Sircy says. "Otherwise, you focus only on answering that next phone call. I wonder, long term, if those things have a large influence."

In other words, the mission drives the numbers, and making the numbers furthers the mission.

BALANCING METRICS

The bottom line is critical, but like the budget, it also has to be considered within the overall vision and direction of the organization. This is more difficult in publicly held companies, because analysts and investors are on guard for any threat that might cause a shortfall in the bottom line or have a negative impact on quarterly earnings. Advance warnings from a company or the analysts who cover it can send a share price reeling, dramatically decreasing the stock's value to shareholders virtually overnight.

However, an organization must be careful that a focus on the bottom line not be perceived as a lack of a long-term agenda. If it is, managers may feel less motivated to actively and accurately contribute to any forward motion achieved by that organization—or less capable of doing so. And Wall Street analysts also prefer to see that short-term results support an overarching strategy.

One organization that understands balanced metrics better than most is Consumers Union, which since 1936 has conducted product testing and provided consumers with information, advice, and warnings based on those tests. Its National Testing and Research Center is the largest nonprofit educational and consumer-product-testing center in the world, comprising more than 50 state-of-the-art product-testing labs. In addition, Consumers Union evaluates cars and trucks at its fully equipped auto-test facility.

If anyone understands the value of translating subjective opinion into quantitative data, it is Consumers Union. The organization is best known as the publisher of *Consumer Reports*, which, with 4 million subscribers, is one of the 10 largest paid-circulation magazines in the United States. Consumers Union is presided over by a board of 18 directors elected by Consumers Union members. As the president of Consumers Union, James Guest is charged with creating the vision—and the metrics—for the organization and making sure the 500 employees understand the mission as well as the bottom line. Says Guest:[8]

> We have to balance between the business metrics and the mission
> metrics. We are mission-driven and our measure of success is not

the financial bottom line, but the financial bottom line is a means to an end. For example, we might make more profit from the magazine by charging a far higher price and serving far fewer customers, but financial bottom-line maximization is not our goal. Our ultimate bottom line is how well we advance our mission of working for a fair and just marketplace for all consumers. To achieve that, we need to be financially sound; we have to pay close attention to finances and the financial bottom line to support the variety of things we're doing.

Our business metrics are easy: financial bottom line and market share and growth in subscriptions. We are now creating metrics for the mission success of our enterprise and will use them in measuring progress and success. Along with developing business and mission metrics, we've also reorganized recently. Previously, no one had full bottom-line responsibility for our information products, so we put all the business functions together in one division under one person. We had two different marketing departments, one for the magazine and print products and one for our Web site (the largest paid-subscription site on the Web, with 750,000 subscribers), so we combined those. We had two editorial departments, one for print and one for the Web, so we moved them together. Now we're a one-enterprise, multimedia information provider, and we start with the customer to maximize what the customer wants. There is clear accountability, and we're pushing decision-making much closer to the ground.

Because of financial pressures in the slow economy, we're using a mind-set of managing for the short term to make changes that will drive managing for the medium and the long term. This year we're doing a lot of short-term things to put us on a long-term path.

It is this understanding of the difference in value of short, medium, and long term that helps an organization move forward, even if only incrementally. When managing for the short term, managers must see the metrics for the daily, weekly, monthly, and quarterly activities in the context of the company vision. How those measurements support what the organization stands for and what it is trying to accomplish must be transparent, both inside and outside the organization.

NUMBERS NOW

It's not only large corporations that must operate by the numbers. Harry W. Souza and Daughters is a dairy farm in Turlock, California. With 15 employees and 1,000 cows, it is twice the size of the average operation in the dairy-rich area. Margo Souza, the farm's CEO, says the numbers, which are tracked by special software for dairy operations, are key.[9]

"Every event that happens to an animal goes in the computer. We have to keep track of that calf from the day the cow gets pregnant. We look at things like how much medicine a cow needs, how we can get it for the cheapest price. We check their milk, because we can tell things about their health from the milk."

Just like managers and workers in the corporate world, the cows must "make their numbers" in terms of producing milk. "Some dairies have the meters going on each animal. We don't have the meters going every day on each cow, but on the days we have them tested, we can tell how much each one is giving.

"Their nutrition is extremely important. There's a computer in the feed truck that sets up all the rations and determines what to put in for each group of cows. Each group is fed a certain way depending on what state they're in: whether they're lactating or waiting to have a calf, and so forth. This lets us quantify how much it's costing us."

Souza's farm also grows feed for the cows and monitors how many tons per acre are being produced, because those crop-yield figures and monthly feed stats will determine whether the farm will have enough feed to last until the next time the crops go in. Souza also must monitor the waste the cows produce. Since the waste is used to irrigate the fields, dairies must keep tabs on chemicals such as nitrogen, nitrates, salts, and phosphorus to make sure that the amounts going into the fields do not exceed allowable limits.

That kind of focus on the numbers is not merely a bean counter's idea of paradise. It is documented evidence of short-term success or impending problems that allows the company to move forward on its long-term goals. Numbers are concrete, tangible, measurable. Verifiable, quantifiable evidence can help a manager demonstrate that interim successes achieved in pursuit of a long-term strategy are of benefit *now,* regardless of whether changes in long-term strategy become necessary down the road. For example, if a multinational company opens a new sales office, sales can be measured almost immediately, as soon as sales personnel begin but before the operation is fully staffed. Those immediate successes can spell the difference between funding for a project and an extensive stay in limbo—or outright rejection.

As we will see in the next chapter, there is too much uncertainty about the future for a project to take years to pay off. Thinking "numbers now" can help keep everyone's attention focused on immediate progress.

6

Incremental
Forward Motion

The days of grandiose, long-term, big-production ideas and programs whose benefits will be realized many years down the road are basically gone. This is not to say there is not a need for long-range planning and multiyear implementations of certain types of projects, such as customer-relationship management, facilities construction, or supply-chain systems. Such projects will always be a part of business. But for the most part, organizations need to be geared for shorter and shorter time frames for delivery, even in the context of multiyear projects.

There are several reasons for this:

- **No one has the time to wait.** Not returns-conscious shareholders, not hard-pressed executive management, and not front-line managers being confronted with metrics that require documented performance.

- **The benefits are needed NOW.** Under increasing pressure from competitors offering customers reasons to switch to their products or services, organizations must create and innovate on a more frequent basis to keep customers happy.

- **Personal advancement requires delivering.** With more demands falling all the way down the management ladder, those who deliver quantifiable results will move ahead. Those who do not deliver can be replaced with those who do.

Coping with these pressures requires executives and managers to think in smaller, more modular terms. Managing for the short term means constantly moving the interests of the organization forward, even if that motion seems to be modest.

In addition to helping satisfy corporate demands, this incremental forward motion can ultimately provide individuals with greater inner peace and the personal satisfaction that is needed in a sometimes-frenzied workplace. Knowing how even a small contribution is advancing corporate interests can help alleviate the frustration of constant interruptions and distractions that pack the average workday. The problem is that managers often do not understand their personal contribution to the organization's ultimate objectives, the true value of that contribution, or the scope of the interruptions and distractions.

SHORT-TACKING TOWARD THE HORIZON

Sailors know that you often do not sail a boat directly toward where you're going. A sailboat cannot move directly into the wind; if the wind is blowing directly from its ultimate destination, it must tack at least 30 degrees to either side in order to progress. The boat goes forward by zigzagging its way toward the goal, heading first in one direction, then another, even though neither tack is exactly dead-on toward the ultimate destination.

The length and direction of each tack depends on shifts in the wind, other boats on the water, and weather conditions. Sailors take this indirect forward motion for granted; it's simply the law of physics.

Managing for the short term is like performing a series of short tacks on a sailboat. By learning to tack back and forth well in response to changing external conditions, the "crew" of a company can move the organization forward. This also forces people to work together as a team.

TACTICS FOR INCREMENTAL FORWARD MOTION

There are specific tactics individuals can use to focus both their own tasks and their team-based activities on the incremental forward motion demanded by managing for the short term. In doing so, these tactics also can help individual managers bridge the gap between calendar-based planning and event-driven planning.

Keep It Simple

In the era of managing for the short term, the more complex something is, the more vulnerable it is. Having clear guidelines that help eliminate redundancy and streamline processes can mean both short-term benefit and long-term support of the organization's overall strategy.

At Marriott International, Inc., there is a high recognition of the realities of the short term within the context of a corporate vision, especially when it comes to principles of operation. "We've found it absolutely essential to have values and principles for computing," says Carl Wilson, CIO of the leading hospitality company with more than 2,300 operations in 64 countries and territories. Says Wilson:[1]

> To give us flexibility and to match shorter life cycles, we've established overarching principles for technology applications. First, can we reuse technology we already have? If not, we look at external markets to see if we can buy the application. We only build an application when it is not available in the market or gives us unique competitive capabilities. We've also found that if you're careful about how you buy and apply off-the-shelf software and do serious due diligence in picking suppliers, you can get to market faster.

To follow those principles, Wilson and his team spent considerable time evaluating technology partners and selected three primary vendors to whom they turn for a variety of needs. Marriott invests time up front for continuing, incremental payback over time. Wilson says:

> When developing our CRM strategy five years ago, we visited several companies. It's not just about picking the best technology; it's about picking the best, true partnerships. We looked at the companies' technology and balance sheets. The other important thing is

enforcing standards across your organization. This gives us a lot more speed and takes a lot of complexity out of the decision process.

Wilson tackles all information-technology projects company-wide with an ongoing focus on short-term benefit. Many companies still extensively plan long-term projects only to find that conditions have changed by the time the project is completed—a costly and disappointing finale with no benefit, either at the end or along the way. Wilson continues:

> It's hard to put together three- to five-year plans. Either the technology or the business changes. Rather than trying to eat the elephant all at once, we break out our major initiatives into phases and make sure we get real business value on each phase. Rather than three- to five-year projects, we look at six- to 12-month programs with very tangible value. This came about by looking seriously at our business model and the best way to present information technology.
>
> We create a three- to five-year vision and update, which we refresh every year when we do the budget. We then update it and move it out regularly. It's not an annual exercise; we do it continually. We now review new initiatives every quarter. You have to match your planning and funding cycles to that.
>
> Most companies' budget process starts six months before the next fiscal year. This means you have to guess on an 18-month cycle, and that's too long. Not all the good ideas for the next year can be figured out by the previous August. Some companies want to lock down the budget eighteen months in advance, and that just doesn't work effectively anymore.

Chop It Up

One of the most important ways to create incremental forward motion is to break whatever needs to be done into smaller, more manageable tasks, each of which can be a subset of an overall strategy or plan. This affects both the budgeting and the planning processes at any organization. The advantage of this managing-for-the-short-term technique is that the organization can receive benefits as it goes instead of waiting for them at the end of the yellow brick road.

Shorter delivery times are being required in every aspect of business. Part of the reason for this requirement is that those for whom a project is being developed might not even be at the company by the time a long-term project is done. "Project life cycles have to shrink to combat the problems you have with larger projects," says Ralph Menzano, CIO of South Eastern Pennsylvania Transportation Authority (SEPTA), the sixth-largest public transportation operator in the United States.[2] "People leave more frequently these days, and at the upper levels executive sponsors leave fairly quickly also."

Like Marriott, the transportation authority has learned to chop up its projects. "You have to have deliverables along the way, and you have to have deliverables at least every 90 days. Nobody has the patience for the longer project anymore," he says. SEPTA has a fleet of 1,500 buses and, when combined with rail and subway services, moves about a million people a day around metropolitan Philadelphia. There are 12 depots to service those buses, but there was no system for maintenance. Menzano instituted a program of incremental forward motion, rather than trying to plan (and get approval for) the "ultimate big-bang" system. Says Menzano:

> We had to get 12 groups to agree. We provided all of them with Net access and e-mail, so everyone could share information. Now the mechanics share e-mails, and it increased communications among all the depots. Then, along the way, we started monitoring fuel efficiency. Over the course of a year, because we ended up setting maintenance standards, we ended up with four million miles of additional bus service to Philadelphians with the same bus inventory.
>
> The American mentality is not matched up. There's no big bang theory anymore—it doesn't work. There is no plan, design, and build anymore—business can't wait. Companies have to think in short bites—this is an MTV world.

Don't Postpone the Important Stuff

This sounds like a no-brainer; after all, the important stuff is what needs to get done first, right? But sometimes things can be perceived as *too* important to tackle right away.

Have you ever looked at a health magazine and thought, "Gee, that looks like something I really need to know about; I'll have to read that later"? Or set aside a brochure about planning for your retirement because "I really need to pay some attention to that; I'll wait until I have time to concentrate on it"? Of course, the time to look at it rarely comes, because more and more items crop up to demand your attention. Even if you do get around to that critically important magazine article, it may be so outdated that you simply toss it, unread.

Though on a much smaller scale, this is the equivalent of the big-bang theory of project management mentioned above. Waiting until the right time comes along so you can focus has the same result as anticipating benefits to come at the end of a long-term project. Too often these days, what you're waiting for never appears, or things change so much that by the time it arrives, it is no longer as relevant. If a task or document is important, it must be dealt with in the short term. It should be broken into manageable segments, or parceled out among several people. Just don't put the task aside and wait until you have time—it probably won't come.

The concept of "spare time" is like the "paperless office" or complete compatibility among computers: It could happen, but don't hold your breath. If something truly seems important, you're probably better off making some incremental forward progress with it right away. Doing so will help you determine just how significant it is, and how to tackle dealing with the rest. If the item is important, it will continue to bubble up enough that you eventually find the time to address it more fully. If it's set aside, it may ultimately reappear on your radar screen, but the time may be too late to do anything about it.

For example, TRW Systems decided that to make its business more effective it should dramatically increase its focus in determining what is important. "We'll pass up business if it doesn't have payback," says TRW's Edward Cypert, Vice President and Deputy General Manager of TRW Systems, part of the $17 billion designer and manufacturer of high-technology automotive parts, and space and defense products.

TRW Systems changed its production methods and now analyzes business before it accepts it. "In the past, we didn't necessarily understand the downside of business we were taking," says Cypert. "Now, unless something is more holistic and linked to other things in our business, we do not do it. This is a real transformation. We had put a premium on top-line growth. Now we're looking at the offerings and the quality of the business. This stabilizes returns and the workforce. It also allows us to crisp up our offerings and get us in a position of looking less for 'one-offs.' The big key is getting away from just top-line growth."[3]

Sort by Speed and Scope

Despite the obvious fallout from Internet start-up companies, there are some good lessons to be learned from them about innovative ways to approach business. Bruce Petro, Chief Information Officer of AmericanGreetings.com since 1995, had spent eight years at parent American Greetings, a Cleveland-based company of about 4,000 employees with annual revenue of $2.5 billion. Petro was very familiar with traditional methods of internal technology development, working with "300 IT people" at the parent company. When he changed to lead the technology efforts of the subsidiary, he found himself rethinking what "moving the organization forward" actually meant.

"There's probably a classical definition of productivity, which is not to be confused with efficiency," says Petro.[4]

> Traditionally, it [productivity] was about greater output per worker, but we've always said that to some extent those things don't matter because little we did in developing information systems was repeatable. However, we institutionalized tracking and management systems to prove to management that we were being more productive, so we could say we were getting better. This had validity at the time.
>
> There were internal people who related strictly to numbers, so we dutifully supplied them with numbers. From a labor standpoint, the bulk always was in the development area. The projects were multiyear.

Petro recalls one company project that had more than 100 people working on it for more than five years, ending up hundreds of man-years over budget. "In those days, if you were on time and on budget, no one cared about productivity."

Being first to market with the latest product, the latest feature, the latest innovation mattered above all else. This was true of many Internet organizations. When Netscape first launched in the mid-nineties, for example, new product revisions sometimes occurred within days of one another. The same was true for AmericanGreetings.com. While the time-to-market issue is less significant as Internet approaches have become mainstream, Petro finds the company still faces other time-based issues. Immediately following the New York World Trade Center tragedy, the greeting card company created an internal SWAT team, including total quality control, to create tasteful remembrance cards within one day.

"Time is our enemy," says Petro. "We still find ourselves against the clock."

His solution for managing for the short term was to change the project times for all projects. Says Petro:

> Our rule is to never do a project that takes more than 30 days. The best way to be productive is to do smaller projects. We figured that out in the parent company. There, short was six months to a year. In the Internet space, however, life cycles are much more compressed and there is so much change. Markets, products, competitors, and customers all change very quickly. If you plan too much, the basis on which you made your decision could be invalidated.
>
> If you defined productivity for us, it's really the ability to deliver. I have a fixed budget and fixed time, so we divide the work into very small projects and phase them in. This puts less capital at risk and we can accelerate the benefit, because we drive a portion of the benefit quickly. We have less money at risk per time, and we have less chance of doing things wrong.
>
> We don't keep track of how much manpower it took to complete a task or project; it matters more that it gets done on the deadline with the correct level of quality. The successful CIO has to figure out who he has to convince that he's being more productive and develop the appropriate definition and corresponding measurement. Smaller is better. Besides, a large part of the satisfaction that I derive from my position is being able to see how my staff make a difference in our business in a short period of time.

Two side benefits of Petro's approach:

- People know not to ask for very big, complex projects.

- Because projects are small, his staff and the businessperson making the request end up working more closely together to achieve quick results that are closely tied to the business.

Petro also has a rule of thumb for whether a project is too big: "If it requires you to put a project plan in Microsoft Project, cut the project scope in half."

Focus to the Left of the Line

For most managers, there are certain things that simply have to be done in a given time frame. No matter what task the deadline is attached to, managers need to keep a mental picture of where all critical items stand while making sure they continue to act in the interest of moving their organization forward.

One way to think about what to spend time on is to prioritize tasks and goals not only by what benefits the organization and what doesn't, but also by what benefits it today instead of what will matter in the future. This may sound simple, but think about how many tasks that occur in a given day or month do virtually nothing to move the organization forward. The result can be frightening. For example, is every hour of every meeting you attend worthwhile and causing your business to move forward?

Think of a box divided into four quadrants. The horizontal axis separates things that benefit the organization (above the line) from things that don't. The vertical axis divides each of those categories into things that matter now (which fall to the left of the line) and things that matter in the future.

While many managers may feel they should spend their time and effort in the top right quadrant (see Figure 6.1), on things that will be important to the company in the future, the reality is that managers and executives end up spending considerably more time, effort, and resource in the top left quadrant. This is because outside factors determine much of today's business reality.

If you're managing for the short term successfully, it's important to remember that time spent benefiting the organization today will ultimately benefit the organization in the future. Part of managing for the short term involves learning to live with this shorter-term focus within the larger context of strategic vision. And remember: Current activities may well affect strategy eventually.

FIGURE 6.1

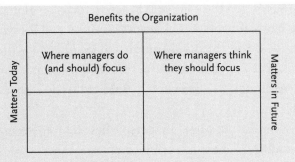

The problem for many organizations and individuals is even more significant than the question of whether to focus on issues that are shorter- or longer-term. Some managers aren't even working in the top half of the quadrant—that is, spending their energy on issues that benefit the organization. This could be because of personal reasons—for example, serious distractions at home or perhaps a job search—or because of business reasons, such as lack of clarity about strategy and company direction.

TEAMS FOR THE SHORT TERM

Incremental Forward Motion with Time-Based Teams

One company that adopted new time frames for new times is Timberland, the $1 billion global lifestyle brand best known for its trademark yellow work boots.

Nathan Swartz founded the company in 1952 when he bought a half-interest in The Abington Shoe Company in Massachusetts. A few years later he bought the remaining interest and, with his sons, made shoes for leading manufacturers for about 10 years.

The company's claim to fame involved the development of truly waterproof boots during the 1960s. The Swartz family changed the company's name to The Timberland Company in 1973, naming it after the brand name of the original waterproof boot.

Sidney Swartz, son of Nathan, was handed control of the company in the '80s, when the company began to focus on global expansion and move beyond boots into women's clothing and footwear.

In the '90s, the third generation moved in when the founder's grandson, Jeffrey Swartz, took the reins of the company as President and CEO. Although the company is publicly traded, the Swartz family controls it.

In many ways, the company personifies the transformation of the ultimate traditional manufacturing company of the '60s—the employees actually made the shoes—into the modern branding company. Timberland now outsources about 80 percent of its manufacturing to other companies in various countries. The inherent skill of the company has become product creation, retail, and marketing.

Facing speed-to-market issues and new competition at every turn, Timberland found itself dealing with a market for which it wasn't particularly prepared. Over the years, the company had evolved a process that took 180 days to deliver a product from product-line conception to launch. The six-month cycle, which involved proper testing and quality control, was ingrained in the culture of longtime employees and managers. Unfortunately, the market had not remained as consistent over the years. Impatient, informed consumers were more willing to try new products and jump on new bandwagons if they saw their peers doing so.

After 19 consecutive quarters of record earnings, why change? one could argue. But top management wanted to scale up the business, and it was not possible with the current product-offering approach. The company decided to change from a product-centric focus to a more customer-centric one. That required major internal transformation, which began in the second half of 2001. The company recruited executives from Nike, Pepsi, and Procter & Gamble to help lead the change throughout the organization.

"We needed a more fundamental view of who our customer is," says Bruce Johnson, Vice President of Human Resources, who was brought in to Timberland to help effect the company transformation.[5] "We want to be a global lifestyle brand, and we weren't measuring ourselves against what the world looked like."

While Timberland creates a long-range plan, which covers three years, its product cycle is 24 months.

"We're also concerned with the culture," says Johnson, who views management at Timberland as a player–coach relationship. "We're hiring people to drive change while understanding the culture we have."

Timberland does not heavily focus on processes. "We're crisis-driven, not process-driven," says Johnson. "This focuses people on getting tasks done. The pace here is frenetic. Sometimes we tend to have to reinvent; sometimes we build small fires to get things done. The people long on analysis will not be very successful here."

To increase managers' and employees' sense of the context of their decisions, Timberland started trying to move those decisions down the organization to the lowest possible levels. To change its product time frames, it created six specific business units in addition to product development, so that a group focused on women's casual shoes would not also have to focus on, say, men's urban boots.

Timberland attempts to get the managers and employees on board in advance by spreading the vision and strategy. "We try to share with them where we want to go," says Johnson. "We want to be a $3 billion company, so we need to fix things at the employee level. We organize around our strategic objectives. There had been lack of clarity and focus."

Timberland wanted to change its planning time frame while retaining its company culture and focus on design and product quality and testing. "We needed to be able to react more quickly," says Johnson. "If a colored boot happens to be selling well, we wanted the ability to be more nimble." Management decided to change the formula for how it makes products. It created three separate teams:

- The Research Team: This group focuses on 365-plus day projects, with a longer-range market view and no need to focus on short-term product sales.

- The 180-Day Team: Since this was the backbone of the company that helped it make its numbers for 19 consecutive quarters, it stayed in place. Its focus remained on creating lines of products, such as an entire line of children's shoes for an upcoming season. The primary focus of this team is product creation.

• The 90-Day Team: This team was created to react quickly to fashion issues or unexpected sales of particular items within a season. The goal of the team is to be able to react to market forces within 30 to 90 days, with modified products. The primary focus of the team is product modification or adaptation. Timberland found that they could create career paths with the other teams.

"People today need a quicker mind-set," says Johnson. "Our business can change tomorrow. We have to be more nimble, because there's more pressure every day."

Timberland's chief executive set a goal for the company to be a "Top Three" employer worldwide, at the same time moving to shorter and shorter time frames in terms of planning and reacting.

Timberland's approach allows one group to focus on more tactical and operational issues while others are focused on the future, assuring that those immediate tactics and operations continue to take the organization in the right direction. In other words, the time-based team approach allows Timberland to focus on longer goals while managing for the short term.

VOICES FROM THE FRONT LINES

Time-Based Thinking[6]

"When I was in sales we were on 30-day cycles—short term was one month, long term was one to two years. The idea of short term and long term depends upon the product and consumer purchase cycle to a large extent."

"The short- and long-term issue is primarily contingent on the business cycle of a particular organization. If the business is in a transition of uncertainty, it will have short-term focus. However, execs rarely are able to balance short- and long-term investments to assure some degree of stability in the organization."

"I'm not consistent in my use of these terms. It really depends on the context—for example, in terms of corporate planning I think of short term as anything less than a year, and long term as three to five years."

The approach has been very successful: Timberland has almost 200 stores in 12 countries and ranks number 54 among "best companies to work for."[7] But there are dangers to this approach if a company focuses only on the short term. At a multi-billion-dollar insurance company with offices throughout the United States, the company created a group called Advanced Systems Labs to ensure that the organization continued to innovate while performing shorter-term operations. Says Karl Schoen-Rene, Second Vice President of the company's Information Systems Organization:[8]

> Management decision processes need to change, but I am not sure these changes are all time-related—that is, that they just need to be faster.
>
> We had bought some of this hype and made several technology decisions based on what the individual who was making the decision knew, and not based on gathering of facts and doing any sort of cost/benefit analysis. We are now suffering through some pain because of the process—or lack of process—used to make these decisions.
>
> This subject is tightly coupled with empowerment and risk taking. In my current culture, we are encouraged to take risks, try new ventures, but don't spend any more money . . . as the reality of the economy takes hold. Luckily we are not driven by the stock market, or these pressures would be very intense. As it is, we can make longer-term decisions than most of our direct financial services competition, which I believe will be beneficial in the long term.
>
> The decision window is no longer three to five years. In some industries it may be down to one year, but for significant decisions, I can't see it going much below that. After all, until they change the financial reporting process, companies are still allowed to produce annual reports upon which they can be compared by the majority of the significant investment houses.

> **Breaking projects into smaller and smaller pieces can help in cost control and produce less failure in a career.**

Schoen-Rene understands the challenges of meshing the shorter-term tactics with longer-term strategy. "Breaking projects into smaller and smaller pieces can help in cost control and produce less failure in a career, which are not necessarily bad by themselves. But sometimes it can cause people to be shortsighted. They need to look beyond tomorrow or they won't be investing in the future. You have to be careful not to lose sight of the vision."

In the case of Timberland, teams that focus on the longer term don't find themselves buried in day-to-day issues, ensuring that the company is always looking forward. The insurance company's advanced systems labs keeps the company on course. The group comprises a core group of people as well as rotational spots.

"It takes a different kind of thinking," says Schoen-Rene. "You get an opportunity to research and understand the direction of the technology and of our industry. They publish information for the company internally. The CEO gives them permission to bring things forward and pilot them."

By allocating people and resources to time-based teams, organizations can optimize the performance of day-to-day operations while making sure they have a future to work toward.

Incremental Forward Motion with Task-Based Teams

Another team approach to managing for the short term involves organizing around tasks or projects. In this approach, resources can be adjusted depending on the size, immediacy, and importance of any given project relative to the given time frame. This allows managers to be more flexible in shifting priorities, and provides incentives for everyone on the team to contribute. More important, customer needs can be met on a more immediate basis, which leaves them feeling better served. One example of this approach is in automotive repair.

The automotive repair industry works on a flat-rate billing basis, an industry standard. If a car owner needs, say, a water pump replaced, a dealer can simply look in a book and see the cost, including parts and predetermined time to repair, and quote that cost to a customer. The key is that the flat rate has a specific amount of time assigned to it. The performance against that flat rate—that is, how many hours were billed compared to how many hours were worked—is called the "efficiency rating." So if one technician worked 40 hours in a week and flat-rate billing that week was 40 hours, the efficiency rating would be 100 percent. Throughout the industry, the number of flat-rate hours billed usually exceeds the hours worked, so that a technician might work only eight hours even though 10 hours' worth of "flat-rate" time are billed. This is a commonly accepted practice; otherwise, costs for automotive repair could be chaotic, with a high potential for overcharging customers.

As in most industries, automotive dealerships are seeking new methods to improve efficiency. In some cases, they increase efficiency by streamlining and improving processes to boost productivity.

For example, at one Mercedes-Benz dealership in a resort area, a tighter linkage between the parts department and the service technicians was created. "We put a repair order printer in the parts department that gained us one to one and a half hours per technician," the general manager told me. "With 30 technicians a day, that's significant." And with a task-based team approach, the results can be even more dramatic.

The dealership wanted to improve its two key barometers, customer satisfaction and productivity, dramatically. By managing for the short term, it got results immediately. Says the service manager at the dealership:[9]

> We used to have our individual technicians working on individual cars and this caused the work to bottleneck in the dispatch department. With the team system, we eliminated the dispatch office because the team leaders do the dispatching. We went from servicing 70 cars a day to servicing 120 cars, with the same number of people. We now have two or three guys on a car at a time.

By moving to teams, the dealership found it could dramatically improve productivity. "Before the team approach, we averaged about 5,200 hours of service a month; with the teams, we hit 7,500 the first month," says the service manager.

The dealership set up four eight-person teams—orange, red, blue, and gray, each of which includes a service manager and an assistant service manager, as well as technicians. If one of them is busy when a customer needs assistance, the other deals with the customer. When a team service manager writes a repair order, he includes the time promised to the client. The skills required are matched to team members, who police themselves. The teams are so self-policing that one team actually decided one of the team members wasn't pulling his weight in relation to the rest of the team. In a real-life version of the television show "Survivor," they all voted him off the team; he was transferred to another part of the company. Team members have a thorough understanding of their contribution to the larger company and they continue to see it in real time.

Probably the best result of the team approach is that clients are in and out of the dealership faster, with a higher probability that the repair is satisfactory, since the team is totally responsible for the work and is charged with promptly handling any "returns," should they be warranted.

Auto dealerships are looking at teams because of the need for increased throughput—the number of cars that can be serviced at a facility. Customers also are demanding better service. However, the most important reason may be the amount of time wasted without the team approach.

"We study the market and current situation, and speak directly with employees (technicians) and find they see a different situation from management; one we refer to as 'the invisible obstacle course' that no one else can see," says Rich Engelage, President of Auto Dealer Direction, based in Richmond, Virginia. Engelage, with 40 years of automotive service experience, designed the team approach and has launched the concept at more than 500 auto dealerships across the United States, including Toyota, Ford, GM, Chrysler, and Mercedes-Benz. Says Engelage:[10]

> This is a flat-rate system. Once the time is gone, it's gone forever. If two people are equally skilled, together they could out-produce three other individuals because the two are a team and they get trained to work together. For example, for a complete brake job, the time standard is about four hours, which means that typically, it would take a technician four hours and it would be billed as four hours. Under a team approach, all the parts are brought to the team by a parts delivery team and four technicians on a team could do the job in 10 minutes today. It is billed as four hours flat rate, but it is ethically and legitimately done and with excellent quality.
>
> Everybody wants to be a winner, so the teams all track their daily productivity. I get calls from all over the country; a team

leader at a dealership wants to let me know they did 240 percent in productivity. We get all the cars in and out quicker.

One East Coast dealership that I visited that adopted the team approach found that only a few salaries of service technicians had to be adjusted. Because efficiency went up, they all got more money. Some get paid for 100 hours a week but they're only working 40 hours. There's also a healthy competition among the teams. They all look at the numbers each night and compare against the other team. At this dealership, when the first team hit 300 percent efficiency, the other team came in at 5 A.M. the next day to beat them. Now all the employees are highly motivated. It's not about cutting corners; it's about increasing efficiency.

It works almost like a doctor's office, where there is one doctor and patients are sent to different rooms and the doctor visits each room. Many more patients can be seen in the course of a day. In this automotive industry, each "office" is a workstation with a lift. In the old system, a car got onto the lift and a technician would find the problem, but the customer wasn't yet at his or her office or wasn't reachable to approve the repairs. The service department would have to put the car back together, remove it from the lift and the service area, and start on another car. Then the approval would come and the car would have to be brought back and the process restarted. Now, if a team-based dealership can't reach a customer, the technician leaves the car on the lift and just moves to the next lift to work with team members on another car. The car never has to be moved. And the results can be impressive: One dealer that booked 4,000 hours a month flat rate moved to a team-based approach and increased service to 6,700 hours, finishing its year with a 30 percent increase in gross profit. Says Engelage:

> This is life-changing money and a real career path. A technician starts young and by age 40 can be making a good living. At that stage, aging sets in and you start to get slower. But because of experience, you get all the hard, complex jobs. You end up making less money because you can't complete as much work. With teams, it's a high yield for all.

A dealership's project-based team approach lets the company be totally open with all managers, allowing each to see where he fits and what he contributes. Individual compensation also is tied to success, so that the strategy and direction are aligned with the people who have to execute it. In this case, the strategy is to match Mercedes's reputation for quality in its cars with a similar reputation for great service through improved efficiency—increasing revenue in the bargain.

Both time-based teams and task-based teams can help work become more modular and more manageable. Getting managers and employees closer to a task or goal that can be managed in the short term has two important advantages. First, both the task and the people involved in it can be clearly seen as moving the organization forward. Second, these more modular tasks provide ongoing information that can encourage the type of flexibility that successfully managing for the short term demands.

MANAGING CHANGE

Changing the Organization

Aligning an organization, or at least getting executive management and management as a whole truly working together, requires change in the organization. Many leaders, consultants, and HR executives have been preaching change for decades; two notable examples of those calls are the concept of reengineering and the Internet revolution, both of which have left lasting marks on organizations. However, sometimes that call to change falls on deaf ears, as managers and employees feel they can muddle through another organizational change proposed or executed either by new management or outsiders.

Lasting change depends on individuals, and individual action is critical to the concept of managing for the short term. The good news for organizations is that when asked to rank the degree to which they feel they have the ability to bring about change in their organizations, most executives and managers feel somewhat empowered[11] (see Figure 6.2). Of course, feeling that one has the power to effect change in an organization and actually effecting that change are two different things. It's the difference between thinking you can rock a boat and actually rocking the boat.

Not surprisingly, managers feel they have less ability to effect

FIGURE 6.2

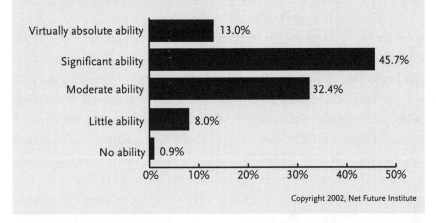

"Rank the degree to which you feel you have the ability to bring about change in your organization."

Virtually absolute ability — 13.0%
Significant ability — 45.7%
Moderate ability — 32.4%
Little ability — 8.0%
No ability — 0.9%

(Scale: 0% to 50%)

change in their organization than do executives. Roughly 22 percent of managers surveyed say they have little or no ability to bring about change in their organizations; just about no senior executives report feeling that way. More than 16.5 percent of senior executives say they have virtually absolute ability to effect change; fewer than 3 percent of managers feel the same power. For managers to feel better able to manage for the short term, they must understand not only what the company's goals are, but truly recognize that the company has empowered them to implement change to achieve those goals.

Changing Crisis by Crisis

As the world's largest hotel franchiser, the largest vacation ownership organization, the largest real-estate brokerage franchiser, and the largest corporate employee-relocation company, Cendant, a Fortune 500 company with annual revenue of more than $8 billion, operates on what Senior Vice President Guy Gray calls "crisis management." For the most part, the businesses, including brands such as Avis, Century 21, ERA, Coldwell Banker, Howard Johnson, Ramada Inn, Days Inn, Travelodge, Fairfield Resorts, and Jackson Hewitt Tax Services, are independently run. Changing the culture happens one manager at a time, one crisis at a time.[12]

"For middle and senior managers, the route to succeeding here is more aligned with how you can manage in crisis rather than process," says Gray. "It's more about getting stuff done and continually improving. It's OK to manage by crisis as long as you're good at it.

"We use crisis methodology rather than process methodology," says Gray. "The model is applicable across industries; what holds companies back are the people and the culture. If you want to change the company, you have to start by changing the culture, and the people changes will follow. Then you can focus on process. Some people simply can't make the conversion. You have to say, 'My company is going to have a kind of people with certain characteristics.' You then need to bring in new people to change the culture. You might have to replace 80 percent of the people to change the culture."

So how does a company change 80 percent of its employees while continuing to make the numbers? "It's a catch-22," says Gray. "You need to do it subtly. You can't deliver the results with chaos within the organization. People know what to do in a crisis; chaos is different. In the short run, you need to implement some of the changes. In a big organization, in a year or two, when some of the people have changed, then you can make major cultural change. The big issue in CEO turnover is they get ahead of themselves, mainly with promises." This notion of getting ahead of themselves with promises is yet another highlight of the difference between the proclaimed "corporate truth" and the reality of execution at the "street truth" level, discussed earlier in the book.

"That's the crux of who will be successful and who won't," says Gray. "There's a significant gap between executive managers, senior managers, and the guys who make it happen. Some of these execs don't see their world for what it is. Subsequently, they make statements that the rank and file can't deliver against. At Cendant, when we were small, it was ingrained that anyone could make a difference. Within a very short period of time you can get an idea to the chairman, from any level. The more stuff you get done, the more you get handed. The survivors figure out that the most important things get done today.

"You can go a week or two feeling like you haven't gotten anything done and then you have a day or two where you get a lot completed, and those are the days you live for. In the old days, you got a reward for completing a task. Today, you get five or six things done and move on; you never take a breather.

"More people have to be involved in decisions. We operate in the mode of getting stuff done today. It's in our culture. You have to find people who can work in this 'live for the moment, plan for the future' culture. If you don't survive the short run, you won't survive the long run," says Gray.

"Here's the challenge. You look at your world trying to manage on a quarterly basis. Given this constraint, if you introduce short-term improvements, focusing on the long-term objectives, you overcome the challenge of selling 'strategic' initiatives to the owners of the P&L. Always attack an opportunity on a small basis, like a trial. All opportunities come with some assumption set that you need to validate. You can usually get folks to buy in if you manage to set a short-term, tactical win. That ultimately can become strategy."

Personally, Gray starts with a daily list with no more than three items on it. On a typical day, he spends six to seven hours in meetings, many with outside companies. "If I get one thing done, I feel pretty good. What my people get done in a day is more important. The more you move down the organization, the more things get personal."

MANAGING FOR THE SHORT TERM REQUIRES INDEPENDENT DECISIONS

With the increasingly short tenure of chief executives, managers who have been with a company for a long time may see moves as short term in the context of their own experience with the company. By contrast, a top executive who may be newer to the company might see the same move as a logical step in a longer-term strategy.

It is incumbent on the chief executive, when articulating strategy, to make it clear throughout the organization that shifts will be required by the business environment, that these shifts are simply a

If short-term shifts are perceived throughout the organization in the context of a larger goal instead of as knee-jerk reactions, they are less likely to be perceived as negative.

given, and that short-term flexibility does not mean there is no long-term strategy.

Businesses are in a difficult position. Wall Street looks to them to present a long-term vision and strategy, but if they do not produce results in the short term, Wall Street is the first to demand a change at the top. Senior executives find themselves simultaneously having to speak for the long term but leading the organization in acting for the short term.

To straddle this divide, the CEO and senior executives must set up expectations that managing for the short term is not in conflict with the overall strategy, and even has positive aspects. If short-term shifts are perceived throughout the organization in the context of a larger goal instead of as knee-jerk reactions, they are less likely to be perceived as negative. Flexibility needs to become a core value for a company if managing for the short term is to be perceived as a genuine need instead of a burden.

Achieving goals through short-term moves means that managers have no time to clear every decision with supervisors; the day-to-day decisions are too numerous and come too quickly for that. So how is a company to avoid simply allowing managers to focus on short-term results without taking the larger goals into account?

For individuals to accept and practice the concept that incremental forward motion should occur regardless of whether it benefits the individual himself, it must be part of a company's strategy. Companies must go beyond simply paying lip service to the concept of teamwork. They must align compensation plans to create a culture that helps people see that any short-term move that truly moves the company forward toward its strategic goals is of benefit to them as well.

Managers must also so thoroughly understand their individual roles in achieving the larger corporate goals that their short-term moves support the long-term direction. That requires that leaders all the way up and down the corporate ladder communicate the vision in modular fashion, in ways that allow each individual manager and worker to understand his or her own function in that context. It also requires that leaders stay in close touch with both their subordinates and the market generally, so they can spot the changes that may affect not only short-term decisions but possibly long-term direction as well.

7

Are We Communicating?

How can an organization bridge the gap between an executive's vision and the reality of the managers and workers who must achieve it?

The increased turnover of top executives doesn't help. A new top executive often is charged with giving the company a new direction, whether needed or not. A company leader also usually wants to leave a corporate legacy, which might involve some sort of broad-brush vision. By contrast, managers who have been with a company for a long time may be skeptical of the pronouncements of a new leadership, and may feel that any strategy is simply one more wave of executive noise to be waited out until that executive team is replaced with another. This is admittedly a cynical view, and by no means the sole factor in reconciling corporate truth with street truth. However, a rapid succession of ever-changing corporate visions can increase the difficulty of rallying the troops behind any one of them.

Most often, both senior executives and managers want to do what is in the best interest of the organization and the shareholders. The challenge is one of interpretation, of how well the message is being communicated from the top, and of how well it is synchronized with the ever-changing realities and immediate tasks at the managerial level.

While top management by and large feels it is doing well at communicating to subordinates the roles of their projects or tasks in the context of the organization's long-term strategy and direction, only 34 percent of managers feel that same message is being communicated better than adequately. Only 13 percent think it is being communicated very well[1] (see Figure 7.1).

This communications gap can lead managers within an organization to draw their own conclusions about aspects of company direction and strategy. Such managers tend to behave according to their own understanding of how to act tactically. That action, even if well-intentioned, can be influenced by many things other than the announced corporate strategy: expediency, customer expectations, self-interest, and individual relationships, to name only a few. And the results of those tactical moves may or may not be translated back up the corporate ladder so they influence the overall strategy and keep it informed by day-to-day reality.

The problem is particularly acute if the executives who are trying to deliver a message are perceived to be communicating only for

FIGURE 7.1

"How well does executive management communicate to subordinates the subordinates' roles in the context of the organization's long-term strategy and direction?"

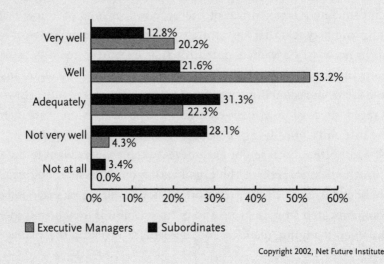

Very well — 12.8% / 20.2%
Well — 21.6% / 53.2%
Adequately — 31.3% / 22.3%
Not very well — 28.1% / 4.3%
Not at all — 3.4% / 0.0%

■ Executive Managers   ■ Subordinates

VOICES FROM THE FRONT LINES

Lip Service[2]

"There is a lot of lip service given to the importance of communication from executive management out to middle management and to the front line. However, the reality is that when the economy began to suffer, and our corporate revenues dipped, the first people laid off were the managers and directors of corporate and internal communications."

"Communication is at a premium. It doesn't happen often enough or with enough clarity. Executive management seems to be quick to let communication go by the wayside. They don't seem to be focused on letting people understand their roles and keeping folks motivated or at least informed."

"The communication is quite poor—both infrequent and inconsistent."

---

show. In order for a message to be delivered, it must also be received, and skepticism about the purposes of the communication does not help people listen well.

THE COMMUNICATIONS GAP

The communications issue can be caused partly by message, partly by its delivery, and partly by its receipt or interpretation. "When executive managers think of communications, they sometimes think it's one-directional," says Tom Murach, Senior Manager at Price-waterhouseCoopers. Murach manages large projects for the world's largest accounting firm, which has 150,000 employees in branches spread throughout more than 150 countries.[3]

"Executives today often are so focused on their 'tops down' role of providing leadership, direction and decisions for the organization that they may lose sight of their 'bottoms up' role of providing the tools and support that management needs to successfully execute this 'tops down' organizational strategy. After articulating the vision and direction, if executives would ask the question 'And what do you need from senior management to do what we've just told you needs to be done?' it could open an entirely new level of dialogue and organizational performance. What senior managers are telling their staffs is not always relevant to what their staffs do every day."

This is the difference between corporate truth and street truth. It has nothing to do with whether executive management's vision is correct or whether middle managers are capable of executing against that strategy. It has to do with perspective, or what an executive or manager sees from where he or she sits.

It also has to do with the direct and personal impact of a particular message that passes from executive management to a manager and how much impact the directive might have on the individual manager's world. "The charge of executing strategy by the manager may not happen as directed because the change causes too much disruption in the manager's world," says Terry Ransford, Senior Vice President of Northern Trust, a major regional bank headquartered in Chicago.[4]

One way to look at the issue is that the corporation is the legal entity and the organization is the people who work for that entity. Says Ransford:

> Businesses are optimized to benefit the organization, or the people, not the corporation. Managers hear a message from executive management and say, "I don't want to do this because I'll lose 50 head count." They're too invested in their traditions. Executives make a major pronouncement to their manager about how they're going to create some great new efficiency and do something a very different way declaring, "We'll do it with technology." The managers, who don't understand the technology, tend to nod their heads, and these guys have no intention of really doing it.
>
> It's like raising kids. They look you straight in the face and agree as you tell them something, then they do whatever they want. Whether they adhere to your wishes is really their choice. That's how corporations work. Managers can rationalize anything back up the chain of command. Ultimately, the guys at the top have the final say, because they can hire and fire and close divisions. The real issue is whether anything gets done at the optimal rate of speed. All of us today really are contract labor.
>
> Executives end up spending all their time in meetings, not out where things really happen. Tactical decisions ultimately have more influence than global, 90,000-foot pronouncements.

VOICES FROM THE FRONT LINES

Problems in the Translation[5]

"Our issues seem to be distortions of the message which occur as it passes through several levels. It's the 'telephone game' in real life."

"A problem exists in seeing how my message ultimately gets down to the next layer of management. People hear what they want to hear. Only if you communicate across levels of management do you find out what is actually received. I try to speak to my staff collectively about three times a year outlining my visions regarding strategy and long-term goals."

"I suspect that executive management has improved 'high level' communication to employees, but there is major pressure at middle management level . . . with more being demanded by employees and more organizational assistance/support needed for middle managers."

"Often we hear the words and understand, but the 'call to action'—the methodology for getting there—does not always translate well. The message needs to be up close and personal."

If the coach draws the greatest play but doesn't have the team to execute it, not much will be accomplished. Executives need to understand the motivations of their managers, which would make it more likely that they can create an environment that will be productive.

It is this gap in communication that causes a disconnect within an organization. The executive may be expertly communicating his strategy to his managers, but his managers instinctively translate what they are hearing into how it impacts them directly. In other words, an executive may be "heard" differently by each. That translation by senior managers—and often, multiple layers of managers—to the troops can cause confusion.

STRATEGY VS. COMMUNICATION STRATEGY

It is commonly accepted that an organization requires strategy and strategic positioning. The components that underlie strategic positioning, as defined by Harvard Business School's Michael Porter, comprise three key principles:[6]

- Strategy is the creation of unique and valuable position, involving a different set of activities. Strategic position emerges from three distinct sources: serving few needs of many customers; serving broad needs of few customers; serving broad needs of many customers in a narrow market.

- Strategy requires you to make trade-offs in competing—to choose what *not* to do. Some competitive activities are incompatible; thus, gains in one area can be achieved only at the expense of another area.

- Strategy involves creating "fit" among a company's activities. Fit has to do with the ways a company's activities interact and reinforce one another. Fit drives both competitive advantage and sustainability: When activities mutually reinforce each other, competitors can't easily imitate them.

However, when it comes to the actual execution of strategy throughout the ranks, the picture can become a bit fuzzy. This is because an organization often will focus rigorously on strategy and vision, but not always pay enough attention to communication and effective execution of that vision. In addition to an operational strategy, executive management needs a well-tuned communications strategy.

As we've seen, executives and managers often do not agree on the effectiveness of communication from executive management. While part of this is interpretation on the part of the manager, another part is the method of communication on the part of the executive. Different managers prefer to digest information via different media. One may prefer the corporate newsletter, another e-mail, another personal presentations from executive management, still another a video. One manager might do better with graphics, while his neighbor might deal best with lengthy text that includes all the details.

"Chances are, the executive is communicating in the style that he or she likes to be communicated with," says PricewaterhouseCoopers's Murach. For example, if an executive is comfortable with short documents and bullet points, chances are that is how he or she communicates to his or her subordinates.

"They presume that style is fine for everyone. The downside is that everybody's interpretation is based on what they did or did not hear, so everybody's interpretation of corporate strategy is different and they end up filling in the blanks and making it up as they go. They're sometimes pulling in different directions," says Murach. "If executives look at communication as both a 'send and receive' function, they can get valuable feedback from their managers. If not, managers will feel that they are being communicated 'at,' not communicated 'to.'"

The cost of that disconnect between executives and managers has great implications across the enterprise. This is one of the most challenging aspects of managing for the short term, but one whose solution can dramatically improve the efficiency of an organization and truly get it in tune with itself.

The disconnects fall into three areas:

- Context. This occurs when changes are explained by executive management but have not necessarily been well-thought-out in terms of their execution or impact on day-to-day operations.

- Perception. Even if messages are well-thought-out, managers may hear a different message from the one being delivered. For example, an executive may be delivering a message about a new initiative; managers may hear it in terms of "new career opportunity for me" or, worse, "elimination of career opportunity for me."

- Language. This involves how the message was delivered. The language used to communicate strategy typically is the language that the executive personally prefers that others use when communicating with him, not necessarily the language that is meaningful to individual managers. In many cases, it is also the language used to communicate to an outside audience, since that often is part of executive managers' responsibility, and may therefore be more vague or less tactical than necessary when communicating with an audience of insiders. Finally, it generally uses a formal medium such as print, neglecting the power of the informal network that exists in every company.

When executives do not communicate clearly and effectively to their managers, the people lower on the corporate ladder find themselves wondering about what they should be doing. "This creates a spiral of confusion," says Sharafat Khan, Partner and Practice Leader,

Human Capital Advisory Services, Deloitte & Touche.[7] "There needs to be a credibility between what they are saying and what they are doing.

"The rank and file is at the water cooler and the executive doesn't understand what is on their minds. As a result, the ROI is not well-crafted," says Khan. "We are all very short-term-oriented, so we send confusing messages which impede achievement of business objectives."

Executives should approach their messaging with internal information in hand before their message goes out. Internal research, including questions sent to every level of the organization from executive management all the way to the customer level, can determine how well key messages are being received and perceived.

"Executives should ask what employees want to start, what they want to stop, and what they want to continue," says Khan. "Executives are not trained to think this way. Informal networks are the way to get things done these days. Executives have to be in tune down below. The managers are the ambassadors who form the perception, and they are the implementers. If they're not convinced or have personal risk, they're not going to advance the business agenda."

This puts the executive in the position of having to walk through the divisions and greet the secretaries and loading-dock workers, who constitute the true pulse of the organization. However, when information is gathered this way on a regular basis, it is important to be careful how it is used, so as not to jeopardize one's information sources.

"Executives today try to get closer by going to staff meetings, where they see nodding heads," says Khan. "As soon as the meeting is over, [those nodding heads] all do something different. Executives need to cultivate and trust managers at the lower ranks, but the filter is in the middle."

Executives may have difficulty getting a message across if they are primarily getting their information from one another instead of taking the time to also listen to the managers on the front lines. The informal networks that exist in all organizations carry a lot of weight, and the savvy executive will take advantage of them to both convey a message and determine how well it is actually getting through.

HEAR YE, HEAR YE

When managing for the short term, it is essential that an organization's strategy and direction and all of its implications be understood from the top down and from the bottom up. The most effective way to do this is to increase interactive communication inside an organization, which can be more difficult than it sounds. For senior executives, this means spending considerable time inside the organization. For managers, it means taking the initiative to understand the organization's goals and objectives and to provide input back up the chain of command. It is not about more memos or meetings, but about creating a culture in which managers and executives truly communicate, both the good and the bad, and then collectively move on.

This means executives and managers must constantly shift between external (such as shareholders and customers) and internal (such as supervisors, peers, and employees) forces. "There's a balance needed, depending on the size and complexity of an organization," says Steven Rudnitsky, President of Kraft Food Service and Executive Vice President of Kraft Foods.[9] Rudnitsky, who was President of Nabisco Food Service and took over the combined food service operations after Kraft acquired Nabisco in 2000, is responsible for all Kraft and Nabisco food products that go to restaurants, hotels, hospitals, and schools throughout the United States. Kraft Food Service is part of the Kraft Foods North America business, which has brands that include such household names as Oreo, Philadelphia Cream Cheese, Maxwell House, and Oscar Mayer.

> **When managing internally, you have to start with a clear understanding of your strategic direction and it has to cascade through the entire organization.**

"Our organization is large and the business dynamics are complex. I'm very customer-focused and enjoy leading from the front by being out with our customers. However, the nature of my job requires that I spend a fair amount of time, perhaps a disproportionate amount, on the inside," says Rudnitsky, who echoed the views of many executives we interviewed. Rudnitsky compartmentalizes internal issues at organizations as either necessary processes or burdensome bureaucracy. "It is good to focus internally to the extent you're managing an internal process to get the right things done."

Part of the role of a senior executive is to manage in both directions. Says Rudnitsky:

> When managing internally, you have to start with a clear understanding of your strategic direction and it has to cascade through the entire organization. In fact, you're doomed unless everyone—from top to bottom—shares the organization's vision and strategic direction. That requires a fair degree of "managing up," if you will, so that people at the very top of the organization understand the business dynamics. This, in turn, helps set proper expectations for the division and leads to support for the strategies for attaining what should be clearly defined business objectives.
>
> Internal management also requires managing across functions. At Kraft, it's a true collaborative effort. At my level, I need to ensure that every discipline—R&D, manufacturing, marketing, information technology, and so forth—and every division employee is working off the same page. We won't succeed unless everyone in the organization understands the business objectives, embraces them and conceptually understands their role in achieving them.

Realizing there is distance from the top to the bottom—the difference between corporate truth and street truth—Rudnitsky created an open and interactive environment to facilitate clear direction down and feedback back up. He started conducting quarterly town hall meetings that include a large portion of his staff. Says Rudnitsky:

> I open every town hall meeting personally. Most recently, in an attempt to provide greater focus for the division, I told everyone there, "If you're doing something that is not consistent with these five strategies, then do not do them and tell your boss." Once you set the strategy, it's incumbent on employees to determine if what they're doing is a fit. I strive to have very little ambiguity about what I want and expect. Directness works best for me. If people disagree, I want to understand why. I have confidence in my managers that the people working for me are as open and as honest with me as I am with them. It's part of a culture. People can be extremely guarded, and it's easiest to continue down a path because "that's the way it's always been done." I want people to challenge the status quo and focus on our clearly defined business objectives. Two-way communication is essential and you have to demonstrate by example.
>
> The key in managing for the short term is to try to make work fun for your team. It's important. Encourage them to look at their assignments and be able to fix, change, or finesse them and, hopefully, have fun doing it. At the end of the day, we are a company with high expectations; however, we all need to find ways of having fun as we pursue our goals.

The effort required to build internal relationships—whether by town hall meetings such as Kraft's or by other means—must compete for top executives' time. Executives must balance it with the effort required to build relationships with customers, investors, and the analysts whose views and words can so dramatically affect a company's stock and, ultimately, the top executive's tenure.

But to communicate most effectively with the outside, it is necessary to really know what's going on inside. Sampling associates at varying levels can be eye-opening. Executives often are startled when they hear the viewpoint of low-level managers, if they ever get to hear it directly.

COMMUNICATING CHANGE

With the constant change businesses face today, continuous and effective internal communication is even more important to keep an organization's execution aligned with strategy and direction.

"If the short term isn't consistent with the long-term vision, it isn't going to get internal support," says Steve Riggio, CEO of Barnes & Noble, the largest bookseller in the United States. The company has hundreds of stores, 50,000 employees, and annual sales of more than $4 billion. Riggio understands that the role of corporate leadership is to ensure that all managers and employees understand where an organization is headed, while keeping an eye on short-term activities and requirements.

"The CEO has to relentlessly communicate why a change is happening," says Riggio. Internally at Barnes & Noble, managers are always kept apprised of the yearly plan and "everybody lives to the budget."

The chief executive also has to balance nurturing the company's culture with delivering financial results. "Wall Street doesn't have the patience for any warm and fuzzy culture stuff," says Riggio. "They want to know where the earnings are going and how you're going to get there. The long-term strategy has to be validated by a financial plan."

Managing for the short term requires this balance of making the numbers while closing the gap between corporate truth and street truth. It is the balance between budgets and company culture, both critical for short- and long-term success. As in the case of Kraft Food Service discussed earlier, the approach at Barnes & Noble is to keep communication open and bidirectional.

"The best way to communicate the culture and vision is to have a management team that is united," says Riggio. "A good culture in a company comes from within."

While communicating from senior executives through the ranks is important, just as important is leveraging information from employees and understanding that any corporate directive will be measured against those employees' understanding of the company's customers.

"Our sales data reflects the lifestyles and interests of our customer base," says Riggio. "The most fascinating information is not from the books at the top of the best-seller lists but from the undercurrents of demand—trends in the marketplace that are just beginning to emerge. The employees will know if something holds true, because they know the customers."

Is the Message Getting Through?

How can executive managers tell if their message is getting through accurately? Here are some of the symptoms of misalignment and disconnect:

- Missed Deadlines/Extended Projects

   This can be an indication that a kind of malaise has set in because managers feel executive management doesn't really understand what is going on in the organization at that level: "If they don't care, then I don't care" is an attitude that is sometimes voiced. Or, perhaps worse, managers see no connection between their project and corporate strategy, and therefore feel little need to meet deadlines they consider arbitrary.

- Missed Performance Goals

   Sometimes this occurs because managers simply do not clearly understand the rationale behind the goals. At other times, conflicting messages may have been sent, with the result that the performance goals originally established do not appear as relevant as they did when they were set or communicated.

- No Feedback

   A lack of feedback on what executive managers are sending out to the troops can be a telling sign. When it appears that everyone simply accepts what is sent out, it might be because the message is not considered relevant. At other times, it may be because of a fear that feedback will be used against managers. When managers feel executive management is open and listening, they talk. On the other hand, when managers notice that someone who questioned an executive directive at the last meeting has since left the company "to pursue other interests," there is less likely to be constructive feedback up the channel.

Communications problems are not the sole reason for shortfalls in performance, of course. But a missed performance goal should trigger an examination of whether or not faulty communication played a part in it. The cost in loss of opportunity is obvious: People are not productive if they do not actively buy in to the message. "If they do, it reduces the total amount of energy an executive needs to expend to fulfill strategy," says Murach.

DEMONSTRABLE RESULTS: SUPPORTING THE INCENTIVE FOR THE CEO

Unlike managers, CEOs have fewer career options. Once you're a CEO, you can later become CEO of a larger company, a smaller company, a better company, a different company, but chances are you're still going to be a CEO (one exception is CEOs of small start-ups who may accept a lower position with a larger company). And a CEO is judged on the overall success of an enterprise. A manager, by contrast, may move up in title, transfer to another division, transfer skills to other industries, or become a consultant specializing in a particular area of expertise.

> The manager who can help a CEO demonstrate and document how well a strategy is being executed is clearly furthering the well-being of the boss, and is likely to be regarded favorably.

A top executive lives or dies by the results of an entire company, yet he must rely on individuals whose personal success may be determined by much narrower criteria. As chief executives live or die by the numbers and are pressured to produce quantifiable success, they push that pressure downward throughout the organization.

But that pressure also creates opportunities that can reconcile the difference between the overall corporate goals and those of the individual, between corporate truth and street truth. The manager who can help a CEO demonstrate and document how well a strategy is being executed is clearly furthering the well-being of the boss, and is likely to be regarded favorably. That should play to the self-interest of any ambitious manager. CEOs need managers who can help them, and managers who help the CEO and top management enhance their career prospects.

Making sure that the information a top executive needs is in the right place at the right time in the right context is sometimes derided as politicking or bootlicking. Clearly, there is some personal incentive at work. But supporting the CEO also goes beyond simple "sucking up to the boss."

To understand what information is important to others, a manager needs a broader understanding of the business than that required by his or her individual job. And the pressure for quantifiable results can help force individual managers to make the link between their own performance and how it affects the organization as a whole. That link can help give a manager that broader understanding that enables him or her to supply superiors with the right information at the right time.

In effect, this connection becomes a virtual circle. The senior executive needs the support of the troops to get anything accomplished. And supporting the needs of the senior executive benefits the manager, not only by attracting attention but also by forcing the manager to gain knowledge—knowledge that will enhance his or her ability to support company strategy even better in the future.

Voices from the Front Lines

What Goes Wrong?[10]

"Communication varies by location in global organizations. Often it is tied to the management style of the region, or even what the current focus of the organization is."

"In our organization, lower and middle management seem to communicate up and down very well. Can't say that upper management does a good job of sending info down in a timely or otherwise fashion."

"Communication from the top down is poor. Also, the communication between departments is minimal despite considerable time and money devoted to team-building. And I am a part of the problem, even though it is against my nature to be in a silo. Under previous management, we did not experience this."

INCREASING TRUST: PROVIDING
THE INCENTIVE FOR MANAGERS

Managing for the short term involves trusting more managers—and trusting managers more—down the line. It also involves supplying the knowledge those managers require to be able to justify that trust. The more the "troops" are truly in sync with their company's leader, the more likely they are to do what top management intends. And that reduces the gap between corporate truth and street truth.

To achieve that kind of understanding, a CEO must honestly confront the extent to which he truly conveys responsibility as well as information. For example, a CEO might "trust" a senior vice president to research and analyze whether the company should expand in, say, London. That SVP might already be in charge of the entire European operation of the global company. The CEO trusts him to conduct the analysis and make the recommendation. The SVP comes back and concludes that the London operation should be expanded. The CEO decides against it for various unrelated reasons. The CEO might have trusted his subordinate to make the right decision, but he trusted him only to make a recommendation. The CEO did not trust him to execute the recommendation.

> If a CEO chooses not to trust the SVP to execute a decision, he must also ask what he can do to increase the chances of the person's being able to do so the next time.

When a CEO feels compelled to make such a call, he must also ask himself a key question: "What information does this vice president lack that would enable him to come to a decision that is consistent with the organization's strategy?" For example, in the example of the senior vice president and the London expansion, that information might be key financial data not previously discussed; it might be a clearer understanding of the strategy itself; it might be a clearer understanding on the vice president's part of his own skills, personality, or organizational role. If a CEO chooses not to trust the SVP to execute a decision, he must also ask what he can do to increase the chances of the person's being able to do so the next time. And if the decision is not based on a lack of information, the chief executive must carefully consider the impact on his subordinate of not being trusted with that decision.

In the above example, we've looked at the issue of trust between a CEO and a senior vice president. But this gap in trust can exist at virtually every level of an organization. Senior managers must address it with their middle managers; middle managers must address it with their subordinates. Otherwise, the cost of the difference between corporate truth and street truth compounds as it moves down the ranks.

With all the business climate issues mentioned thus far, it is imperative that senior executives trust more people with more issues and more actual decisions. As many have come to realize, the old economy method of "information is power" is being replaced by "sharing is power." The days of hoarding information to increase self-worth are gone. For example, the boss of the past might be the only one who knew how his division or part of the organization worked, by keeping direct reports distinctly separate and discouraging information sharing across groups. Only he would know *all* the parts. This approach cannot work effectively today, because the business-customer-supplier-shareholder relationships are too intertwined.

In the complex business world of today, no one can have enough information to do everything that needs to be done. A manager is not an individual; he or she is the sum of his or her contacts, and the knowledge they can share. And having such a network requires a manager to share as well, with superiors, peers, and workers.

The kind of broad understanding of a company's business goals and constraints is critical to a manager's being able to earn trust. And a manager need not rely on a supervisor to impart it; indeed, it is most effective when pieced together from a diversity of perspectives. The clues about what is important at the company-wide level are everywhere: in a company's annual report, in executive speeches, in newspaper articles, in conversations with colleagues in other departments.

And the more managers can tie their thinking to those goals, the more persuasive will be their arguments for why a pet project should be adopted or a priority changed. Quoting the corporate priorities as outlined during a recent talk by the top executive to employees can

---

VOICES FROM THE FRONT LINES

Taking Responsibility[11]

"It is not executive management's job to 'communicate . . . the roles of their daily, weekly, monthly, and quarterly projects and tasks.' Executive management's job is communicating the organization's long-term strategy and direction. Figuring out what that means for my division (projects, tasks, linkage) is MY job."

---

remind others that your project is in tune with what the big guy wants—and even subtly suggest that if they veto it, the big guy won't be happy.

Being able to trust managers to both make decisions and execute them is critical to an organization's managing for the short term. If it does not, it will find itself moving too slowly; moreover, it will find those managers leaving for environments where they *are* trusted.

It is not only managers who must earn trust; corporations must do so as well. At both the corporate and individual levels, earning trust involves setting an example and being consistent in supporting that message with actions as well as words. One study found that a company's ability to develop trusting relationships among coworkers, leaders, customers, and business partners was an indicator of its employees' job satisfaction and organizational effectiveness.[12] The survey identified five aspects of organizational trust:

- An ability to rely on coworkers' and leaders' effectiveness and competence

- An atmosphere of openness and honesty

- The company's concern for employees as expressed by empathy, tolerance, and safety

- Consistent and dependable actions by employees and managers

- Shared goals, values, and beliefs

Leading by example is a principle that a parent understands well. How can you expect to be followed if you're perceived as not living by your words? To get managers to buy into the idea of managing for

---

VOICES FROM THE FRONT LINES

Walking the Talk[13]

"Listening to others is the first step in successful communication. But in ongoing periods of change management, this specific quality falls short just too often. Executing promises is step number two to move on in communication. But with ever-shifting strategic goals, there remains not sufficient room for making the keeping of a promise transparent."

---

the short term and moving forward incrementally and quickly, executives must communicate that vision to the rest of the company by doing so themselves. By focusing on what really drives the business, based on the information communicated by executive and senior managers, senior executives can help demonstrate how the company's strategy is connected to the real-world environment.

INFORMATION FLOW: THE ENABLER

It is important to remember that information flow is critical in the context of enabling a company and its managers to function better in the short term. Nonetheless, when information flow becomes information *overload*, it becomes counterproductive. Information is important only to the extent that it is available in the right place at the right time for the right people—and increasingly, in the right technology—to take action.

And as we will see in the next chapter, that information must be accompanied by decisions on how those actions will be measured to determine whether or not progress has been made toward the company's ultimate goals.

8

Communicating Down the Line

Having a vision, strategy, and objectives—plus the metrics to measure progress toward those objectives—is not enough. To successfully manage for the short term, each executive and manager has to understand his or her individual and departmental contributions and how they relate to the ways in which the success of the organization is measured. This knowledge has to be spread throughout the management ranks, all the way down to the individual level.

It is not enough for executives and managers to communicate the organization's strategy, no matter how well the message is communicated. Unless they also explain how performance is quantifiably measured against that strategy, there is no personal and departmental context for the strategy, and it cannot be fully realized.

Without that individual context for corporate progress, the distance between corporate truth and street truth widens. The middle manager may hear the message, perhaps even agree with it. But unless he or she sees a clear way to contribute, the individual often just goes about his or her business. There is no clear corporate incentive for that person to do anything differently to support that strategy.

Each individual has to be made to understand how he or she affects those measurements that are tied to the strategy. This is not to say that quality takes a back seat, because even quality is increasingly being measured. Sharing those metrics, and helping managers and employees deeply understand where and how they fit into the bigger picture, is critical in managing for the short term.

For example, when Jill Bemis came to Metropolitan State University in St. Paul, Minnesota, in 1995 as the budget director, it was difficult to put together a budget. Her predecessor had what Bemis describes as a "knowledge is power" approach: "At the end of the year, the budget had a nice carry-forward because she could hold money back. No one knew it was there."[1]

The budgeting process has since become more open, says Bemis, who is now finance director. The criteria for approval of projects are not only clearer but also are based on the organization's strategic goals. The university has a two-year budgeting cycle, with monthly management reports and quarterly updates. The planning and budget council, which makes the budgeting decisions, cuts across lines at the university and includes managers from a variety of functional areas as well as union representatives. The process requires everyone who submits a spending proposal to fill out a form justifying the request. Managers have to not only document what resources are needed for the project but also outline which specific strategic goal or goals the project is related to and how it can help the university meet that goal.

This is part of how an organization keeps everyone focused on the successful implementation of strategy in the short term. Every budgeted item must be viewed in context of the overall strategy, resulting in greater understanding and commitment to deliver on those projects that are funded. The department heads also can then be held accountable to delivering on both project and strategy. The two become intertwined.

At Metropolitan State, the planning and budget council assigns a

> Managing for the short term requires communication not only of the company's destination, but also of how everyone in the company is doing while getting there.

numeric ranking to the various projects based on how well each suits the university and how closely it matches the organization's goals. Only after doing that initial sort does the committee look at the cost benefit to the institution and the resources required. Finally, the committee ranks the projects on a scale of 1 to 10. "As long as people stay with the rating and they're consistent in the way they rate all the projects, it doesn't matter what the exact score is, because it will be tied to the overall goals," Bemis says.

This sharing of metrics and information on how every part of the plan contributes to strategy is key. Managing for the short term requires communication not only of the company's destination but also of how *everyone* in the company is doing while getting there. That requires that employees up and down the line understand the metrics as well as the department heads do; they have to know what mile markers are being used to measure progress.

VOICES FROM THE FRONT LINES

What Works: Tools[2]

"The organization, as a whole, is not very effective at relating organizational goals to the process, or 'task,' level. My area has been more effective in this regard through the use of cascading scorecards. The scorecards tend to provide a clear line of sight to the divisional objectives, as they are bucketed under consistent themes."

"Ironically, we just had a team looking at ways to better communicate these topics across the wider organization. They ran across a new tool to allow instant feedback via computer poll during Webcasts of important messages. I am looking forward to its first trial."

"We utilize the process called 'Policy Deployment' for deploying our company objectives; in addition, we have a well-articulated set of values and beliefs that are used as guidelines for all employees. The Policy Deployment process allows for defining the company objectives but also has a regularly scheduled review of the objectives at all levels of the company so that feedback is available almost immediately. This allows us to take remedial action if the objectives are not being met."

SHARE THE METRICS

At many companies, the concept of "making the numbers" is deeply ingrained. For example, at Cendant, even though its businesses are varied and most are independently run, certain functions are leveraged across them. Two such services are worldwide telecommunications and the 50 contact centers in 17 countries.

Responsibility for managing those centers, which includes 15,000 employees, falls to Guy Gray, Senior Vice President of Cendant.[3]

"We live and die by the quarter," says Gray. It's not just the financial numbers that affect managers there. "The first thing you do is stretch your day," says Gray. "Eight hours is unacceptable in today's world."

To encourage his managers and their employees to be more adept at making their numbers, Gray spends a lot of time making sure his team understands the implications of their actions on the organization as a whole. He set two major goals, or vision statements, for his managers. The first was for them to run their businesses like true businesses; the second was to convert the call centers to contact centers. The two went hand in hand.

Part of managing for the short term involves attitude and how something is perceived. It is not enough to tell a manager or employee to do something, which might have worked in days past. Now it is more important for the managers to understand the greater implications of what it is they are being asked to do. Those managers and their employees also have to be made to feel good about what they are doing. Cendant utilized both these dynamics in Gray's operations.

Previously, call centers were where a phone representative would take an incoming call from someone who wanted to, say, place a reservation at one of the company's many hotels. Call centers at Cendant were viewed as cost centers, and managers and employees were not necessarily encouraged to view them as more than that. Cendant was certainly not alone in that attitude; most companies have tended to view phone centers largely as the primary contact point for a company's customers[4] (see Figure 8.1). As a result, the objective for call centers generally, including Cendant's, was to be as efficient as possi-

FIGURE 8.1

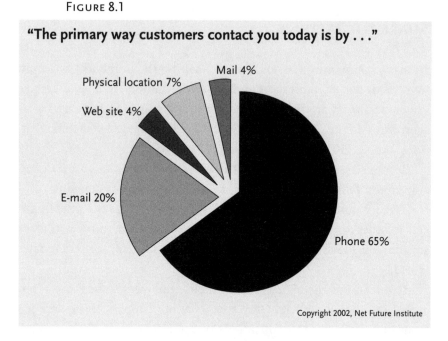

"The primary way customers contact you today is by . . ."

Mail 4%

Physical location 7%

Web site 4%

E-mail 20%

Phone 65%

ble, which usually meant stripping out any unnecessary costs. Maximum number of calls handled per employee, shorter time frames per call—it has been a culture of volume and efficiency.

With the exponential growth of the Internet and e-mail, companies increasingly are facing a changing world, with potentially large impact for call centers. This will involve a move away from telephone to more interactive, electronic communication, including e-mail and company Web sites (see Figure 8.2).[5] Because customers now have more ways to contact the company easily and cheaply, call centers can potentially become more sophisticated relationship-builders.

"We want to evolve call centers to contact centers," says Gray. However, he is tackling this long-range project by managing for the short term. "By utilizing pilots it may take an extra year to get there, and you may end up spending a bit more, but you get the right result. When people are managing some businesses, how many large, strategic projects end up being successful? The world is changing. So if you start a big, long-term initiative, when and if you complete the project, the objectives have probably changed. With shorter-term projects and time frames, and smaller trials, you're delivering value along the way."

FIGURE 8.2

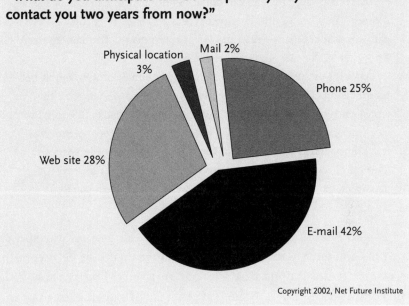

"What do you anticipate will be the primary way customers will contact you two years from now?"

Physical location 3%

Mail 2%

Phone 25%

Web site 28%

E-mail 42%

Gray wanted to position his managers for the future; if he could not do so overnight in a technical sense, he could at least do so psychologically. He renamed the call centers "contact centers" to start refocusing people on their role in the organization.

Gray then began educating his managers on their overall context in making the numbers. Gray got his managers and their employees to understand overall corporate impact of the contact centers, both from a revenue and an expense standpoint. Ideas were solicited for increasing revenue, whether by increasing productivity per call or handling greater numbers of calls. He also solicited ideas on cutting costs. Employees offered ideas and were asked to qualify them on business terms and net impact to the organization, right down to earnings per share. Says Gray:

> It's about maximizing revenue and minimizing expense. It's not more complicated than that. Now when my managers think of impact on revenue they build it into their tactical decisions that roll up into improving the business. It's amazing now that everyone is managing the business as a business, versus managing an

efficient call center. We now measure our people on margin on revenue that we directly effect.

All our people now know our EPS and how our business makes money. They know the revenue drivers and they now look at "How can we impact those revenues?" It's important for managers to know what the marginal contribution is.

When you give people the context, they make much, much better decisions. They appreciate that you acknowledge that they're smart enough to understand how the company works. People then can understand their relative position within the organization. It's more important to set that platform than to tell people what to do. The employees here are expected to deliver a lot more results. It causes some pressure and stress, which isn't necessarily a bad thing.

In addition to setting overall direction for his group, Gray spends his time and energy trying to help his subordinates to be successful at what they do. "I don't have a lot of time to go tell people how to do their jobs," says Gray. "I take pulse checks from time to time and don't get super-involved in determining what projects we should be doing.

VOICES FROM THE FRONT LINES

What Works: Frequency[6]

"I set monthly targets for both sales staff and trainers. We hold monthly branch meetings and weekly sales coaching meetings, aimed at maintaining a constant eye on quality and professionalism for each branch."

"We hold bimonthly information sessions, which are very relaxed. The purpose is to communicate goings-on with the teams from the corporate level, or to share a team's current project successes with other teams. These sessions work really well right now, as our division is fairly small (less than 100 people). As we grow, this will become difficult to sustain."

"Executive management has quarterly meetings to communicate short- and long-term strategy and how current projects are linked to and aligned with those priorities."

"Strategy is communicated well, changed often!"

"It's about empowerment and people having an idea of how they impact the business and knowing that they can make decisions. Then the empowerment is powerful. At Cendant, all decisions are made on economics. It's all about the numbers. You've got to be able to deliver. If you don't, you're not going to survive or thrive here. It actually simplifies things."

This viewpoint is not limited to headquarters and top management. At the contact center in Phoenix, Christine Parren is the site manager. Ten supervisors and 130 staffers field phone calls for reservations with Cendant's nine hotel brands.[7] Parren, who has worked at various divisions of Cendant for more than 10 years, is responsible for all operations at the center.

"I think a lot about how to keep my staff well-connected," says Parren. She keeps her staff informed by weekly staff meetings and one-on-one meetings with her 10 direct reports every other week. However, it's not the fact that Parren holds the meetings that's important, but what she focuses on during them.

"We show everyone how our team fits into the whole division's performance," says Parren. "We conduct a lot of exercises and show how even a point-eight percent change might impact the overall plan. We keep everyone focused on the results and the contribution to the entire division."

Parren spends considerable time and effort making sure everyone understands their role in the company more or less on a relatively real-time basis. Says Parren:

> We drill down to their individual agent-group performance. We point out their strengths and opportunities and try to point out things—for example, that your team is one-third of the group's performance. The supervisor group is well aware of performance, so much so that you could call any one of them and they could tell you what our performance was yesterday and whether their agents had a good day or a bad day individually.
>
> We utilize sales boards and we post daily performance. We rank it versus a year ago and relate it to goal. There used to be a focus on whether someone missed their numbers and punishing them if they did. Now we're working to assist people with making their goals. Agents are now much more aware of their goals and focus.

When people feel like they're exceeding their goals, it's a motiva-
tor. It also creates friendly team competition. People often pass me
in the hallways and say they're doing better today than yesterday,
and I share their enthusiasm with them. I feel I make a difference.

Much like Guy Gray thousands of miles away, Parren in many
ways is really working for her team. "This is a very fast-paced environment, and my role is to remove obstacles." As a result, the
Phoenix center had the company's greatest numerical increase in
employee improvement scores between the years 2000 and 2001.

One way to measure whether you are personally involved with
your company's numbers is to stop for a moment and write down
what you personally contribute to your organization's performance
on a daily, weekly, monthly, and quarterly basis. If you cannot determine this because of a lack of information, set up a meeting with your
immediate supervisor. If that supervisor doesn't have the answer, you
may be able to find out by moving up the chain of command or
checking with others in the organization. To effectively manage for
the short term, it is imperative that personal metrics be understood.
You must know precisely where you fit and how your contribution is
measured.

This understanding of "fit" and contribution provides a clearer
picture of personal and departmental value as well as individual self-
worth. That knowledge can be particularly useful in tough times,
when being able to document individual contribution can sometimes
mean the difference between employment and a job search.

REWARDS BASED ON METRICS

Helping everyone understand how they personally can affect the
company's metrics includes providing tangible rewards when those
measurements show success. Those rewards should be as concrete
and measurable as the metrics themselves. For example, if a company
promises to share with its employees the savings from efficiency
improvements, issuing a separate check to every employee for his or
her share of them makes those savings tangible. The gesture then has
a much bigger impact than adding the amount to a regular paycheck,

---

VOICES FROM THE FRONT LINES

What Works: Size[8]

"We have a small enough organization (21) that communication is much easier and more effective. Having experienced executive management in larger organizations, there is a difference. There is more complexity involved when your people are spread out in different offices. With a smaller organization that has four different office locations, communication is more organized, and each person takes more responsibility for their projects and results."

"Even within our small group of under 50, communication is poor, and work tends to get done in silos."

"Historically, engineers and upper management have been cordial, but true understanding has been sorely missing. In my own job, I fill the role of the 'communications bridge' between the technical forces of my company and its upper management. This is the proper role of a CTO—that is, not to invent things but to get the whole organization leaning in the same direction while continuing to get the day-to-day job done."

---

where Social Security and unemployment insurance deductions will minimize the amount and make it far less noticeable.

The individual manager has to clearly understand that "if I do this, then here is the impact on the organization and this will be my personal payback." Doing so provides the personal incentive that can help reduce the gap between corporate truth and street truth. Too often, compensation plans are not connected to the performance that will deliver on an announced strategy.

MOVING EXECUTIVE FOCUS TO THE INSIDE

Ensuring that individuals understand their personal contribution to the overall goal requires intensive focus on an organization's internal concerns. When managing for the short term, it is necessary for the CEO and executive management to achieve a better balance between internal issues and external necessities. This is not done primarily to benefit executives so much as it is to help the management team

become a living part of the organization's strategy. A dramatic benefit is that the vision and strategy of the executive can more easily be
realized, delivering what is being promised to (and expected by)
external forces, including investors.

Kevin Callahan is President and CEO of Exeter Health Resources,
which comprises Exeter Hospital, Exeter Healthcare, Matrix Health,
Core Physician Services, Synergy Health and Fitness, and the Rock-
ingham Visiting Nurse Association and Hospice, all in New Hamp-
shire. Callahan finds himself in an industry that, like many others,
has a unique set of challenges.[9] Says Callahan:

> Health care is an industry whose growth and demands are very dif-
> ferent. It's the single largest consolidated industry, and an industry
> where everybody wants the service. Forty to 50 percent of the
> service is controlled by the federal government and insurance.
> There also is a significant role by the employer as the sponsor. It's
> a trillion-dollar industry where the customers have no economic
> appreciation. This is an industry that's facing an aging population
> moving into the time of peak health care consumption. Technology
> has proliferated and driven areas from cardiac pumps to pharma-
> cology. A typical expense was hospitalization; now it's pharmaceu-
> tical. And looming out there is the genomic and biotech impact on
> health care.
>
> There's almost unlimited demand for health care in this country,
> but there are major limiting factors. Human resources is the first,
> where the average age of a nurse is 45 with plans to retire in the fore-
> seeable future and lack of technical personnel. So we have 80 million
> baby boomers coming of age and a health care workforce that is
> being depleted. The other rate-limiting factor is the ability to
> respond to unrelenting demand with capital, because it is facility-
> intensive. Because of the depression in reimbursements from the fed-
> eral government, there is negative impact on availability of capital.

As Callahan's words indicate, Exeter Health Resources faces challenges as strenuous as those of any industry, so it is critical that the
organization run at its peak. And peak performance requires each individual to perform at his or her best, all focused in the same direction as
the organization. "A struggle in this environment is, 'How do you find
competent leaders and staff and retain them?'" says Callahan. "We
have to keep these people engaged and enrolled in what they do."

Exeter Health Resources discovered, in probing communications with its entire management group, that middle management in particular was highly frustrated. Managers felt they were being placed in the position of managing day to day and with scarce resources. It was a combination of the type and amount of work being asked of them. Once that problem was identified, the CEO consciously decided to focus internally for the sake of the long-term direction of the organization. Says Callahan:

> The constant focus of middle management of the past was to keep the trains running. We found that the managers could not self-actualize. We started working with the middle management ranks. I try to meet with each manager individually and listen to them. I found that a CEO's jobs are in some ways easy compared to what middle managers have to deal with.
>
> We were forced to start looking at issues, such as has the skill set that's required changed? What is the new skill set? It's not compensation issues for retention; for us, the employee group is looking for a level of intimacy with their immediate supervisor and with the corporation, which is what they feel they don't have. They lack the intimacy, the purpose of the corporation. Because we all can feel at times that we're on a treadmill, we have begun to use focused retreats with middle management to explore the tactics of creating this intimacy within the organization. What we are seeing is people want a work–life balance. We found they have an inability to leave the job at the work site when they go home. They feel there's no solution. Managers have lost the connection to the future goals.
>
> With a looming shortage of health care professionals coming in, we have conducted a series of employee alignment surveys over the last four years. The workforce said we don't have an intimate relationship with our management force. The number one factor that contributed to the lack of alignment is communication. Those who knew the strategy were aligned, but we found that the majority didn't know the strategy.

It was at that moment that Callahan decided to shift his focus to dealing with internal issues and aligning the management team. As is the case with most chief executives, Callahan continually faces challenges and opportunities to change course, or at least change focus. He likens his role to going down a river that has many tributaries. "As

---

Voices from the Front Lines

Problems with Focus[10]

"Sometimes it feels that executive management gives more significance to the demands of the outside stakeholders than they do to those inside of the organization. The amount of PR is amazing, and it seems to bog down their agendas to a point where they have little time to get back to working with the employees."

"Reporting often gets discouraged when managers and supervisors either do not read it or, even more likely, do not consider acting on it!"

"My superiors don't seem to care how my projects are going until they are forced to be involved by the top executives. Once my projects hit the executive spotlight, I am allowed the resources to get it done."

"In a partnership-led professional service organization, it seems there is great communication amongst the partners but little with the remainder of staff—even senior staff. Similar organizations structured as regular business corporations seem to communicate far better both up and down the ladder."

CEO, you get pulled into tributaries and you have to keep your sight on the river," says Callahan. "A lot of CEOs get sucked in and never come out."

Callahan's focus has to be remarkably versatile, since like any manager he is pulled in many different directions. And like many CEOs, he feels responsible for staying focused on the outside forces that will impact his organization, even as he faces the realities of his company's internal challenges.

> My swing to internal was really not by desire; it was out of necessity. I view my role as thinking outside our operations and try to focus on seeing around the corner. However, 61 percent of our production cost is labor, and since I have accountability for the revenue stream, I have to deal with this area of this human-services-intensive business.

Although Exeter Health Resources is privately held, Callahan must deal with bondholders, bond-rating agencies such as S&P and Moody's, Medicare, and massive regulatory oversight. Callahan reports to an outside board of directors, and while the various external factions are primarily looking at the numbers, the CEO has to make sure his employees can deliver those ongoing results.

"We're intensely financially driven on one hand, but the quality of our service has to be excellent," says Callahan. "This requires a sophisticated set of skill sets in a manager. We created a balanced scorecard to communicate to our managers the relative value of issues dealing with goals and objectives. The balanced scorecard helps us communicate effectively."

Managing for the short term is all about balance. In the case of managers and employees at Exeter Health Resources, there is the balance between work and home life. For the chief executive, it is the balance of internal and external forces, the balance between making the numbers and delivering value to customers—in this case, patients.

Once it becomes second nature for managers at all levels to measure themselves within the context of the corporate measurements, the organization can start to move forward on successful execution of strategy. And since managers' actions are tied to the health and development of the overall company, those that deliver will be well-positioned to take on increasing responsibility in that broader context—in short, to become the company's leaders.

9

Leading for
the Short Term

Not every executive has the luxury of leading only during the best of times. During the great prosperity of the mid-nineties, many executives found their companies faced with nonstop growth and increasing market size or share. Under the circumstances, concern for costs often seemed relatively unimportant. Dramatic increases in revenue and stock price kept most stakeholders happy. However, during economic downturns, corporations tighten their belts and executives feel more pressure to deliver positive results— by any measurement. The economic fallout of the World Trade Center attack on September 11 accelerated the challenges of coping with an impending recession, and in 2001 there were few companies that were not in some way affected.

Despite annual sales nearing $30 billion, The Dow Chemical Company was among those that were not immune. Headquartered in Midland, Michigan, Dow Chemical is the largest chemical company in the United States, and is the world leader in the production of chemicals, plastics, and agricultural chemicals. Leading the global entity, with its approximately 50,000 employees, is Michael D. Parker, who became President and CEO in November 2000, just as the overall economy began to deteriorate.[1]

"This is the toughest environment the chemical industry has faced in more than 30 years," says Parker. "Dow is 104 years old and very strong in a mature industry that is very big."

The chemical industry, including pharmaceuticals, represents approximately $1.7 trillion in sales annually. During the previous decade, Dow had transformed itself from a geographically organized company to a business whose strategies and operations were totally global. "We look outside for best practices and leverage work processes across our global structure," says Parker. "We believe in operational excellence as a fundamental model. We are a very good company getting better all the time, and we're trying to get bigger." As is the case with many large companies, growth has been primarily through acquisition. "The key is synergies after an acquisition," says Parker. In addition to absorbing its acquisitions, Parker is looking for "truly new things" for sustainable, long-term business growth. "I'm trying to get a whole organization to focus externally on the marketplace."

Like many top executives, Parker finds himself facing various constituencies. Parker fully understands how key understanding and serving all of the stakeholders in the company is to leadership when managing for the short term. From the start, he has focused on establishing a heightened sense of teamwork, leadership at all levels and outside-in focus, to enhance performance and ensure the needs of all stakeholders are well understood. "The organization will look to me, so I must role-model the behavior I expect," says Parker, who always keeps an eye on each set of stakeholders.

We have four sets of stakeholders. First, there are the shareholders, so I have to spend considerable time with analysts and those who own, or might want to own, significant shares of our stock. Then we have our customers, and I spend time there because it's a signal to our organization that we have to be more market-focused. Third, there are our employees, and my role is motivating them. I think they need to see the leader is a hardworking guy, who believes in the company, is highly motivated and is having a great time. And fourth, there are the communities in which we operate, whether here in Midland, Michigan, or Freeport, Texas, or Stade, Germany—all of which are small towns that keep us highly accountable for our actions.

As is the case with many chief executives, Parker's emphasis on when and where to focus on which set of stakeholders continually shifts. He sees communications with his direct reports as critical, especially in closing the gap between strategy and execution.

Parker has the benefit of understanding his industry inside and out, having worked his way up at Dow since he started his career there in organics research and development in 1968. Parker knows how critical information-sharing and knowledge of the corporate mission, values, strategy, and direction is to the company's future. That understanding is the basis of his goal to enhance high-performance teamwork and leadership at all levels. Something, he concludes, must be modeled from the very top. That is why he created the Corporate Operating Board, a 16-person team comprising his direct reports.

> **People want to be good team players, but if they don't see the whole picture, they can't be.**

So, for one week each month, Parker's Corporate Operating Board, which includes eight business group presidents, six corporate functional heads, and one geographic head, all work with Parker, meeting as the most senior leadership team in the company. Says Parker:

> We run the company during that week. We work together setting the strategy and direction. As an example, we've just finished creating a comprehensive People Strategy, to ensure we are consistently developing our most sustainable source of competitive advantage—our people. Key to the Corporate Operating Board's success is the opportunity it provides Dow's senior leaders to elevate to the big picture level one week a month and to focus on their particular area of responsibility for the other three weeks of the month. It provides transparency and clarity as well as alignment.
>
> The key is to take the noise out of a big system—through transparency and by creating a common level of knowledge and understanding. Doing this over time, a lot of the noise goes away. It also creates great teamwork. People want to be good team players, but if they don't see the whole picture, they can't be. Business is about people.

Parker finds industry experience invaluable. "You need to know a lot about your subject; industry experience is critical," he says.

"The other key to leadership is consistency of purpose. Change must be purposeful. It doesn't come free of charge. With change, the idea is 5 percent; implementation and real effort is 95 percent."

Like many top executives, Parker finds himself working "a huge number of hours; you can't do a job like this and not put in a substantial number of hours." But successfully leading for the short term requires a greater time commitment both from the chief executive and managers in more of the operational matters. By bringing together his top executives one out of every four weeks, Parker ensures that knowledge gets back to the divisions, increasing the odds that leaders within those divisions also are closer to seeing how their actions fit within the greater context of Dow as a whole.

COMMUNICATING FOR A REASON

As Dow's example demonstrates, what's important about communication between senior management and managers is the reason that it's

---

VOICES FROM THE FRONT LINES

What's Involved in Good Communication?[2]

"Organizational communications tend to fall into two categories: (1) Periodic management team updates, which require considerable time commitment and become inefficient over time. (2) Issue-related—more focused and efficient, but reactive in nature. Finding the right balance between these two forms seems to be more of an art than a science. We don't seem to have many good artists in our midst."

"With so much under way in a dynamic environment, the need to be targeted and disciplined in communication is critical."

"Operationally, feedback on communications has been excellent. Personally, I would like to extend communications to also confirm movement in terms of strategic targets and goals—we cover those well, but fighting fires is the priority."

"Does the organization *value* upward communication, or merely tolerate it?"

being done. It must give senior executives and managers such a thorough understanding of how they can advance the organization's goals that they can make decisions independently that are consistent with those goals. That understanding should help them spot new opportunities or obstacles that the CEO, being generally more removed from day-do-day customer interactions and daily operations, might never be aware of.

Companies that want to make those connections sometimes set up multiday retreats to discuss corporate direction in an attempt to align senior management's vision throughout the organization. Unlike Dow's process, in which senior executives work at headquarters one week each month, these efforts are often sporadic. Unless the strategy and vision are made relevant to the ongoing realities of the managers' daily lives—essential to managing for the short term—we've found from the companies we've talked to that such meetings often have little impact.

Like Dow Chemical, Vandenberg Federal Credit Union, which serves Vandenberg Air Force Base and seven other California locations, has found, too, that making regular connections works better than larger, infrequent sessions. "We've all tactically run into the same problem," says Diana Dykstra, President and CEO.[3] "We have a three-day offsite to go over the strategic plan and vision and then we go running off and get a disconnect really quickly because everybody gets so caught up in the day-to-day. Life is what happens when we go back to our desks."

Dykstra has found that ongoing brief reminders using the company's intranet help keep the company vision top of mind. For example, if the organization is introducing a new checking account, there will be a notice on the front page of the company's intranet that not only discusses the introduction but, more important, explains *why* the account is being introduced in terms that tie it to the company's overall goals and strategic plan. Vandenberg's customer base now tends to be older, and part of the corporate strategic plan is to attract younger customers. The discussion of the new checking account might explain why attracting younger customers is important to the company's financial health, even if the product doesn't appeal to the existing customer base that the staff is used to dealing with.

"We're starting to develop small vignettes that don't take an hour to read that explain why we're going to do something, why it's going to be important. With the ivory tower, people tend to look up and say, 'Don't you know what we do every day?' It's not so much 'This is where we're going to go,' but why. It gives people a better sense of where a decision sits in that vision.

"People are starting to say, 'I get it. I've worked for this company for years, and I always thought you guys were idiots.' With an explanation, it's not just something that came out of a board of directors."

> **Breaking the strategy into communication components that mean something to middle managers is key when managing for the short term.**

Dykstra hopes that by pushing information down the pipeline, the flow of information will begin to travel both ways, with the front-line troops linking up their experience with the strategic direction to find new ways to advance the overall vision on a day-to-day basis.

"What I hope to have happen is that it empowers them to be creative and make decisions on their own that support the vision. I want to be getting information from them about how we can do that, instead of them waiting for us to give the direction. I can look at data and I can talk to people, but my customer contact points are the most powerful. I want my teller to be able to say 'It's really important for us to bring 18-year-olds in, and this is why.'"

Breaking the strategy into communication components that mean something to middle managers is key when managing for the short term. When the strategy seems theoretical in the context of day-to-day management, day-to-day managers have a difficult time making it personal. There also has to be an overarching set of principles, which can be viewed as "the way we do it here." It comes down to corporate culture. The tone has to be set at the top.

For example, part of a company's culture might allow for failure as a way to success. In such instances, senior executives must make people understand that in pursuing the vision, it's okay to fail sometimes. "I get frustrated by 'we've always done it that way.' My biggest successes have been my biggest failures," says Dykstra. "Don't just bolt on new processes to fix old problems.

"When staff understand why we're doing what we're doing and can stand up to me and say, 'No, that doesn't fit the strategy,' the strategy is closer to what's actually going on. As CEOs we can get a little wild; we can jump on something with no tactical idea of what's involved in actually doing it. I catch myself saying, 'We must have this new widget.' We don't want to go tearing after implementing that without seeing if it fits the strategic vision.

"As a CEO, it's hard to tell the board, 'No, we're not going to do that.' It's easy to say yes; that's why the plates get full."

CEO As Bridge Between Inside and Out

Sometimes events create dramatic changes both inside and outside an organization—changes that the top executives are forced to deal with in one way or another. Such was the case at Delta Air Lines when the events of September 11 left the airline industry in dire financial straits. "You have to live in the short term while you're seeking the long," says Leo Mullin, Chairman and CEO of Delta Air Lines.[4] "At Delta, we were in an immediate term crisis beginning September 11. After that date, it was not clear from a financial standpoint how the industry would get through this." Says Mullin:

> How fast would traffic come back? In October, we were scheduled for a board update on strategy, but we spent the time on liquidity analysis. We are highly oriented toward cash flow, but at the same time, we had to be looking at what kinds of environmental and competitive pressures were developing. Our goal was to have Delta come out stronger than when it went in. The crucial ingredient was to keep both the short-term crisis and the long-term strategy front of mind. To succeed, you can never lose sight of your compass and sense of where you want to go and you must also keep in mind what the competition is doing and how the market is changing. We realized this could be the biggest strategic opportunity to achieve our market objectives. When you encounter a crisis like September 11, you don't turn to the textbooks. You either have it, or you don't.

Before September 11, we concluded there would be no major airline mergers for four or five years. After September 11, we found that the government's policy regarding government loan guarantees might actually be aimed at aiding industry consolidation.

Internally, Mullin quickly created a significant internal communication effort so that all managers and employees understood the company's plans for the short term. "We took a massive approach towards internal communication, including daily status reports as to how and what we were doing," says Mullin. "You have to be prepared to put yourself out into the forum so the organization understands what the company is doing to advance the cause."

Mullin also found himself involved in external aspects of the airline industry, including trips to Washington and battles on behalf of all the airlines. As a result, Delta employees were able to watch their CEO on television, arguing for help for the airline industry and for Delta. "The employees had the sense that the CEO entered the battle in the external arena on their behalf." Delta will receive a total of $654 million from the government, winning Mullin additional support from many Delta employees.

CEO LEADERSHIP FOR THE SHORT TERM

In addition to being the facilitator between the inside and outside arenas associated with the corporation, CEO and top management must juggle a variety of tasks in helping managers lead for the short term. He must:

- Conduct Internal PR

    The CEO can define and communicate the strategy, but without a solid plan for communicating that strategy to the people responsible for implementing it, the potential for disconnect is enormous. Successful leadership for the short term means setting up an effective formal employee communications effort and understanding and making use of the informal ways in which employees gather and exchange information.

- Act As Chief Culture Officer

   If the CEO is not vigilant about making sure that the company's strategy takes into account its culture—and that the culture is shaped so that it supports the strategy—the disconnect can lead to catastrophe.

   Executive leaders must take charge of implementing change and helping employees understand the company's values. In some cases, companies create a formal culture officer; in others it is simply part of the role of the CEO and executive team to ensure that the company culture is aligned with its business strategy.

- Create Strategy with Input from Throughout the Organization

   A chief executive must be able to develop and refine strategy on an ongoing basis to accommodate the realities of the organization and the marketplace. Senior management must walk a fine line between being able to implement strategic initiatives quickly, and ensuring that those initiatives take into account their implications for all parts of the organization.

- Align Performance with Strategy Through Compensation and Incentives

   Incentive planning should not be considered simply a human resources function or a frill. Unless people are compensated in ways that reinforce the organization's priorities, performance can become disassociated from strategy. A CEO can have a powerful effect on how incentives are perceived. For example, a CEO who has decided to reward employees if the company meets certain performance standards must do so in a way that links the reward to the goal. Rather than simply adding a bonus to a regular paycheck, where the impact is diminished by deductions, the bonus could be paid out in a separate check specifically identified as the employee's share of the money the company gained by meeting a specific goal. Rather than being an afterthought, incentives should be overseen by someone in senior management who can make that connection between performance and reward clear.

- Make HR Strategic

   As the economy increasingly becomes knowledge-based, hiring the right people becomes more and more important. In some cases, it may be more useful to think in terms of hiring a person and tailoring the job for their unique set of skills rather than hiring for a job that requires having to hunt for just the right person.

• Make IT Strategic

One study of 420 information technology professionals found that 52 percent of those surveyed felt their largest IT initiatives were directly linked to the business goals and objectives of their organizations. That means that almost as many—48 percent—*didn't* agree that their largest initiatives were linked to business goals.[5]

Because of the rapidly changing nature of technology, it's especially important that senior management stay in close communication with their technology and finance people when developing strategy. Not only can they stay more informed about technology capabilities that can enhance the business, but they can align IT spending plans more closely with the business cycle. Many executives already realize the strategic importance of technology. An understanding of technology is the leadership skill managers would most like to enhance in themselves[6] (see Figure 9.1).

FIGURE 9.1

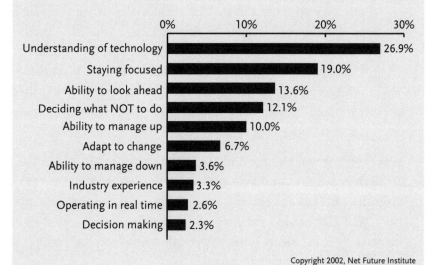

"Which of the following leadership qualities would you most like to enhance in yourself?"

Quality	Percentage
Understanding of technology	26.9%
Staying focused	19.0%
Ability to look ahead	13.6%
Deciding what NOT to do	12.1%
Ability to manage up	10.0%
Adapt to change	6.7%
Ability to manage down	3.6%
Industry experience	3.3%
Operating in real time	2.6%
Decision making	2.3%

Copyright 2002, Net Future Institute

- Act As COO for the General Managers

  Senior management is responsible for ensuring that the next tier of managers is clearly communicating the corporate vision to their respective subordinates. Unless that link is strong, communication of strategy becomes like a giant game of Gossip. The message becomes distorted by every person who communicates it until, by the time it gets to the individual worker, it is unrecognizable.

- Conduct Internal Communication

  Even having a good formal internal communications department is not enough to make a difference in achieving high performance. A study by the International Association of Business Communicators[7] found that even in high-performing companies, having a good communications program was less important in determining the success of a corporate initiative than several other factors that stem from the culture of the company itself.

  Those factors included:
    - **Clarity of purpose**. Successful companies concentrated on a limited number of key messages and made sure that they were really driven home consistently.
    - A corporate atmosphere of **openness and trust**. Successful companies had an environment in which people were allowed and encouraged to ask questions.
    - Effective **information sharing**. Successful companies tended to use both formal knowledge-sharing devices such as databases and printed material, and informal devices such as networking events and job-swapping programs.
    - **Consistent behavior** by company leaders. Companies where executives were not perceived to practice what they preached experienced less success with their initiatives than did others.

- Leverage Internal and External Information More Efficiently

  Both executives and managers need to identify the sources of essential information and the most direct route for that information. Half the battle of communicating either up or down is in identifying who needs what information and how best to get it from its source to the right people.

Gaining Support for the Vision: The Senior Executive

Executives and managers clearly rank the ability to recognize and adapt to change as the leadership quality most important to them[8] (see Figure 9.2). Interestingly, the ability to manage down is viewed as the least important in terms of personal leadership.

However, recognizing and adapting to change isn't enough. Neither is communicating the business plan or strategic vision for adapting to that change. Even if executives have conveyed the company's business plan, they may not be successful at helping managers and employees understand how it applies to their business unit or work group. In one study, two-thirds of workers said they understood the business plan and their personal role in achieving it, yet fewer than half said their manager had explained how the plan affected their work group or communicated well with the staff.[9]

Even when executive management is communicating well, the message often doesn't get through. While there is a greater need for communication between executives and their managers, it is essential

FIGURE 9.2

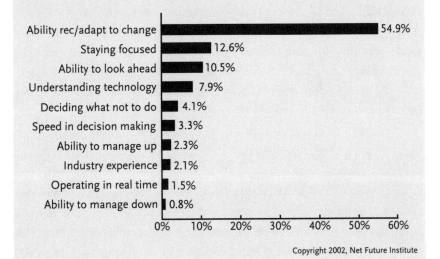

"Which of the following leadership qualities has been most important for you personally?"

- Ability rec/adapt to change — 54.9%
- Staying focused — 12.6%
- Ability to look ahead — 10.5%
- Understanding technology — 7.9%
- Deciding what not to do — 4.1%
- Speed in decision making — 3.3%
- Ability to manage up — 2.3%
- Industry experience — 2.1%
- Operating in real time — 1.5%
- Ability to manage down — 0.8%

Copyright 2002, Net Future Institute

that the communication be perceived as relevant. When there are not enough hours in the day, every communication must be significant to the recipient. A message that isn't significant or personally relevant will be ignored.

In my experience, every executive would be credited with better communications skills if he or she were to meet with every manager and employee on a one-to-one basis every day; obviously, that's not practical. But using some form of effective two-way communication is critical for managing for the short term. Executive managers find themselves caught between the chief executive's strategy and their subordinates' execution. Whether or not they realize it, they act as translators in two directions. The chief financial officer is interpreting financial metrics for both the CEO and for managers who must prepare budgets. Chief marketing officers are converting strategy into marketing messages and customer information into marketing plans. Information-technology executives mediate corporate desires, technological capabilities, and timely implementation.

"I see myself as the conduit of knowledge," says Antonio Monteiro, Chief Information Officer of Internet Securities, a New York–based provider of emerging markets business information in the United States, Europe, Latin America, and Asia.[10] "I find myself in the role of translating business into technology and the other way around."

It is generally simpler to communicate up than down, primarily because there are fewer people to communicate with when communicating up. After all, an executive or manager generally works for one or two people, while there may be dozens or hundreds or even thousands working for those same executives or managers. For example, at Internet Securities, a subsidiary of Euromoney Institutional Investor in London, the CIO reports to one or two executives but manages 80 people scattered throughout 20 countries.

"We have to communicate down in different languages in different cultures," says Monteiro. "I communicate by phone, e-mail [Internet instant messaging], and in person. But the most effective is face-to-face. With 80 people in different parts of the world, we mostly rely on e-mail, so managing down is not as effective as managing up. The best would be if I had them all in one room, being able to react to one set of emotions, but that's not going to happen. Talking to people individually is the best form of communication. Sometimes people have the impression that they have a job to do and management are just figureheads to them, so they listen and then they move on. It is important to involve them in the decision-making process so they're involved in as many ways as possible."

COMMUNICATING UP THE PIPELINE

Being a Mind Reader

With the increased pressure on senior management to have far more complete, up-to-date information than ever before, managers are simultaneously more important and less important than ever before. Senior executives used to be able to simply delegate to their managers; now, because they are being held more accountable by their boards, shareholders, and stakeholders, they must know much more about exactly what is happening in each division.

That means that a senior manager must not only make that information available in an ongoing, constantly updated way, but must also be able to communicate the information in a way that the top management can use effectively.

If a manager goes to an executive with an issue, it had better be for a good reason or it will likely be handed right back. (For that matter, if an executive goes to a manager, there had better be a good reason as well. Even if the issue doesn't get handed back, it might get buried under everything else the manager is juggling. As we will see later, most things that are critical tend to bubble up on their own.)

Managers have to figure out exactly what the boss needs to make better strategic and tactical decisions. The flip side of good communication from the executive level is the ability of managers to understand their individual roles and how those roles can advance the corporate goals, even if a given task lies outside their specific assigned responsibilities.

In essence, managers must become mind readers. The better they understand the challenges that the boss faces, the better they can supply the information needed to cope with them. The role of the executive in this process of mind reading is to make it as easy as pos-

VOICES FROM THE FRONT LINES

Obstacles to Upward Communication[11]

"There seems to be a great deal of fear [about] talking with senior management and an insistence that the presentation get 'spun' in a positive direction—it doesn't seem that anyone wants to hear the truth, at least if that has any possibility of being perceived in a negative light."

"Proximity (less than 150 feet or visual connection) is influential. Being officed on the other side of the floor makes informal updates much more difficult."

"In a lean organization, less than 80 employees at the head office for a 40,000-plus-employees organization, it is hard for a VP to get access to a level above, since the amount of reporting increases drastically from one level to the other."

"I have tried to provide status of what I believe my manager should know, which includes all of the many assignments for my team, but have been instructed by my manager to report only those tasks [for] which my team has the lead role. This reporting also needs to be a certain way so that he could easily roll up a status to his manager without having duplicate entries. In the end, this might be okay, but it also could overlook some of the mission-critical tasks that my team has worked on."

"Building open-minded and outspoken teams is always a long-term and complex project, even more complex in an ever-growing organization which is undergoing many motions of reorganization."

sible for subordinates to read his or her mind, allowing subordinates to be proactive about anticipating the effects of their actions.

In a way, the process functions almost like a neural network. The senior executives need to set up the metrics and help build pathways of communication with managers, who can use them to convey the needed information. That information flow needs to be adaptable in real time, using whatever pathways are most effective. To know what warrants that escalation, it's important to know the executive's own priorities, the role he or she plays in the larger organization.

Here are the questions every manager needs to ask about higher-ups to improve his or her mind-reading ability:

Voices from the Front Lines

Communicating Up: The Boss's View[12]

"The openness of communication seems to be at my encouragement—I have to be proactive to keep the channels open, or they don't communicate well. They communicate the routine matters well—what they don't communicate well are 'signals and symptoms' of emerging issues or problems. Those tend to get escalated when they are at a 'problem' mode, not in advance—thus the interviewing from top down."

"Weekly status reports are important, but not necessarily for what is said. What is *not* said in a status report tells you what is really occurring in your organization."

"It is difficult for some managers to communicate bad news to me [as their CEO]. I have tried to coach and train them to say it 'as is' in a timely manner. Sometimes the bad news can also be good news, I always say to them, if it is dealt with honestly and timely."

"Communications is a challenge in the best of times and circumstances. Today more than ever, people are distracted and a major part of managing is interpretation of the words, acts, and deeds of the different people who work for me. Creating environments for them to make comments [knowing] that they won't be punished or chastised for their opinion is a priority."

"Communication gets filtered through other levels of management. I like speaking directly to the front-line and back-office associates . . . they tell me what is *really* happening. Their messages are usually very straightforward, and I have to be thick-skinned to hear it all, but it gives me a chance to respond to misconceptions, respond truthfully (which is sometimes 'we cannot do this, and here is why'), and to even say 'I don't know' or 'I had not thought of that.'"

- **Exactly what do they need?** Is it information? New ideas? Detailed reports or highlights? Statistics or an overview? Or are results alone enough? What company priorities is the boss charged with furthering?

- **Exactly when do they need it?** Is it enough to provide information on an "as needed" basis, or does the executive need reports at regular, defined intervals?

- **How will I make sure he knows I have what he needs?** What is the most effective way of shaping the information so that the executive knows where to turn?

"You Can't Handle the Truth"

A large company I once worked for had a very intelligent and dynamic chief executive who was charged with turning around a very staid organization in a relatively short period of time. He staffed the company with a few loyal followers from his previous organization and brought in several top-level executives from the outside. Included in the mix was a top lieutenant who, for whatever reason, ultimately soured on the strategy. For the next year, in lower-level staff meetings and private conversations, he totally undercut the chief executive. It got to the point that in staff meetings the chief executive did not attend, this lieutenant would publicly criticize the strategy and openly berate the chief executive.

After about a year, it came out that the lieutenant was leaving the company to join another. This was announced officially in an extremely laudatory memorandum to the entire staff from the chief executive, who greatly praised all that the lieutenant accomplished in his tenure. After the going-away party, I was alone with the chief executive at one point. I mentioned in passing that it seemed awfully gracious for the chief executive to write such a memo and say such nice words at the going-away party, considering everything.

He looked at me, puzzled, and asked, "What do you mean, considering everything?" I said that I had thought the lieutenant really had been fired and that the chief executive was being very professional about it. "Why would I fire him?" the executive asked. "For all those things he has been doing and saying about you," I said. He responded: "What things?"

As I began to relay many, many instances of undercutting, from comments at staff meetings to private discussions about, in essence, a mutiny, it began to dawn on me that the only person in the entire management team who was unaware of the departing lieutenant's ill will was the chief executive.

He finally looked at me and asked: "Why didn't you tell me?" I answered, "I thought you knew."

This is a fairly dramatic example of a situation in which a chief executive is not totally connected—not only to his direct reports but to the "street truth" activities within his own organization. In some cases, many surrounding the chief executive are aware of what's really going on but don't jump at the chance to tell the executive. Why?

- **Self-preservation.** Who wants to be the one to tell the boss the bad news? The "I-can-do-anything" attitude managers so often feel they must demonstrate just doesn't seem to lend itself to approaching an executive with something that could sound like "let me tell you about your shortcomings."

- **Fear of the news sounding like sour grapes or ratting someone else out.** How plausible is it for a manager to go to the executive and say, "I love what you're doing, boss, but let me tell you about what someone else thinks about you that is not so good"?

- **"It's not my place."** "Who am I to tell him what everyone thinks? He's surrounded by people smarter than me."

- **"He's a loser."** The manager feels he knows what's best for the company, and it's not the strategy announced by the executive. Believing the strategy won't work, the manager not only does not buy in, but also expects he will still be at the company after the executive and his strategy are long gone.

The senior executive who focuses only on externals out of a desire for self-preservation should be aware that those same self-preservation instincts should be directed internally, as well. This does not mean a top executive should be paranoid. It does mean that a senior executive who doesn't focus internally and encourage two-way communication risks missing important information that can ultimately affect the externals—that is, the company's performance—and help align the organization in a united direction.

Keeping Senior Management Informed

To keep corporate truth and street truth in sync, senior management need to hear street truth from their managers. When managers figure "I'll let someone else give him the bad news," they're usually not alone; everyone else is figuring the same thing. As a result, a senior executive can be isolated from what is really going on, even if everyone else in the company knows what the deal is.

The good news is that both managers and executives seem to feel that the flow of information upward is fairly good. Asked about how well they feel they communicate important issues to their superiors in terms of how those issues may affect the organization's strategy, 60 percent of managers felt they did either well or very well[13] (see Figure 9.3).

It's not surprising that individuals reporting about their own behavior would perceive that they do well. However, that assessment is not dramatically different from the 67 percent of executives who responded that their subordinates do well or very well at communicating upward[14] (see Figure 9.4). In fact, executives' assessment of their subordinates' communication was slightly higher than that of the managers themselves.

FIGURE 9.3

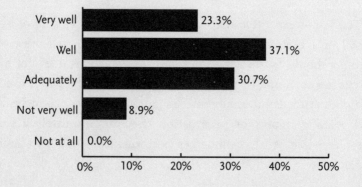

Managers: "How well do you communicate to your superiors important issues concerning the progress of your daily, weekly, monthly, and quarterly projects and tasks in relation to your organization's strategy?"

Very well — 23.3%
Well — 37.1%
Adequately — 30.7%
Not very well — 8.9%
Not at all — 0.0%

Copyright 2002, Net Future Institute

FIGURE 9.4

Senior executives: "How well do your subordinates communicate to you important issues concerning the progress of their daily, weekly, monthly, and quarterly projects and tasks in relation to your organization's strategy?"

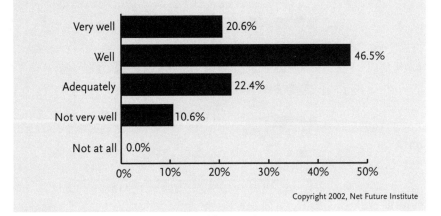

Granted, these executives and subordinates do not necessarily work at the same company and may be talking about different environments. However, it's instructive that the difference between executives' and managers' perceptions of communication from subordinates is not nearly as wide as the gap between their perceptions of how well executives communicate to the troops.

Regarding downward communication, our research showed that more than 73 percent of executives felt they were communicating well to their subordinates, while only 34 percent of managers reported feeling the same way, as discussed in Chapter 7 (see Figure 7.1). When it comes to communicating up, managers and senior executives are more in sync with each other[15] (see Figure 9.5).

Based on these results, the responsibility for the disconnect between managers and executives would seem to lie in the executive suite. Granted, the farther down the corporate hierarchy the message must travel, the larger the number of people involved and the greater the potential for distortion. However, meeting that challenge is clearly one of the major tasks top executives must address if an organization is to successfully manage for the short term.

Information is useful only if it gets to the right person at the right

FIGURE 9.5

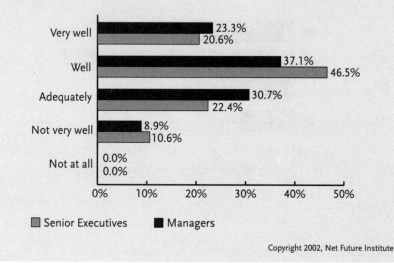

"How well do managers communicate to senior executives important issues concerning the progress of their daily, weekly, monthly, and quarterly projects and tasks in relation to their organization's strategy?"

Very well — 23.3% / 20.6%
Well — 37.1% / 46.5%
Adequately — 30.7% / 22.4%
Not very well — 8.9% / 10.6%
Not at all — 0.0% / 0.0%

■ Senior Executives   ■ Managers

Copyright 2002, Net Future Institute

time to enable the person to make the right decision. In some cases, that's the chief executive, who has to use the company's formal communications channels as well as the informal channels. And it has to be clear that bringing bad news to the right ears won't incur a penalty for the message bearer. Making that clear is not just a matter of lip service; as we have repeatedly stated, managers also must understand that delivering unwelcome news is part of their role in helping the company. Too often, problems, bad blood between individuals or divisions, or mistakes get deep-sixed because no one wants to rock the boat or address uncomfortable truths.

A senior executive must ask the right questions and assure others that he or she has a truly open ear. And that openness must be part of the company's culture. Dave Carlson, Programming and Internet Development Manager for the Antioch Company and Creative Memories, says that executives at the worldwide direct and retail seller of photo albums, scrapbooks, and bookmarks establish a comfortable environment for questions and opinions:[16] "It starts with our corporate values, including the ones about 'safe environment for introducing ideas' and 'tolerance for failure.' I have heard several executives state publicly that it's okay to come to them with bad news. My experience with each of the company executives is that they are compassionate people who don't punish the messenger. . . . They make it clear through their words and actions."

It helps that at Antioch strategic decisions are extensively discussed at various levels before any pronouncements are made. "Whenever possible, people involved are given the opportunity to express their opinions. Many strategic decisions are developed by group consensus. When the CEO or another executive makes a less-than-popular decision, they do a good job of explaining the reason for their decision. People still may not like the decision, but they accept it and support where they can."

Being employee-owned helps, Carlson says. "Except for infrequent executive sessions, board meetings are open to everyone in the company. Two voting members of the board are elected from the working population. These employee-owner board members ensure there is a two-way flow of information and opinions." In addition, the CEO gives quarterly updates in the workplace at a variety of times and locations so any interested employee-owner can attend, and monthly birthday celebrations give additional opportunities for interaction.

Regardless of the method used, that kind of open atmosphere is essential if managers are to put themselves on the line to deliver the fullest possible picture of what's really going on.

COMMUNICATING IN REAL TIME

The true, two-way communication required in managing for the short term can take many forms. Because technology has enabled the free flow of information to anyone, anywhere on a real-time basis, there is opportunity to tap into vast knowledge sources throughout (and even outside) an organization.

At AT&T, executives and managers in many divisions make use of this technological capability and involve managers in real-time decision making. "To succeed as a leader, you must foster communication

VOICES FROM THE FRONT LINES

Encouraging Upward Communication[17]

"E-mail has helped tremendously in keeping team members advised of progress on current projects."

"Communications [are] usually in e-mail form for daily and weekly items—feedback is usually missing. Communications [are] usually face-to-face with presentations for monthly and quarterly items."

"Matching or synching the strategy to the objectives and its progress is expressed not only to senior execs but to direct reports. Direct reports must understand the coupling of business strategy to their work. Great ideas and suggestions that may shape the business can surface due to a proper environment."

"The key to obtaining and receiving an appropriate amount of information from the team is to have regular one-on-one sessions which are adhered to. Time must be made to make subordinates feel that their updates are important to you, and feedback must be given to ensure that the right level of detail is provided. Also, the team must feel empowered to take responsibility for their updates and have the autonomy to [act on] agreements from the one-on-one."

"I work on the same principle that I expect from my direct reports: I communicate on an as-needed basis. I don't want to have to stand looking over someone's shoulder, and I don't want someone to stand over mine. But when there is something to be communicated, good or bad, it should be as promptly as possible. Outside of that, subordinates and supervisors should agree up front how they want to handle communication, including how often and in what format."

"Regularly scheduled status meetings are great for relationship building, but tend to be counterproductive. If you are spending significant time preparing material for your regular meetings and your superior is taking time out of their schedule, you both should have more to show for it than warm fuzzies. The key is trust based on meaningful reports that identify specific areas of concern, the causes, and corrective scenarios. Trust is given and trust is earned."

"We have weekly one-on-ones where we discuss all the issues and actions required. We also have biweekly cross-functional meetings [at which] we discuss the issues and get cross-functional feedback. We also utilize policy deployment that provides the enterprise direction to all levels."

"Good communication exists on project status but not in relation to strategic implications.

"Complexity of organization, links in the chain of command make little difference in communications flow in any direction. . . . The critical factor is the listening factor—that is, how easily and well superiors and subordinates listen. It is a critical skill."

among employees and embrace the technology that improves the frequency and quality of communication and collaboration," says Pat Traynor, Vice President in charge of Web Hosting Services at AT&T.[18]

Traynor and her group used to have weekly and quarterly meetings at which pressing current and future issues would be discussed. As in many other large companies on the scale of IBM and GE, AT&T found that with the growth of its corporate intranet, it was more capable of sharing information with managers all the time rather than at predetermined intervals. Says Traynor:

> Today, Web-based forums enable real-time and near real-time discussion and debate across the organization. And debate is a healthy way to elicit participation among team members. When the implications are strategic or are deeply going to impact financial results, that's when you see a natural culling out of issues. The decisions to be made or topics that matter most are quickly identified, becoming obvious to all involved.
>
> Technology as a facilitator for communication removes not only geographic and time barriers, but also barriers often associated with level within an organization. In my own experience, the key to successful use of technology for communication is a leader's openness to new ideas, discussion, and diversity of thought. I've found that by opening myself up to information from a variety of sources, rather than a select few, the end result is far better. I receive thoughtful information from multiple sources, sooner and without mediation, enabling me to come to decisions more quickly and on a more informed basis. This method of communication has also had a tremendously positive impact on man-

agers. With this openness of communication, people are engaged and empowered.

We're quickly moving toward a model of self-facilitation, where more executives will become dependent on real-time, Net-accessible information. We'll recognize the need to seek diverse views. Each of us will do our own knowledge gathering, and we'll trust our own sources based on learnings and experience with those sources over time.

What I suggest is not unique to any size of company. The technology, the tools, and the ability are available to all; it just takes enlightened leadership to make it work. This is much broader than any individual. You have to have the right leaders who are willing to practice this method of communicating to make it work. Through a process of information sharing, collaboration, and communication, where managers are engaged participants in the decision-making process, consensus is reached when the decision is made, resulting in a much more cohesive organization.

As a practitioner of her viewpoint, Traynor not only shares decision making with her managers through an open exchange of information and active discussion, but also includes business partners and vendors. This ensures that the decisions being made have internal support before execution and are in tune with the current market conditions.

IT'S STILL ABOUT THE NUMBERS

Part of involving leadership at all levels in the corporate vision is helping everyone better understand why the numbers are important to all, as discussed earlier. The numbers usually reflect organizational priorities, and can serve for managers as a good indicator of not only where the company is heading but also what executives are focused on.

"You have to drive everything back to the numbers," says Terry Ransford, Senior Vice President of Northern Trust.[19] "You have to be P&L-driven to take the emotion out. Nobody's going to stand in front of the chairman and say 'I want to do it this way because we'll make less money.'

"The more that the actual people doing the work can invest in the idea that they'll be out of a job if they don't continually improve, the better they will perform," says Ransford.

When all managers and employees understand the details of how a company makes money, see the impact they personally can have on those numbers, and are held accountable, executive management is empowered by their knowledge. That empowerment not only enables better decision-making, but it creates a company atmosphere that is attractive to the type of leaders that all companies want to have on board.

10

Managing People for the Short Term

The same shortened time frame that applies to CEOs also affects the expectations of employees. Unless companies find a way to provide quick and ongoing rewards, impatient employees—usually those that companies most want to keep—are likely to start looking elsewhere.

The increased mobility of the workforce has been well documented. The average turnover rate across all industries is 15 percent, but in some functions it is even higher, ranging from 31 percent in call centers to 123 percent in the fast-food sector.[1] Almost 10 percent of all new college hires leave their job within 1 year; 25 percent leave within five years.[2]

The problem is not limited to entry-level employees. Of 6,900 managers in 35 U.S. companies surveyed about their difficulties in hiring managers, only 44 percent agreed that their company had enough talented managers to take advantage of the most promising business opportunities (only 7 percent strongly agreed).[3] And 90 percent believed it was more difficult to retain managers than in previous years.

And consider these statistics from a study of 500 North American managers and senior executives:[4]

- More than 40 percent reported that they expected to leave their job within two years.

- Twenty percent expected they would leave in six months or less.

- More than 20 percent planned to leave their present position to work for companies in direct competition.

- Twenty-five percent expected the turnover rate at their respective companies to be higher than 20 percent, and 12 percent expected turnover to reach 30 percent or more.

During the economic frenzy experienced during the rapid networking of the 1990s, employers found themselves hampered by a shortage of workers. That frenzy has passed, but employers still must compete for the employees who really matter.

In addition to boosting the cost of replacing people, turnover can affect the bottom line even more directly. More than 44 percent of the managers in the study reported that employee turnover and the resulting lost expertise had cost them customers.[5]

The level of job satisfaction seems to be dropping—one study[6] showed less than 51 percent of respondents being satisfied with their jobs in 2000, compared to 59 percent in 1995. (In another study, the percentage was 48 percent.[7]) And the problem seems to be slightly worse for baby boomers; workers between the ages of 45 and 54 were the least happy among the groups surveyed. The percentage of boomers who considered themselves happy in their jobs dropped from 57.3 percent to 47.5 percent between 1995 and 2000. Gen Xers, by contrast, ranked first in overall job satisfaction; 58.1 percent of those surveyed reported job satisfaction in 1995, compared to 55.6 percent in 2000.[8]

Just as there is a disconnect between top executives and managers, there often is a disconnect between workers and their companies. In one study, 47 percent of respondents believed that their company supported the idea that "what is good for the company is good for the employees"; only 39 percent believed their company also felt that "what is good for the employees is good for the company." Of those who felt their company was employee-focused, most felt that way because of perks, benefits, and employee discounts. Less important (though only slightly) were salary, bonuses, an enjoyable work environment, and recognition, in that order.[9]

Salary would seem to be a baseline for employees; if salary is not competitive or perceived to be appropriate, they will go elsewhere. But a company that wants to be perceived as truly employee-focused can't achieve that just with salary. Executives and managers who responded to a Net Future Institute survey about the most effective means of retaining employees cited autonomy and challenging work as the key incentive, followed by pay increases and advancement opportunities[10] (see Figure 10.1). With one exception—pay increases—this ranking is not dramatically different from the ranking of factors executives and managers said were important for themselves personally (see Chapter 2). Executives and managers rated pay increases as the second most important retention tool for employees; for themselves, compensation and performance-based bonuses came in behind not only autonomy and challenge but work environment and advancement opportunities.

EMPLOYEE TURNOVER: WHEN IS IT A PROBLEM?

Companies spend a great deal of time trying to increase their employee retention rates, with the cost of replacing someone reaching as much as an employee's annual salary. And the higher the level of the

FIGURE 10.1

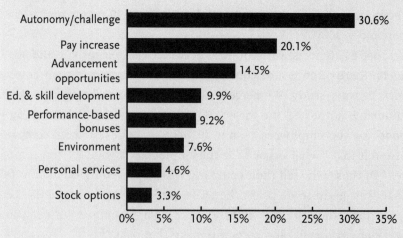

"What incentive for retaining employees has been most effective at your organization?"

Autonomy/challenge — 30.6%
Pay increase — 20.1%
Advancement opportunities — 14.5%
Ed. & skill development — 9.9%
Performance-based bonuses — 9.2%
Environment — 7.6%
Personal services — 4.6%
Stock options — 3.3%

0%   5%   10%   15%   20%   25%   30%   35%

VOICES FROM THE FRONT LINES

Motivating with Challenges[11]

"In our organization, a challenging work environment, with responsibility and ownership for their work, is the biggest source of employee satisfaction. Combined with that is recognition of the individual and the team through compensation, training, and advancement. Money alone will not keep employees happy. That is usually not the reason an employee leaves a company. They leave because they are bored or they do not feel that their value is recognized."

---

employee, the more knowledge exits with him when he leaves. Though turnover rates tend to fluctuate with the state of the unemployment statistics, turnover of valued employees remains a major concern for most companies.

But are companies asking the right question of themselves? Are they beating their collective heads against a wall in an era when companies reshape themselves with mergers and acquisitions, when the demands of technology require ever-changing skill sets, when employees have been conditioned by rapid changes in their job environment to always be on the lookout for their next job?

One study of 107 companies concluded that 40 percent of financially troubled firms reported extremely low employee turnover. At these distressed firms, executives in finance, human resources, manufacturing, operations, and distribution averaged 8 years of service. In healthier companies, that average was 5.2 years.[12] The results can indicate several things, such as that the rapid changes of the business environment mean that it can be useful to have periodic infusions of new thinking about old problems. It also could mean that employees stay at unhealthy companies because of fear, uncertainty, or even lack of confidence. In addition, companies searching for winning talent may not be searching at "losing" companies.

And a Net Future Institute survey showed that managers feel that retaining employees is easier by far than finding the right new employees, even after an economic recession sent unemployment rates higher[13] (see Figure 10.2).

Retention strategies can have mixed results. It's important that pay

FIGURE 10.2

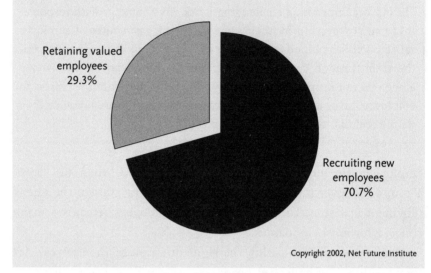

"Which is more difficult for your organization: recruiting new employees or retaining valued employees?"

Retaining valued employees 29.3%

Recruiting new employees 70.7%

is competitive, but it isn't necessarily the highest-paying firms that have the best retention. Even when those salaries are forced upward by stiff competition, raises alone do not constitute a retention strategy.[14]

There is widespread agreement among executives and managers we interviewed that retention of valued employees is beneficial to the organization. Consider these comments from three different managers at both small companies and large corporations:[15]

- "As the saying goes, 'People first, strategy second.' It is impossible to drive business value without top talent retention. Strategies are just as good as people who are able to execute with a degree of skill."

- "Retaining is the key to greater productivity, and thus higher profits for the company."

- "Companies that want to retain their best people need to have a strategy in place. There is too little proactive retention. *Reactionary* is the word I would use to best describe our retention culture."

Retention clearly is a worthwhile goal, but it is not necessarily the best strategy across the board. In some cases, managers might do better to focus their efforts on retaining the employees who matter—and that might be not just individuals but an entire division. For individuals and areas that do not fit those criteria, managers will need to manage to maximize the efficiency of the turnover process. In those cases, managing for the short term may mean recognizing the realities of employee turnover and structuring hiring, training, and even outplacement procedures to make the most of the short time an employee may be with the company.

As one Net Future Institute survey respondent said, "The key is to assure that the incentives are aligned with business strategy . . . this is the most important aspect."

RECRUITMENT CHALLENGES

Every type of organization faces various challenges with recruiting, as highlighted by the comments from three survey respondents (see page 190) concerning different aspects of employee retention.[16]

VOICES FROM THE FRONT LINES

Rewards Tailored to Goals and the Individual[17]

"A combination of short-term, smaller incentives for reaching short-term goals, and larger incentives for reaching long-term goals, are the most appropriate."

"The determination of a short-term incentive versus a long-term incentive will be based on the type of employee. All employees are impacted by short-term incentives. For employees that are critical to the operation, both long term and short term are important."

"The difference in impact is primarily dependent on the attitude and education level of the employee. Better-educated, administrative, and professional employees will be more influenced by long-term incentives. Unskilled, lesser-educated, production, and particularly organized employees are more attuned to immediate gratification."

"Long-term rewards tend to be financial through items such as stock options, bonuses, and promotions/salary increases. The short-term rewards focus more around recognition—names published, etc.—rather than financial."

- **Availability of talent.** "As an IT organization within a large research university, recruiting great folks is hard—even after the 'dot-bomb' era. Our threefold approach, beyond advancement, is a copious supply of technology, travel, and training opportunities."

- **Ability to screen candidates.** Recruiting at different levels of an organization requires different skills. Says one survey respondent: "We use recruitment firms for top management positions, and that works fine. But we seem clueless when it comes to mid-level skill positions. It takes effort to recruit properly. That effort always seems to have a low priority."

- **Market conditions.** In a tight economy, some employees feel safest where they are while riding out the storm. "Most currently employed workers are not interested in changing jobs, and as a company needing additional employees, it is harder to find suitable candidates. The downturn of the economy has set candidates' expectations of income to a more realistic mode than [during] the height of the boom in technology a couple of years ago."

ALIGNING HIRING WITH EXISTING NETWORKS

Possessing great skills in recruiting but not addressing the issue of losing valued employees is like pouring water into a sieve: There's never enough water in the basin.

At SAP America, the North American arm of Germany-based SAP, the world's largest inter-enterprise software company, there is a holistic approach to employee recruitment and retention. Larry Kleinman, Senior Vice President of HR for SAP America, and a member of the executive team, leads a 120-person HR staff serving the 5,000 employees throughout the Americas. He works on trying to understand and optimize the organization's dynamics.

Kleinman views his role as one of making sure the company's managers can manage people.[18] Says Kleinman:

> I believe in viral networks involving informal communications rather than the planned communications. The most effective are the informal networks. You have to identify that network, who

talks to whom and when, and who is important. You have to make sure you message to them first.

Employees are disenfranchised about vision and strategy. People end up working on things that matter to them. The desire in people is that they always want to be worthwhile.

There are two schools of thought. You can either get a clear sense of where we're going or you can get a vision that's just enough to keep chunking along. I opt for the first. If you can get a clear sense of purpose, people can share in it.

Things change so fast, especially in the technology world. Technology really is a different industry.

It's a challenge to make HR strategic. Retention has become a strategic issue because it is the biggest limit to growth. Hiring and keeping people is the mantra of what will make a company successful today.

At SAP, we're quantitative in terms of what drives the business. There are big outcomes for people who match the profile, which drives our ability to do market research. We have a good profile of what kind of person can succeed here, and we have linked that to economic outcome. We know that if we hire a certain kind of salesperson and if they are in the top of our measurement, they will produce 60 percent more than another person.

The glue in the middle is the manager; it's the glue that makes everything come together—or not. It's real basic stuff that has to happen. Management matters. For us, we found it involves basic things: make sure expectations are crystal clear as to what is expected of people every day; make sure you have the right person in the right job; craft jobs around the individuals; and give recognition.

The manager of the future is a very different animal, because things are getting so complex. Managers need to communicate better and relate to people in different ways.

Part of the problem in recruiting has been in the way the role of human resources has traditionally been viewed within the corporation. Raj Singh, CEO of Toronto-based Brainhunter.com, which offers Web-based recruitment systems and staffing services, says recruiting might be more cost-effective if internal HR people were compensated more like the outside recruiters companies now hire to find talent— in other words, on an incentive basis, or salary plus incentive, rather than straight salary.[19]

"Companies have to take a strategic view of HR, as opposed to seeing it as an operational cost center. Historically, emphasis in human resources has never been placed on recruiting. The emphasis has been on payroll management, compensation, and benefits. There has never been somebody in charge of the attraction and retention of talent."

Companies may need to create titles like "chief talent officer" to emphasize and strategically manage the attraction and retention of talent. And they also need to come up with better strategic alternatives to bad economic times than simple layoffs, since recruitment costs will rise when many of those dismissed are once again needed when the economy picks up.

ALIGNING TRAINING WITH INDIVIDUAL DESIRE FOR AUTONOMY

Companies are struggling with balancing the demands of managing for the short term with employees' needs for long-term professional development. In one study, although the lack of career development opportunities was high on the list of reasons for people leaving their jobs, less than half of those companies in that study offered multiple career paths or adequate career development for their IT professionals.[20] And it's safe to assume that if that's the case for IT, an area in which workers are generally in great demand and turnover rates tend to be high, career-development opportunities are probably even more lacking in areas with less competition for employees.

Only 28.2 percent of employees in one study reported being satisfied with educational and job-training programs, and 22.2 percent expressed satisfaction with promotion policies.[21] Only 50.9 percent of companies have set formal career paths, and 28.2 percent of those have established formal career-development processes.[22]

How can companies balance employees' demands and needs for training that keeps their skills fresh with the fact that the company may have to watch money spent on training walk out the door when the employee takes a job elsewhere? How can companies train for the short term when training implies a long-term perspective?

One answer is to become a facilitator of employees' own training efforts. As employees become free agents and companies structure their workforce needs to be more flexible and dynamic to accommodate changing needs and economic conditions, workers will increasingly have to rely less on structured company training efforts and more on themselves. Rather than prescribing career paths, companies will increasingly find themselves in the role of enablers, helping workers pursue the skills necessary for their futures. One reason companies face the difficult decision about training is the investment versus how much the employee or manager "returns" to the company.

Consider this response to a Net Future Institute survey by a manager at a mid-sized company:[23]

> We invest so much time and money in training. However, because employees are less loyal than in the past (partly a Gen X issue), we are finding that we are training people well who have no problem moving to a new company or industry with the skills we've trained them in. That is causing us to rethink how much training these new recruits get and how quickly we give them all we've got. We will train them well enough to do well and let them earn more training opportunities as rewards.

Company-specific training efforts—for example, training on specific products—will always be needed. However, at least some of the need for that training will be off-loaded onto technology. As wireless devices make data more accessible, workers will simply tap a database for information that would once have required specialized knowledge. Employees may be trained in how to use the database, but understanding the value of the information it contains and how that information can be used to help customers may be up to the individual.

This sort of training also does not provide the higher-level skills that make an employee both more marketable outside the company and more valuable inside the company. For example, in managing for the short term, managers determine how they best receive information and how they can most effectively disseminate it. Many companies have implemented formal testing strategies, such as the Myers-Briggs personality inventory, to help managers and employees profile themselves and understand how they take in and process information.

For those skills, a company may encourage individual development, but the individual is often responsible for obtaining the skills he or she needs, since it ultimately rewards the individual more than the company. Making the right choices will influence how well an individual is able to do his or her job and produce results.

Companies are more willing to train people in some of the technical skills of a job, says Carol Rohm, Vice President of PrideStaff, Inc., a Fresno, California–based staffing company with 33 offices in 13 states.[24] In many cases, those skills are simply easier for people to pick up than such things as communication and a sense of accountability. "A lot of those soft skills need to be taught at a young age; it's often a question of whether they get them at their first official company they work for. I've seen kids coming out of college never having utilized a checkbook and assuming they'll make $50,000 a year. Often they're not even trained to send thank-you notes after an interview."

This ability to self-select training options and paths, facilitated by the organization, provides managers and employees with the autonomy and freedom of choice that is so important to motivating them long-term. Managing for the short term in this case may not only help the company to "make its numbers," but also provide individuals with greater ability to chart their own destiny.

ALIGNING OUTPLACEMENT WITH THE REALITIES OF TURNOVER

In a study of more than 500 managers in North America, three-quarters of them reported knowing employees within their company whose unique knowledge would be lost if they left the company.[25] Yet the same study showed that most companies have no established plan for capturing knowledge from departing employees and passing it on to others. Part of managing for the short term is acknowledging that key employees may not be around forever under the best of circumstances, and that it is important to retain as much knowledge as possible. Some companies work formally with employees leaving the company to do a "brain dump"—to get as much as possible of what's inside an employee's head on paper before the exit. Others encourage "alumni" to stay in touch with people inside the company, on the theory that even though they have left the company, they can serve as valuable resources, as informal salespeople for the company's products, or even as customers.

Downsizing is another area in which the need to balance short-term concerns about cost with long-term strategy is strong. A company struggling to make its numbers often must decide whether to eliminate people it may have spent a great deal of time and money to get into the company. And companies may have to do so knowing that when the economy or the specific industry picks up, many of those positions and the expertise those employees have will be needed once again. At that point, the scramble to fill positions starts over.

The constraints of having to deliver in the short term cannot be escaped; at some point costs simply have to be cut, and layoffs may become inevitable. However, managing for the short term points to the need to create a strong hiring pipeline and maintain a broad base of contingent workers. Such options can provide flexibility in the short term while keeping in view the overall direction in which the organization wants to move.

Voices from the Front Lines

The Value of Short-Term Incentives[26]

"I think it is unrealistic to think we can motivate the troops with long-term incentives when our outlook/perspective is so short-term. Another point: To the extent there is a 'clear line of sight' from behavior to reward, performance improves. Short-term incentives make that linkage clearer."

"With the recent economic developments, employees are more interested in what they can get in the short run. Long-run rewards work well at retaining people in a tight employment / booming market (e.g., stock options), but aren't very useful in more difficult times."

"Every executive clearly knows the impact that short- and long-term incentive comp has on their motivation and productivity. Why wouldn't the same apply to the entire employee base? This will soon become normal practice."

Companies also are exploring ways to reduce the impact of hard times on their employees, to make their numbers while still trying to keep their employees' good opinion. For example, some companies are offering their employees a choice of taking unpaid vacation time, a pay cut for a specified period of time, or some combination of the two. Such strategies can help address short-term needs while allowing employees some degree of control over how those needs affect them personally.

KEEPING THOSE YOU WANT

The retention problem is particularly acute in areas where the demand is highest. Take information technology as an example. Among IT professionals, four years is the average stay in a job; for newer hires—those who have been with a company less than two years—it is even lower: less than three years. The demand for IT professionals outstrips supply by 20 percent, while the volume of work that IT departments will be asked to complete is expected to increase by 50 percent by 2005.[27] Increased workload and high demand for certain skills combine to create a recipe for a highly fluid workforce in an area considered increasingly strategic.

As might be expected, the reasons for turnover vary. Among younger IT workers, the most mobile, the most frequently cited are promotions and higher salaries offered at other firms; for those forty-six and older, the number-one reason cited was retirement.[28]

Net Future Institute research shows that, though it is not necessarily what they desire, managers generally believe they have been most successful at increasing employee productivity by motivating and rewarding them on a short-term basis[29] (see Figure 10.3).

Examples of short-term incentives—both financial and nonfinancial—that Net Future Institute members have found effective include:[30]

"Incentives that focus on quarterly time frames."

"Remuneration [that] follows the project life cycle—for example, bonuses in connection with milestones."

"Programs that have made working for the company a fun and dynamic experience, from Fun Fridays, to employee appreciation week, to 'Spot' awards, to quarterly awards."

FIGURE 10.3

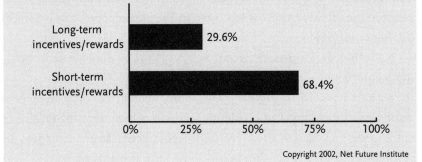

"Excluding salary, my organization has been more successful at increasing employee productivity by providing employees with . . ."

Long-term incentives/rewards — 29.6%

Short-term incentives/rewards — 68.4%

Copyright 2002, Net Future Institute

"Incentive compensation."

"Paying attention to workplace environments, company philosophy, and effective benefits packages."

"Challenging them to solve hard problems, empowering them to make decisions, supporting them if it wasn't quite the right decision and getting them back on track, having fun in a safe and caring environment, making sure they have career growth and opportunities and fair compensation. Sounds like pie in the sky, but it really works."

"Stability and corporate track record . . . in a volatile market."

"The prospects of the business as [an] incentive to remain part of an organization that has a future."

"A program called '9/80,' [in which] employees work nine hours a day Monday through Thursday, then work eight hours on one Friday and get the next Friday off. This results in a three-day weekend every other weekend."

> It makes little sense to ask people to wait for long periods for their rewards when they are being asked to deliver in the short term.

In managing for the short term, it makes little sense to ask people to wait for long periods for their rewards when they are being asked to deliver in the short term, day by day, week by week, month by month. Instead, the entire organization needs to adopt some of the mentality of the traditional sales force, which has always been focused on immediate results. Salespeople are frequently given incentives for reaching their short-term goals, whether the prize is a trip to Hawaii or a week's vacation with pay. Such immediate, competitive incentives can be a key way to keep everyone's attention on the here and now.

Nonetheless, long-term incentives continue to play a role in helping a company to achieve its long-term objectives.[31]

As can be seen in Figure 10.4, senior executives and managers both view autonomy and challenge as the top incentive for retaining employees.[32] Consider these verbatim comments from managers in response to a survey on short- and long-term incentives:[33]

- "Compensation is not the key driver of productivity—short- or long-term. Productivity is best enhanced in organizations: with the right people, rewarded properly, in an environment where decision making is speedy and high quality, where work processes are efficient and rational, where information and knowledge flow is open and honest, and where the management structure is supportive and goal-specific."

FIGURE 10.4

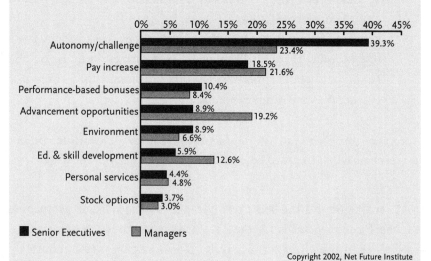

Senior Executives vs. Managers: "What incentive for retaining employees has been most effective at your organization?"

Autonomy/challenge: Senior Executives 39.3%, Managers 23.4%
Pay increase: Senior Executives 18.5%, Managers 21.6%
Performance-based bonuses: Senior Executives 10.4%, Managers 8.4%
Advancement opportunities: Senior Executives 8.9%, Managers 19.2%
Environment: Senior Executives 8.9%, Managers 6.6%
Ed. & skill development: Senior Executives 5.9%, Managers 12.6%
Personal services: Senior Executives 4.4%, Managers 4.8%
Stock options: Senior Executives 3.7%, Managers 3.0%

■ Senior Executives   ▨ Managers

- "Years ago when I worked for a company that provided computer software for the apparel manufacturing industry, we found that, in the manufacturing facilities where employees were paid on a piecework basis, the quicker they were able to see their earnings and receive them, the more efficient and productive they were."

- "Immediate rewards for positive performance have had a dramatic impact on our productivity and employee-satisfaction measurements. Additionally, we have found that awarding quarterly bonuses, based on profitability, keeps our employees focused on profit-generating initiatives."

Executives who believe that employees really work only for the money need to reexamine whether they have missed opportunities to make nonmonetary factors more significant to their employees. A more independent, mobile workforce may place a higher value on autonomy and latitude in decision making than has been the case in the past. And that autonomy is precisely the kind of reward that managing for the short term can and should provide. In this case, that requires making sure that employees understand how they can further the company's goals in very tangible ways—ways that may also earn them financial reward—and enabling them to take action to do so.

Pushing decision-making ability down the chain of command does more than offer workers some of the autonomy executives find so important for themselves. It also frees up time for a manager to take on higher-level tasks personally. And those higher-level tasks can mark the manager as a leader.

11

Using Information to Navigate Through Decisions

Sometimes managing for the short term can seem like driving from Chicago to Orlando in the dark. You can see ahead only as far as the beam of the headlight; nonetheless, you ultimately can make the whole trip that way. You know where you're going, but you just aren't able to see very far ahead during the course of the trip.

This is exactly what managing for the short term is like: taking the steps necessary to reach a goal while recognizing that you can't know everything about the route in advance, and that circumstances and directions may change before you get there. In fact, they may even change the destination of the journey.

ELECTRONIC NAVIGATION VERSUS THE ROAD MAP

The traditional metaphor for corporate strategy is that of the road map, a tool to guide and direct the company on its ongoing journey. Road maps are created based on all the information available when the map was last updated by the map company.

Today, a road map may be a good tool for planning a journey, but it breaks down as a navigational tool once you're on the road. It can't take into account the impact of weather conditions. It can't factor in how traffic conditions will affect travel times.

Information-based decisions are like driving with an electronic navigation system. It, too, has the original map data built in, but also takes into account current traffic, weather, and other real-time conditions. The system constantly plots a new route based on what the driver does. If the driver chooses not to follow the suggested route, it immediately adjusts and plots a new route. Both the traveler using a map and the one with a navigational system may arrive at the same destination, but the "wired" driver will arrive more efficiently by adapting to conditions as they arise. In addition, based on information not known when the original destination was entered, the driver may make a call and decide collectively with others to go somewhere else entirely.

Managing for the short term involves leveraging this new information as legitimate input back into the planning process. Its use once the journey has started can provide an organization with a competitive advantage, even if only for a limited time. However, enough short-term advantages can add up to consistent leadership in any given market.

BALANCING PROACTIVE AND REACTIVE

Most managers like to think of themselves as being strategic thinkers, and many are—when they have the time to stop and think. Yet increasingly, being able to act quickly and intelligently on information from outside the company—the most important being information derived from customers—is also coming to be considered strategic. As we discussed earlier, event-driven planning must be guided and informed by the reactions of the marketplace, on more of a real-time basis.

Companies find themselves making reactive decisions every day. But there are different types of reactive decisions:

- Passive reactive. These are reactive decisions that are based only on expediency. These would fall into the category of short-term

VOICES FROM THE FRONT LINES

The Budget As Road Map[1]

"The budget is the budget is the budget."

"A budget is a target and, conceptually, should not be revised—that becomes a game of 'chasing the numbers.' If the point is to 'always have operations meet budget, even if I have to manipulate the budget figures to do so,' then revise the budget constantly. Otherwise, prepare a budget based on the best information available at the time, understand why you missed the budget targets during the cycle, and make a more precise budget next cycle. If you want more accuracy, keep the cycle short but review more."

"While things change throughout the year, we do not revise our budgets in *any* case during the course of the year. We either make budget, or we do not make budget (or we exceed it at times). However, the budget itself is not changed. We do go through a formal reforecasting process at the beginning of the last quarter to project where we will be against budget at year end. But the targets are still the original budget numbers."

"We are a small department, so we bend over backwards to stay within our official budget. Larger departments are constantly pushing the edges of their official budgets based on 'new priorities.'"

"We review our budget at predefined times, outlooks. We review and revise up or down dependent upon revenue versus expense actuals. These outlooks replace the plan for the remainder of the fiscal year."

"Too many companies do not really understand and properly use the budgeting process. That is, they have company and departmental budgets, but they are not dynamic, they are not well defined in terms of facts and assumptions, they are not flexible enough to meet changing conditions. They respond far too slowly and not in a team-based way. Heads roll, and virtually always the wrong heads—those at the top are usually the last to go."

"We negotiate annual corporate and business-unit budgets with our parent. These budgets are generally in line with the forecasts we specify in our five-year strategic plan. We are not given the opportunity to revise them at any time during the fiscal year."

management; that is, they are made not necessarily with the impact on the end goal in mind, but out of necessity.

- Strategic reactive. These are reactive decisions that are productive in themselves, because they provide interactive input into the decision process. They are not just information-based; they also produce useful information. Strategic reactive decisions are those that enable additional information to be factored back into planning and direction. In that sense, the process is more like traditional proactive decision-making.

For example, let's say an overseas manufacturing plant burns down at a critical time in the production cycle, just when the company is attempting to penetrate a new market. A passive reaction might be to quickly find a company to which production can be outsourced. A strategic reaction might be to not only find a way to outsource production, but to use the opportunity to evaluate whether vendors and other materials suppliers can adapt quickly to changed circumstances. Knowing how resilient the supply chain is can help determine how quickly the company can change its strategy when it needs to—for example, if it wants to expand more quickly in the new region.

Customer input filtered quickly back up the line does not constitute a strategy. The strategy still has to be set by the organization's leaders, tuned in to both market forces and changes perceived on the horizon. A company's leaders might foresee these changes before a company's customers realize the changes are coming.

INFORMATION AND DOING WHAT IS RIGHT

While the Internet brought with it the ability for anyone to connect with anyone else at any time, it also brought expectations beyond what could be realized within realistic time frames. Collaborative commerce between suppliers and customers can make the distribution chain shorter, but it has not always taken advantage of the total amount of information available from customers. In addition, some companies in the distribution chain move too quickly, while some move too slowly. As a result, the right information is not always in the right place for the right person or division to make the best decision. When that happens, it creates another disconnect.

"Without good information from the customer to the supplier, your inventory goes up and there's a lot of confusion, which leads to the way business used to be," says Brett Strouss, Director of Channel Marketing at SAP, the $6 billion Germany-based software company.[2] "It's process and people, and now the technology is enabling entirely new business processes and taking out the inefficiencies." SAP, as do many large organizations, conducts collaborative selling with its customers, using the Internet as the conduit. Says Strouss:

> Immediate customer needs require immediate response. The focus of many companies is to keep up with the expectations of their customers. We all live in the instant-gratification world, where you can check on anything in real time, with a lot more customer self-service going on than ever before. The drawback is, there's a lot of chaos that goes with it.
>
> When you're moving quickly like this, people often are making decisions on insufficient information. An executive has to make a decision on the information he has. Some don't understand the complexities of some of these things. The real world is that the executive believes he's making the right decision. The problem is that the middle manager doesn't necessarily understand the direction of the company. We almost need an education just in this.
>
> We're seeing companies move too quickly. The rapid-action mode seems to be driven by agile competitors, though I haven't seen market conditions change that dramatically.
>
> The quandary about customer information is that because some companies have long product cycles, they have to be thinking ahead of the customers. In the software industry, we have to balance the needs of the customer going whichever way the wind might be blowing with what we know is right. We have to build something that is for more than one or two years.
>
> It ultimately comes back to the top executives. If you have top people with vision and strategy, then the overall organization benefits and you can build momentum. That's the difference between the top CEO and the mediocre CEO. Leaders do the right thing.

VALUING CUSTOMER INFORMATION

Many of the executives and managers who responded to one Net Future Institute survey already are using customer information to help drive development and modification of new products and services. However, substantially fewer also use that information to help drive either short-term or long-term strategy, or to help determine how best to allocate resources[3] (see Figure 11.1).

Managing for the short term requires a constant flow of information to ensure that decision makers get the feedback they need to make changes before proceeding to the next short-term move. This focus on information also requires increased focus on customers, whose needs are immediate rather than long-term.

But too much information can be as problematic as not having enough. When managing for the short term, executives must determine three key aspects of information:

1. What information is most important to capture, manage, and distribute?

2. Where in the organization is information needed, and by whom, for it to affect decision making?

FIGURE 11.1

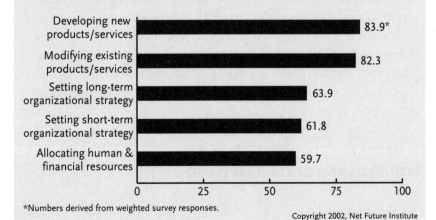

"In your organization, how important is information from customers to each of the following areas?"

Developing new products/services	83.9*
Modifying existing products/services	82.3
Setting long-term organizational strategy	63.9
Setting short-term organizational strategy	61.8
Allocating human & financial resources	59.7

*Numbers derived from weighted survey responses.

Copyright 2002, Net Future Institute

3. What is the quantitative value of information, and how is that value measured?

The reality is that information has different meanings and values to different people at different times. "Not all information is created equal," says Laurence Bunin, CEO of Handshake Dynamics.[4] Says Bunin:

> More and more, companies are realizing that they actually need an "information strategy" that makes it clear what types of information are most important, and where these pieces of information need to get to. This is because information flow is critical to the successful implementation of many business strategies.
>
> Managing and distributing information costs money. To make good decisions about how to apply resources against the management of information, companies must know what information is most important. One way to do this is to determine what information is most essential to supporting a company's strategy and activity system. Another way is to determine what information is most important to key internal and external stakeholders. Regardless of the methodology, one thing is clear: CIOs are looking for quantitative ways to determine the relative value and importance of particular types of information.
>
> Information questions used to be more basic: How do I collect all this information? Manage it? Store it? Who needs it and where does it need to go? But quickly, information management challenges became overwhelming. Now CIOs need to ask, "Okay, what's most important?"
>
> Smart companies use portfolio analysis. They select a "basket" (portfolio) of projects that together "balance" their short-term interests against their long-term interests. There is an increasing demand by smart CEOs in determining how to prioritize the importance of various types and pieces of information. They can't do everything, so they had better determine what's really important.

IMMEDIATE CUSTOMER NEEDS REQUIRE IMMEDIATE RESPONSE

It is no secret that the ability to interact with customers has increased dramatically, giving companies an unprecedented ability to be truly customer-focused. That, in turn, has increased the need to manage for the short term. As the number and size of online transactions grow, they raise customer expectations about how quickly a company will respond. That applies not only to orders but also to any sort of inquiry.

Managers are recognizing that speed in getting back to customers is vital. Senior executives and managers rank "quick response to inquiries and complaints" as number one in importance to their customers[5] (see Figure 11.2).

In these executives' view, it is not the product, or even information about the product, that matters. The key issue is how a customer expects a company to interact with that individual. That interaction is not about the product; it is about the customer relationship. In fact, the ability to compare products, including those of competitors, ranked dead last in perceived importance to customers. These managers seem to recognize that when it comes to connecting with a company, customers want interaction, they want help, they want it to be easy, and they want it when they want it.

Managers not only rank rapid response as customers' current top priority; they also say it will be their customers' top priority in the future. Rapid response is seen as even more important[6] (see Figure 11.3).

FIGURE 11.2

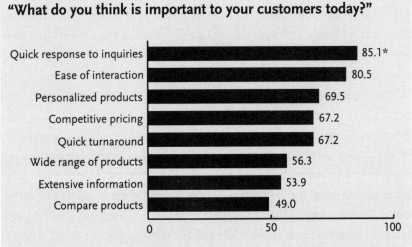

"What do you think is important to your customers today?"

Quick response to inquiries	85.1*
Ease of interaction	80.5
Personalized products	69.5
Competitive pricing	67.2
Quick turnaround	67.2
Wide range of products	56.3
Extensive information	53.9
Compare products	49.0

0   50   100

*Numbers derived from weighted survey responses.   Copyright 2002, Net Future Institute

FIGURE 11.3

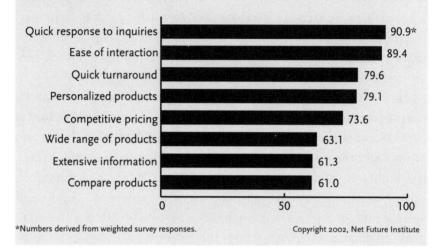

"What do you anticipate will be important to your customers two years from now?"

Quick response to inquiries	90.9*
Ease of interaction	89.4
Quick turnaround	79.6
Personalized products	79.1
Competitive pricing	73.6
Wide range of products	63.1
Extensive information	61.3
Compare products	61.0

0   50   100

*Numbers derived from weighted survey responses.

Copyright 2002, Net Future Institute

As companies realize the importance of being customer-focused, they increasingly face having to provide the information customers want, which is much more easily said than done.

"These companies are realizing how difficult it is to do this," says Handshake Dynamics' Bunin. "Large companies often have many customers, and a tremendous amount of information stored in systems. But it is very difficult to figure out, in a consistent and strategic way, what information is really most important to customers. Customers often don't know how to ask for what they want, but they are very quick to switch suppliers when they don't get the information they want."

Each piece of information is different from every other piece, and the correct piece is needed at the correct time. Consider this scenario: Residential builder Agnes Theriault is ordering hundreds of thousands of dollars of components from her plumbing, electrical, and heating suppliers. She wants to know not only the delivery date of each component, but also the sequence of the delivery dates included in the order. She also wants this information tied to her company's billing systems, so that payment is scheduled in the same sequence as the deliveries. If her suppliers do not offer that information, a competitor with such capabilities can take the business away from the supplier before that supplier even knows that the buyer desired the information. A slightly better or even comparable component that is not available to finish a house on schedule can cause the builder additional costs.

"Companies need to get proactive about valuing their information types from the perspective of customers or other key stakeholders," says Bunin. "They need to use an information prioritization methodology that takes into account the relative importance of certain customers and types of customers, and the ability for certain types of information to help those customers, in order to determine which information assets should be ultimately made available to the customer and at what cost."

Though customer relationship management (CRM) initiatives began to slow when the economy turned sour, the results of the surveys above indicate that projects may have been postponed, not abandoned. Indeed, CRM has the potential not only to increase sales to existing customers but also to identify a company's most profitable customers so that sales efforts are more productive.

For example, representatives of Marriott International who deal with the hotel chain's group bookings now proactively contact corporate customers in advance of trade shows and conferences instead of waiting for a group representative to call and arrange for rooms. The more proactive approach, coupled with a robust CRM system that gives each account executive system-wide information about facilities and room availability, has meant a higher closure rate and little price negotiation, both of which have boosted revenues.[7]

CRM AT THE CUSTOMER LEVEL

Casinos have always rewarded high rollers with free hotel rooms, meals, and other perks. But who gets what, and why, has traditionally been undisclosed and discretionary. Las Vegas, Nevada–based Harrah's Entertainment, Inc., the world's third-largest gaming company, uses real-time information to better quantify the value of a customer and tailor a player's rewards to that person's demonstrated gaming behavior. Tim Stanley, Harrah's Vice President of Information Technology Development, has found that being able to use real-time information about customer behavior increases repeat business; same-site sales increased 12 percent from 1999 to 2000, and earnings before interest, taxes, depreciation, and amortization rose 21 percent.[8] Moreover, it has been able to help its bottom line in other ways.

The company integrates real-time individual gaming behavior at all of its 25 hotels and casinos with aggregated information about its 25 million customers. That lets employees at any property, regardless of whether the customer has ever been at that property, predict which rewards and marketing offers are likely to be successful at encouraging the kind of behavior that is most profitable to the company.

Harrah's Total Rewards card helps take the mystery out of what is needed to qualify for perks. A customer takes the card to a kiosk in the casino, gets an immediate reward based on his gaming behavior that day, and instantly sees what else he might qualify for. But the real power lies in the system's ability to modify a Harrah's customer's behavior on an ongoing basis, Stanley says:

> The system comps both on your tier status and on a daily rewards basis. It allows us to measure across the brand your value to us, and we can change our behavior accordingly. If you do a behavior—let's say you spend a certain amount of money at the slot machines—you get rewarded for it on the spot. But we can also do predictive modeling that lets us say, "We think this customer probably is this kind of player, and we want him to come back."
>
> Let's say you're a high roller, but you're staying at one of our competitors and spend a lot there. Then you wander across the street and spend $30 with us at one of the casinos. That probably doesn't look like much, but we can look at your play model—things like your address, the location of the property, and your play behavior—compare it to our database, and say, "We think this customer probably is this kind of player." We can create a reward structure so it's to your benefit to consolidate your play with us, based not only on what we see you do but also on what we predict you might do. And that can happen before you even leave the property, which gives you an incentive to come back.

An added benefit of capturing and using customer information on a real-time basis is that an organization can use it to track internal performance from department to department. Though not every company has the business metrics of a casino, the lessons of using real-time information are totally transferable. Says Stanley:

> It also gives us the ability to create standardized approaches to customers, though individual properties still have the ability to do things on their own initiative. We can match them and compare them. If our predictive models are working fine in 18 properties but not in two others, it's probably not an issue with the models but with local execution. It gives individual properties the ability to fine-tune their operations.
>
> Rewards are part of what we call reinvestment in the customer. If we typically reinvest $30 out of every $100 a customer spends, how can we continue to maximize the difference between that investment and what a customer spends? If we change an offer so that we reinvest 25 percent instead of 30, we can test what impact that will have on that type of customer's behavior. If they still come and still spend that $100, that difference goes directly to the bottom line.
>
> If your behavior changes [in the opposite way], we can know that quickly and adjust. Individual properties often tend to reward their same customers over and over, when the reality is that some of these customers will probably come to you even if they get nothing. If you can adjust the profitability of a customer based on your reinvestment strategy, it goes directly to the bottom line.
>
> We can go into planning cycles with better information about the impact of what we do. We know if we invest in X, it has this effect across the entire company. It makes it a heck of a lot easier to know what works and what doesn't, and how we should be spending our money.

Harrah's ends up with a very granular view of its customers and its internal operations on an ongoing basis, with the ability to constantly compare performance at any level. That information and the knowledge it brings allow the company to quantify virtually any aspect of its business, one of the prime imperatives of managing for the short term. The company has also found ways to leverage that information to achieve more strategic goals, such as promoting the Harrah's brand and extending the life cycle of existing equipment.

We have the ability to look down at individual slot machines at each property and see how they perform against different customer profiles, based not only on the type of customer but the time of play, the property, etc. It allows you to adjust fairly strategically how you use those machines to maximize the revenues from them. That has also let us leverage the information to get exclusives on new games that are just coming out.

If we do a big promotion of a new game—getting celebrities in, doing a special mailing—we can measure the impact of spending that kind of money on that kind of promotion. We can also take a game that's been on the decline and look at what customers like to play on it, where it does best, what time of day it does best, and do a new promotion or add additional ways to win on it or promote it to a specific type of customer. That helps us increase the profit well beyond what it might otherwise do. And every one of those that we do circles back and we get more data.

We do a P&L for every single offer, so we can match what has been predicted around a given offer and see how we've done.

This method of managing for the short term has allowed the company to adopt a strategy of yield management, similar to those the airlines use to maximize revenue per flight. For Harrah's, it's all about getting the right person in the right room at the right time at the right price.

Depending on the channel we use for the offer—direct mail, telemarketing, Internet, or e-mail—we can adjust the offer itself if it's not working, or adjust the availability on the back end. Our new yield management approach is based on what kind of customer you are; we can yield you a room based on your value to us as a gamer. If you're trying to get into the Rio for the weekend and you have no history with us, you're probably going to pay a rack rate, but if we know you're a very good gamer, you will get a real-time rate quote based on your Total Rewards value and gaming behavior. If you have an offer in your hand, the system may make a yield-based decision. It may put you in a room, but limit the number of rooms available for that kind of offer, and award them based on your gaming behavior, for example.

Automating those decisions takes them out of the hands of the call center. It cuts down call time and does a much better job of yielding the right customers.

For Harrah's, customer information has been translated into bottom-line results. When managing for the short term, every piece of information that can be used to improve the numbers must be leveraged.

Using the Information Stream for Immediate Results

Information alone doesn't enable managers to manage effectively for the short term—or, for that matter, for the long term. To enable effective management for the short term, information has to be readily available and absolutely up-to-date, and provide a three-dimensional picture of the customer. To use it effectively, a manager needs to have a good sense of what he wants to get from the information. And all of this has to be done in the context of the organization's strategy and long-term direction.

Lands' End, the Wisconsin-based direct retailer, demonstrates the power of using interactivity to direct the company's activities day to day. The company is revamping its product-development process, using customer information to guide purchasing, inventory levels, and even product design. Bill Bass, the company's Senior Vice President for E-Commerce and International Catalog Operations, says the launch of a custom-design initiative, which enables a customer to design a pair of pants for himself, is the first step in letting real-time customer information drive what the company develops for mass consumption:[9]

> With our normal product-development process, we come up with ideas for products. The designers go to Milan, Paris, Hong Kong, and bring back ideas. Then they design products that will be going into the catalog twelve months out. What is produced is based on our best guess about what will sell.
>
> With the Internet, we're able to put some of those items online prior to their appearing in the catalog and see what customers are buying. Pocketed T-shirts or without pockets, black versus blue— we can get an idea of customer preferences earlier. For example, we're selling different sizes of tank tops than we thought we would. It gives us a better read on inventory. We can do tests online to see which sells better, which can help us adjust our inventory.

As with AT&T and its residential long-distance service, processes that took decades to build are being altered in only a few years. In the case of Lands' End, this means adapting the product-development process to become more iterative. When you have a catalog that goes out to 10 million people—what Bass calls "the big bang"—one wrong guess about how popular a particular item or color might be can leave the company with a bottom line that reflects unsold inventory.

Implementing procedures that enable managers to manage better for the short term is itself an iterative process, Bass says.

> We've evolved this system over 40 years so that we're very efficient at doing what we do. Adapting that cycle is a complex process. If we want a product to be ready six months, 12 months earlier so we can test it online, it changes the product-development cycle. Designers have to get their ideas out earlier. We've got fabric companies who have to have the fabric to us sooner, manufacturers who have to get us the product earlier; they're all accustomed to a certain product cycle, and it's difficult to change overnight. Everybody knows that's where we want to go, but it takes a while.
>
> To do a new pair of pants—say we wanted to add a pleat to a particular model of pants—it takes a year to go from designer to putting the product before the customer. By comparison, we developed the entire custom-made apparel process in nine months. Right now we're essentially doing one-offs; we've only done a few items that have been treated as exceptions to see how they affect the system that's in place. To do many more products involves much more change in the process itself. You have to get to a critical mass. Once you've got a system in place, then you migrate more products over.
>
> With custom-made apparel, we're not developing products anymore. We'll make whatever you want. It helps us see what people want, so it definitely will have an impact on the catalog business. But it means dramatic cultural change.

To achieve that cultural change, the company has to ensure that its managers are all aligned behind the corporate vision of providing its customers with the greatest flexibility possible in their transactions with the company. Managers are compensated based on company-wide sales; there is no incentive to impede progress, because a move toward customized apparel sales might affect, say, catalog sales. At

Lands' End, the pay structure is geared to getting everyone in sync with the overall company's goals.

Immediate results are particularly important in the retail industry, where conditions change day by day. "Retail is detail," says Scott Bauhofer, Senior Vice President and General Manager of BestBuy.com, the online arm of Best Buy Co., Inc.[10] The parent organization, a nearly $20 billion consumer electronics specialty retailer with more than 450 stores in 44 states, is set up to monitor inventory closely and provide buyers with rapid information about how individual products are moving. "Inventory turns" are key for Best Buy; the higher the number of inventory turns, the less inventory needs to be stored and the lower the company's carrying costs. The company works closely with its vendor partners to ensure that the products that are in stores are those that will perform best for both the vendor and the retailer. Says Bauhofer:

> Both sides can see immediately with new products and ongoing products whether they are meeting the goals set for both vendor and store in terms of inventory turns and sales. We are able to flex with what we know. Forecasting's very important, and we have processes to get that close to right, but we also have the ability to respond quickly to what we see when it's not what we expected.
>
> In particularly volatile categories—computers and video games, for example—we generally will know the Monday after a Sunday ad runs what those sales are going to be for the life cycle of the product. Knowing that, you can make adjustments, either to the order quantities or to the price, whatever is best for both partners. You can quickly work that out. In a longer-life-cycle product, like a refrigerator, it will take longer to know; there would be likely more changes during the life cycle.
>
> Merchandise managers and senior buyers, who have responsibility for some subset of products, have a fair amount of latitude over managing their product category, in partnership with their suppliers. You can't get this all done on your own, both in the good times and the bad times. They are tasked with managing their business to meet their financial plan.

Best Buy also offers products online that the brick-and-mortar stores may not choose to carry. However, good online performance can influence whether a product gets picked up by the stores. "Because it's in the early stages, that process is more entrepreneurial," says Bauhofer, meaning that individual managers now take it upon themselves to check out the information provided by online sales. However, he anticipates that the information will be useful enough so that the process will become more widespread.

In the case of both Lands' End and Best Buy, monitoring sales in something close to real time has helped managers adjust quickly when they receive information different from what was contained in forecasts.

The New Planning Time Frame

With more information available to more managers, it is time to view employees as assets and highly leverage those assets. Rather than focus on simply sending goals and objectives to employees, managers must tap into their wired workforces and retrain them to send back information about customer demands and needs. In this new era of customer service, departments that have traditionally been considered cost centers will be revamped to provide greater immediate competitive advantage in terms of increased sales and greater customer knowledge.

Projects can be managed to provide constant feedback and opportunities for course correction based on customer needs. This has huge implications for the planning process. The traditional business process of Vision to Strategy to Planning to Operations becomes more of an iterative process. Information at the transaction level from customers will have to flow through employees to managers to executive management in real time. That in turn will affect the time frame and frequency of the planning process itself.

At Brotherhood Mutual Insurance Company, a $124 million property and casualty company that primarily insures churches, there is tight linkage between planning and operations. As in many companies, the annual planning cycle starts in August and culminates with a November budget. The company keeps its planning group down to seven executives, with a larger operating committee that includes all the company officers.

"The department heads have to know what the yearly schedule looks like," says Mitzi Thomas, Assistant Vice President of Corporate Communications.[11] "We reprioritize as we go, so the planning committee had to be open to this. It has learned how to do that. When you do the planning process, you can't always anticipate opportunities."

When the operating committee identifies an opportunity after the plan has been created, the new information and recommendations are brought back to the planning committee. "That's where the delays in projects come, and that's good," says Thomas. It's a positive because the opportunity that is seized upon has to be considered substantial enough to delay a previously planned project.

This is how interactive events can be fed back into the planning processes to successfully manage for the short term. The added value is that the employee or manager who identifies the information and causes it to be sent back to planning eventually may see the impact of that on results. That can give the individual a better understanding of his or her value within the organization.

The Dynamic Budget Cycle

If an organization's strategy is its navigational system, the budget is the control panel that provides information about how the car is running: how far it has gone, how much gas is left in the tank, whether the engine is running hot. But the process of projecting what an organization will take in and how that money will be spent is just as affected by the need to manage for the short term as anything else in the organization.

It used to be that the budget was sacrosanct. Weeks and months would be spent in the budget planning and approval process, and, once approved, it basically was the law. Now companies begin reviewing their budgets shortly after adoption, based on new information about changing conditions. Many companies adopt budgets but plan to modify or reforecast throughout the year.

Seventy-one percent of senior executives and managers say they begin revising their budget within the quarter or less[12] (see Figure 11.4). Thirty-one percent said they begin revising the budget within one month or less after it is approved.

Managers have found many different ways to adapt their planning cycles to accommodate the pressures of the short term. Examples cited by Net Future Institute members include:

FIGURE 11.4

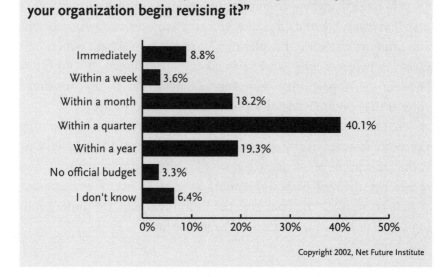

"How soon after an enterprise-wide budget is adopted does your organization begin revising it?"

Immediately — 8.8%
Within a week — 3.6%
Within a month — 18.2%
Within a quarter — 40.1%
Within a year — 19.3%
No official budget — 3.3%
I don't know — 6.4%

- Using forecasts as a means of updating a planned budget. Rolling forecasts use current figures to constantly adapt projections

- Comparing variances to the projected numbers rather than revising the budget itself

- Using longer budgetary cycles for the overall organization and shorter ones for departments within the organization

- Keeping budget cycles shorter and reviewing them more frequently than once a year

- Starting the yearly budget planning process nine months before the next annual budget is due

GETTING THE BENEFIT TO THE CUSTOMER

Of course, all of these ways of using information to drive the business must ultimately translate back into benefit for the customer. Many managers recognize that customer service is not a necessary evil but a strategic weapon[13] (see Figure 11.5).

Voices from the Front Lines

The Budget As Navigational System[14]

"Technically the budget does not get revised, but practically it is adjusted via a monthly forecast with variance explanations—over the course of the budget period (one year), the adjustments will generally net out within a reasonable range (± 5 percent) of the base budget."

"Budgets are guidelines at our organization. They are not cast in concrete. Sometimes we don't need to revise, sometimes we do. It's dependent on Federal Reserve actions, interest rate changes over which we have no control and could not have seen in our crystal ball when the budget is put together."

"It is customary in our business and from my experience at other companies to officially revise budgets twice per year at the reporting level. However, original plan is used as a measurement against objectives, with the latest update budget as the latest thinking for stockholders."

Figure 11.5

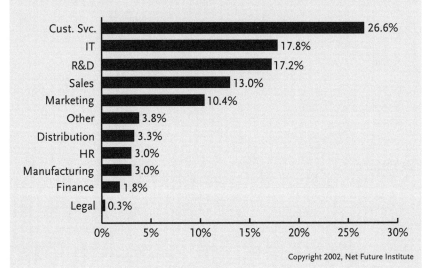

"What department do you believe provides your organization with the most strategic competitive advantage?"

Cust. Svc. — 26.6%
IT — 17.8%
R&D — 17.2%
Sales — 13.0%
Marketing — 10.4%
Other — 3.8%
Distribution — 3.3%
HR — 3.0%
Manufacturing — 3.0%
Finance — 1.8%
Legal — 0.3%

Copyright 2002, Net Future Institute

As with Guy Gray at Cendant, managers who have to deal with information overload still recognize that information is vital to staying in close touch with the customer. Keeping closely connected allows managers to be able to address a problem in the short term so it doesn't become a long-term catastrophe.

III

MANAGING YOURSELF FOR the SHORT TERM

12

Getting to What Matters

It's no secret that many people do not feel totally fulfilled at work. They want to add value, but feel that the things they are forced to do from day to day prevent it. Even though they spend most of their time on tasks they consider relevant, some feel those tasks should be done by someone else.

It's not that there's some sinister plot to keep workers and managers from being empowered. It's just that many managers are so focused on what they need to do at any given moment that it's not always that easy to look up and recognize workers as being unhappy. People typically want to feel that their work makes a difference. Unfortunately, a disconnect between executive management's corporate strategy and middle- to lower-level managers sometimes prevents those workers from having that satisfaction.

Managers need to alter the way they think about what some may view as the tyranny of the work environment. They need to be able to manage their jobs in ways that allow them to feel better about both their roles and how they're spending their time. As we saw earlier, managers are inundated and frustrated—inundated by all the demands placed on them daily, and frustrated by the feeling that those demands push what many consider to be the important activities to the periphery of the workday: early morning, evenings, and weekends.

GETTING IT DONE

A newspaper has one goal each day that takes precedence over everything else: to get out that day's paper. The day starts with a news meeting where each department head details content planned for each section, and linkages are made among sections. As the day progresses and news events happen, stories are reported, written, and edited until, ultimately, time runs out. The newspaper has to be printed and delivered, and the news is shaped by that deadline. The content may change during the day, but the time frame for performance remains the same.

A newspaper also provides a good example of the way in which the relative importance of various occurrences shifts. Every day there is a "lead story." Even on what could be called a slow news day, there has to be one story that gets the biggest headline on page 1, the one considered most significant that day. However, on a different day that same story could be on page 18. It all depends on what other news is happening. This constant reevaluation of the relative importance of a story carries throughout the entire newspaper; the sports section leads with the most significant sports coverage, the most significant business story is at the top of the business section, and so on. However, it usually is not any individual story but the overall "package"—that is, the newspaper itself—that really matters to the subscriber. The value of the newspaper is that the editors place things in perspective for the reader. All of this is done, on a recurring basis, day in and day out. It is what the newspaper has to do to succeed.

> **Managers constantly have to judge priorities within different contexts, often simultaneously.**

Similarly, both managers and employees must learn to view managing for the short term not as a negative or positive but simply as a requirement, something that must be dealt with. "Getting the paper out" means identifying key tasks and making those the top priorities. A story has to be selected as the lead story, the next story in priority has to be chosen, and so forth; this has to be done within each department and then across departments until all priorities are established. In addition, newspapers have "breaking news," stories that occur sometimes immediately after the organization of the newspaper has been set. Breaking news can change everything, with ripple effects throughout the newspaper's various sections. The same is true in business.

When managing for the short term, there are distinct methods and tactics to get through the day, week, month, and quarter. Much like a newspaper staff, managers constantly have to judge priorities within different contexts, often simultaneously. Every manager has a "front page" to focus on, while not forgetting those "inside sections" from which front-page stories sometimes come.

Newspapers also have had to adapt their news cycles to the immediacy of the Internet. They now post news articles on the Web site between the regular cycles of the paper, just as managers now have to recognize and deal with occurrences and the connections between them over shorter periods of time.

LET THINGS BUBBLE UP

Part of the answer to feeling inundated is being able to recognize what really matters in the overall corporate context. There is always more than you can do within the time available. The reality is that managers still can and do get a lot done. To be most effective at managing for the short term, you need to be flexible in changing priorities.

The important issues rise to the top, almost by themselves. If you think about what you are working on right now, it often is not what you planned to do when the day or week began. Something happened—an event, a market shift, a personnel change—that reordered the priorities. This is neither good nor bad; it just *is*. As with the daily newspaper process outlined above, the most significant or lead story of the day tends to make itself evident; events in work life do the same.

Managers sometimes fight that process, trying to continue working on a task they had already committed to completing first. That can be a mistake. The solution? Rather than filling every minute of your week or month with meetings or appointments, allow some flexibility for priorities to shift and rise as events require.

Sometimes there are conflicts between what a manager perceives to be his most critical immediate tasks and what others perceive to be critical. When such conflicts occur, you need to ask yourself: "Does this really matter?" If the answer is "No," then let the task drop lower on your list. It also may be important to explain to your superiors or direct reports how the task you're selecting is significant to the company's goals.

BE RUTHLESS

When managing for the short term, it is necessary to have an overall master plan and stick to it rigorously. This may sound like a direct contradiction of letting things bubble up, but it isn't. Flexibility within a given time frame is essential, but managers must constantly be centered on tasks that are critical to success. It might be as simple as "I have to move this project forward, no matter what," to "I must develop or recruit a very strong number two." Basically, you need to be ruthless in identifying those one or two things that need to be always top of mind.

It may be the one project you've been working on for a while, even if that work is done only incrementally (as is often the case, given all the interruptions of the business day). It might be a task with a pressing immediate deadline. Whatever the case, this over-arching focus can help you to say "no" as tasks cross your path that are less important, or pressing, or which fall more and more outside of that area of concentration.

"I'm a believer in laserlike focus. It's critical to establish the vital vein—that is, what are the five things I've got to get done in the next 18 months," says Barry Herstein, Chief Marketing Officer of the London-based Financial Times Group.[1] "This is the foundation, and then you stay focused on them. I try to be as ruthless as I can against those five screens. Then you have the vital few things you have to deliver strategically."

Herstein, formerly the chief marketer for Avon, learned early on to get as close as possible to the customer so he could prioritize his focus. He spent a significant amount of his time at Avon with district managers and in the field. At the Financial Times Group, Herstein also spends as much, if not more, time with the staff in marketing as he does with his departmental peers. Says Herstein:

> The more I can share the message, the better it works. That's what helps catalyze reactions. The more I can touch the people on the shop floor, the better it is. Communication is everything. People want to be engaged, and they want their senior management involved with them. This management by walking around really works. If you connect with the person who touches the customer, it really works. It's so simple and so basic. You have to determine what are the five things that matter, then say them over and over again. Employees want to know the "why," and they want us to give them the tools.
>
> Compensation systems also have to be changed to match the strategy. Many people in companies want to have input, but they also want direction. When they're included in hearing their leader's path and direction, they respond. People want to be aligned and they want leadership. But there's a fine line between micromanagement and empowerment and participating in that process on the part of management. By working together, we find the new programs and create the environment and framework for people to deliver.
>
> The people who get promoted are the people who deliver. It's all about shifting the units. Senior management has to be engaged in the process of employees and managers of delivering those numbers.

Being ruthless really is about staying totally focused on what really matters—driving efficiency and productivity on a personal as well as an enterprise-wide level. "To be more productive, organization is the most important skill," says Kathy Ball-Toncic, Vice President, Capital Markets, at Financial Fusion, Inc., a Sybase subsidiary that builds

The people who get promoted are the people who deliver.

and serves financial institutions through a global support network with 60 offices.[2] Ball-Toncic spends about half her time traveling, working 10 to 12 hours a day.

Being ruthless for Ball-Toncic means sometimes closing her door with a Do Not Disturb sign and, to make sure no one catches her eye,

Voices from the Front Lines

Being Ruthless[3]

"One of my mentors years ago told me to 'do work that only you can do'! All else should be delegated."

"I establish an entire to-do list in priority order. This includes people I want to call, ongoing projects, written reports, letters, etc. Although my list is perhaps 20 items, I anticipate only the top five will get done in a given day. If I am writing a report, for example, I might accomplish half this task."

"We use tracking software for client contact (sales/marketing) and project scheduling software for development. We have milestone points for development. Sales have no set contact numbers; just make sure to meet sales objectives. Individual sales managers have different tools they employ (at their discretion) to meet their objective. At any time, tasks are stratified based upon necessity. Some on my list just don't get addressed due to changes in business environment, overall business objective."

facing away from the windowed door. She also is ruthless about what she tackles in the course of a day. "I use the 'above-the-line' and the 'below-the-line' concept. All of the above-the-line things simply have to get done. It's an iterative list." Like many executives, she is highly productive off-hours, including early mornings and late nights.

Be a Player-Coach

It is almost impossible to find an underworked manager in business today. When companies face tough economic times, everyone knows the typical action: lay off people. But as organizations shed people, they do not typically shed work. This is one of the reasons employees and managers feel so overwhelmed by workload these days. The sheer volume of work is being spread among fewer and fewer people.

There are two approaches for managers who find themselves in this situation. The first is to play the role of the supervisor and try to keep everyone moving. But the lower in the organization you go, the less effective this approach will be. The days of telling a subordinate to finish the project while you head home early are over. It doesn't take much for a lower-level manager or employee to figure, "We're doing all the work here."

Of course, the reality from the boss's perspective is quite different. The senior manager might be spending considerable time shielding his troops from external problems, such as moves to cut staff in a specific area. The lower-level managers and employees are not always privy to these behind-the-scenes activities and may have quite a different view of what to them looks like golf and dinner.

When managing for the short term, you need a second approach that makes behind-the-scenes activity more public.

"I manage, but now I also do as much as those who I manage," says Carolyn Dickson, Municipal Marketing Manager at BFI, a subsidiary of the $6 billion waste-management company Allied Waste Industries.[4] Dickson finds her staff to be more productive as they see her working with them. "The general manager is here also, from sunrise to sunset, so we feel we're all in the same boat," she says.

Becoming a player-coach means not just sending in the plays from the corporate sidelines but also helping to run them. Nonetheless, each decision or task should prompt a manager to ask whether it could be handled by someone else; you can't afford unnecessary drains on your time. If not, the manager's next question should be "What can I do to prepare someone else so that they can make this kind of decision next time?"

One major benefit of rolling up your sleeves with your subordinates is that they come to understand your issues—in effect, the broader issues of the business itself. "They see my concentration and focus, so they help me get there," Dickson says. "You have to be a player-coach these days. We find that the ones who have made us a success are the team players. I try to keep the day flow going, and my staff ends up knowing more about how they contribute to the whole."

RECOGNIZE THE VALUE OF DAILY TASKS

In some cases, downsizing is not only a question of fewer people to do the work; it's a question of the type of work that's left to do by those who remain. In companies that have chosen to reduce lower-level staff and retain more seasoned managers, those managers may be saddled once again with tasks they spent years trying to get promoted out of having to do.

However, managing for the short term involves recognizing the value of those seemingly menial tasks to the organization. Having to handle something yourself instead of handing it to a now-nonexistent staff person can open up its own opportunities for moving the company forward. If a process is burdensome, having to perform it can spur someone who manages for the short term to find a way to streamline it.

For example, one senior manager we spoke to, whose department at a U.S. manufacturer and supplier of steel to auto, construction, and other industrial companies, has five fewer people than it did five years ago.[5] In a department that had 13 people, that's a substantial reduction. As Materials Manager, she supervises longtime managers who in many cases are now having to do routine tasks previously performed by clerks, such as keying in data and hand-carrying paperwork between the office and the shop floor.

> Everyone is doing a multifunctional role. The company made a decision that there would be X number of people in the company. The sales department was left intact and wasn't affected by the numbers. Unfortunately, quality control and materials and operations were. I'm not sure they understood the demands they'd be putting on the individuals remaining.
>
> Short-term staffing ups and downs are being eliminated. If we started to get totally busy and weren't sure we could handle it, we would bring in temporary people to fill gaps. Now even the contract person has gone by the wayside. You try to make do. I don't think there's anyone in the management group who works less than 50 to 60 hours a week. We've lost our legs; therefore, we're kind of half-managers in the traditional sense.
>
> Everyone who reports to me has more seniority than me by at least 10 years, and they're older than me. The next person under me is where he wants to be in the organization; he's been here 43 years. Their goal is to not have their quality of work life affected. They didn't anticipate that their roles would change so dramatically.
>
> The steel buyer also now is doing claims; he doesn't have the

time to spend with the vendors. If he is going to socialize, it has to be after work. What free time you have is now filled with necessary, day-to-day activities that have to get done. Our steel buyer had a clerk who worked for him; she keyed in orders and did the running around the plant for receiving paperwork. That's something he now has to do.

It's one thing to do it to cover for someone when they're on vacation; it's another for that to now suddenly be the norm. It affects their perception of themselves in the organization. They're no longer the person the vendor comes in and visits with. When you've worked in a company for a long time—he's been here 30 years—to suddenly feel you've stepped back is difficult.

It's difficult to teach people, to give them the support and make them feel that they are still as important to the organization. I'm trying not to have them feel that their roles have been lessened. Sometimes human resource departments don't understand that. They say, "Yes, but you're still the buyer." The response is "Yeah, but I didn't have to run around the plant and pick up paperwork."

However, the situation is not necessarily as bleak as it might appear. Sharing the workload has increased cohesion among the people remaining. "The team dynamics are extremely good," says the senior manager. "Everyone appreciated that they all kind of got knocked down a bit. They're a great group of guys to work with. That probably is what makes it work well." She manages both union and nonunion workers, and finds that even the union members "understand what things need to be done. As long as you don't blithely violate something in the agreement, they're willing to work with you." She continues:

My predecessor was much more into the office atmosphere, into purchasing. I did the legwork, and he was able to stay focused more on the budgets. He was always at those meetings. When he opted to retire, they took his role and combined it with mine. That is the problem of managers these days. When I talk to other managers, they face the same thing. We don't have the same number of people reporting to us. We have to be the day-to-day people as well as the long-range planners.

Though she works in steel manufacturing, a cornerstone of the traditional economy, the senior manager articulates a situation common to managers in virtually every industry. The challenge is not only to bridge the gap between the corporation and its employees, but also to ensure that the resources that are left are focused on helping the company day by day, week by week, quarter by quarter—in short, that they are focused on what really matters.

It is that kind of comprehension that helps make the connection between individual interests and corporate goals, a connection that is needed to align the entire organization. And personally, getting to what matters is a key task-management skill that can mean the difference between moving up in the organization and being moved out.

13

The More You Do, the More You Do

Picture yourself on a tennis court near the net, facing an automatic ball machine on the other side of the court. If you turned on the ball machine at its highest speed and started trying to hit the balls back, you might feel overwhelmed watching the balls whiz by you. But if you start to hit the balls you can, you'll find yourself hitting more and more balls. You adjust to the faster pace and the machine seems to slow down. The machine hasn't changed; the individual has.

It is this capacity to adapt to surrounding circumstances that can provide an edge when managing for the short term. Managing for the short term is not about trying to hit all the balls or slowing down the machine, but about hitting the balls you can and hitting each one well, improving the percentage of balls you try for as you go along.

In managing for the short term, managers should seek an even greater amount of responsibility. The time to take on a greater workload is when you know you can't. It is not so much the workload that matters as it is the perceived willingness and capability a person has to help the organization. And that perception comes not simply from doing more, but from doing more of what truly helps the organization.

When Janice Hayes, Executive Director of the Bibliocentre in Toronto, Canada, wants to reward a member of her staff, she may give them an extra day off attached to a long weekend or take them out to

---

VOICES FROM THE FRONT LINES

Obstacles to Productivity[1]

"Perhaps I'm underestimating the 'productivity' of the many interventions that I am called upon to make between 9 and 5, but it's hard to point at any real progress from these 15-minute encounters."

"Need isolation from fire-fighting activities to be truly productive. Must let other managers manage the chaos."

"As executive management I view 'productive' time as time actually spent moving something forward versus the administrivia of day-to-day operations."

"I can get more of the paper-related tasks done in the morning without anyone around. Once people find out you are in and available, you might as well put the files away until 5:30."

"Meetings (productive or senseless) are consuming more and more of our time during regular office hours. With chronic resource constraint, we continue to extend our working hours just to meet our basic responsibility, not to mention the increased load we all now carry."

---

lunch. However, she also may give them more to do by putting them on another committee. Her organization administers centralized purchasing and administration for 80 campuses and 25 colleges and most of her staff is unionized, so "we've had to get creative about how we reward people," she says.[2]

As the organization focuses on knowledge management and becomes more of a learning organization, she says, "this is a way to recognize their accomplishments and give them the skills to lead others collaboratively. We push the staff out into these different areas when they've demonstrated achievement. It enhances their employability."

Recognizing the importance of "the more you do, the more you do" increases a manager's need to make sure that priorities are clear,

> By focusing more on what truly matters, both corporately and personally, you can find yourself with more available time to deal with more.

and that taking on additional work truly and—even more important—demonstrably contributes to the company's bottom line. By focusing more on what truly matters, both corporately and personally, you can find yourself with more available time to deal with more.

Part of the problem comes when managers and workers find themselves doing a lot of work that does not matter, to the organization or to themselves personally. Some work results in neither forward motion for the organization nor forward motion for the individual. And work that is perceived not to matter is debilitating for both individual and organization. Being able to link priorities to business goals is essential.

THE LIST APPROACH

Task management is a critical skill for doing more by doing more, and lists are a key tool used by nearly all managers. If you find yourself

---

VOICES FROM THE FRONT LINES

Where Are Managers Productive?[3]

"The nature of my job is such that I must be 'inspired' to creativity. Often a coffeehouse, the beach, etc., with a notebook produces the best results."

"Work at home is most productive for me personally, away from meetings and the interruptions that come from running a large department. As a manager of people, I spend most of my time strategizing, directing, and leading, and therefore have to be in the office."

"It used to be that there would be some downtime due to traveling or perhaps a day in between two trips that would be wasted. Now my most productive days are when I am in a hotel for a day between meetings. As long as I have a decent Internet connection, I am working away."

"Generally, I'm very productive at the office. However, I'm also extremely productive when I'm away at a conference, due to the nature of our business."

"Strategic-thought planning is best at home. Tactical stuff is best handled in the office due to availability of people and faster system response times."

creating daily and weekly lists for work, take comfort—you're not alone. It turns out that 95 percent of executives and managers keep a list of things to do for business, even though they realize they will not accomplish everything on it.

We found that most executives and managers have anywhere from six to 20 items on their list of things to do at any given time[4] (see Figure 13.1). The good news is that the largest percentage said they get to somewhere between half and 70 percent during the day[5] (see Figure 13.2). However, less than one percent of them manage to accomplish everything on their list during the day; even getting through about three-fourths of the list is accomplished by only 17 percent of the managers surveyed.[6] (And you thought you were the only one with this problem!)

Lists are perhaps the most widely used method for managing tasks, and the variety of ways to use them is nearly endless. However, when managing for the short term it is necessary to keep a list, either physically or mentally, containing those items that matter most to you and your organization.

The 20-Item List

This is a list that includes virtually all the priorities of the day, with virtually no hope of getting all of them done. Typically, three to five items on a master list might be completed, with the remainder rolling

FIGURE 13.1

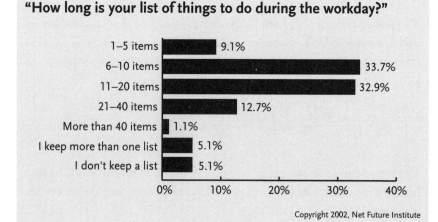

"How long is your list of things to do during the workday?"

1–5 items	9.1%
6–10 items	33.7%
11–20 items	32.9%
21–40 items	12.7%
More than 40 items	1.1%
I keep more than one list	5.1%
I don't keep a list	5.1%

Copyright 2002, Net Future Institute

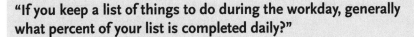

FIGURE 13.2

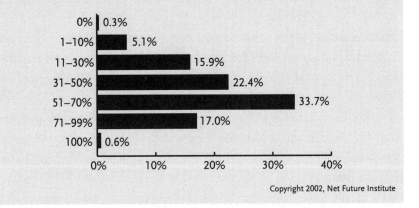

"If you keep a list of things to do during the workday, generally what percent of your list is completed daily?"

0%	0.3%
1–10%	5.1%
11–30%	15.9%
31–50%	22.4%
51–70%	33.7%
71–99%	17.0%
100%	0.6%

Copyright 2002, Net Future Institute

over to the next day. The advantage of this approach is that the master "list" is always top of mind. The downside is that you might get depressed seeing a growing list on a daily to weekly to monthly basis.

The Rolling List

When John O'Brien worked at a corporation, he had a secretary and support team to arrange e-mail in a binder for en route action and coordinate project logistics. Combined with his Harvard Planner, the system worked beautifully.[7] When he became an independent consultant, he was "seeking a more fluid, less controlled environment."

VOICES FROM THE FRONT LINES

Long Lists[8]

"When I established my first 'to-do' list here I counted over 100 distinct items—some of them catchalls for multiple-step deliverables. I recently celebrated when my list dipped below 30. It is now at 54 items representing a blend of activities, from simple tasks like 'write a memo' to 'Employee development plan,' covering team skills matrix definition and the development of training P and P. In terms of accomplishments, some of my most productive days are strictly on short-term fire fighting."

However, without those support systems, he realized that he was overwhelmed by having to juggle all the tasks his staff had previously handled. "The supposed freedom became an abyss. I completely lost control. Instead of controlling my environment, it had begun to control me."

After about a year, he hauled out his paper planner again and ordered updated refills: "It's the framework that gives you the freedom." The system shows a week at a time on a double spread and allows him to keep a rolling action list. He puts a slash across the specific day on which he plans to do a given task. If it doesn't get done that day, he can put a slash on a new day; once it's accomplished, it gets a slash in the opposite direction to complete an "x," indicating that it's done.

"I don't have to write down everything all over again," says O'Brien. "At the end of the week, I can look back and see how much I planned to do that I didn't get done and how much I did. I can look at what else was going on that day and see whether I was perhaps misjudging how much time I had planned, or whether I had looked to see whether a given task was incompatible with other tasks scheduled for the day.

"You may plan to do something on a given day, but life has a way of sneaking up behind you and doing away with that plan."

The Nightly List

One list approach involves planning for the next day just before going to sleep, anticipating that there will be little time in the course of daily office life for planning.

"My days at the office are spent running around from thing to

---

VOICES FROM THE FRONT LINES

New Items for Old Lists[9]

"By the end of a normal workday I have completed a good percentage of the priority items, while adding at least as many new items to be done as have been completed."

thing," says Robert Copple, Senior Counsel in the Motorola Law Department, where he has worked for six years.[10] "I have pushed away the things that don't matter, and I deal with the things that are important that day. My whole day is tactical and strategic, with no bureaucracy involved. Basically, I play war games all day long."

Copple plans for the next day after his children have gone to bed. "I don't go to sleep at night until I know what I'm going to do the next day. I will write an ongoing list of about 30 items and constantly refine it. It keeps in front of me the things I need to be aware of," Copple says.

He doesn't concern himself with trying to accomplish any specific number of items on the list. "I have many days where I won't get anything done on my list, but if I didn't get to things on the list, it means they didn't have to be done that day. Things bubble up, but you can't spend your entire career reacting."

Copple also believes in keeping others on his team constantly apprised. "In complex litigation involving many internal constituencies, I make extensive e-mails to keep those constituencies informed and to quickly get de jure or de facto consensus," says Copple. It helps me to keep things moving, and to avoid claims later that part of the constituency was not informed and would have done things differently. I am fortunate to have a very qualified and motivated litigation team. As such, we are all fairly obsessive/compulsive. We make it a point to cc: each other on e-mails regarding all developments in our cases. As a result, I know what is going on, have a higher level of trust, and can give more focus to my responsibilities."

The Weekly List

This approach involves a bit of foresight and advanced planning, but forces you into a broader view of your business. It also requires focus on longer-range goals, eliminating smaller issues that may get in the way.

"I do a lot of things that matter; there's not a whole lot that doesn't matter," says John Madden, owner of Contemporary Audio in Michigan.[11]

Madden works 50 to 60 hours during his Monday-through-Saturday schedule, and he saves Sunday night for planning.

VOICES FROM THE FRONT LINES

Working by the Week[12]

"I generally work off a longer-term list and work items in priority order and by due date. I do set goals for what I'll get done in a week, but not in a day."

"Every Sunday night I come into the office and plan for our Monday sales meeting. I set up my week in advance, and I allow for surprises," says Madden. "You have to be careful not to book yourself solid, because you're guaranteed something will come up. We were planning for an expansion; then the place next door decided not to move and, boom, everything changed."

Madden subscribes to the rolling-list approach. His usually has 10 to 15 items a day on it, of which he generally accomplishes half and rolls the remainder to the next day. "I absolutely love what I do; it's a passion," says Madden.

Double or Multiple Lists

Another approach to lists is to keep one weekly list in addition to a daily list. Generally, the daily list items would come from the weekly list, which is an overview of total items on the radar screen.

"I create a weeklong list on Monday with about 20 items, then do a daily list first thing each morning with three or four things and get them done," says Michael Hayes, Integrated Marketing Communications Lead at IBM.[13]

Hayes keeps 8 A.M. to 9 A.M. and 5 P.M. to 6 P.M. open for unanticipated items and focuses most on accomplishing his short, daily lists. "It gives me a sense of accomplishment," says Hayes. "If I get it all done and still have time, I go back to my weekly list. There's always a little work left to get done on the weekends. I used to make longer lists, but then I'd get discouraged." Hayes's long-term list (kept in a spiral notebook) might have projects that must be completed as far out as six months, while short-term items are steps toward accomplishing the longer-term goals and generally are completed on that day.

A variation of this is keeping multiple lists for various time frames, or separate lists for home and work.

The Folder List

Like many managers, John Ogrizovich, Vice President of Waste Management, Inc., has a weekly meeting with his direct reports. And each week he finds that not long after the meeting, something inevitably comes up that he needs to address with one or more of those direct reports, something he would have brought up at the meeting had he known about it at the time.[15]

Ogrizovich's solution: "I keep separate folders for each person that reports to me. I throw notes in those folders whenever something comes up, because I know that person's liable to show up well before the next week's meeting. That way, instead of waiting until the meeting, the next time I talk to one of them, I can open that folder and say, 'While I've got you, let me check with you on this.' In my experience, most good information gets shared in an unplanned meeting."

Ogrizovich also makes a point of looking at each new e-mail before he goes home for the day. "I will not go home till I've at least looked at every e-mail. I at least want to know what's there." However, he finds that electronic communication is no substitute for personal contact. He has a monthly luncheon with new employees: "It's not so important that they meet me; it's most important that they meet the 10 to 15 other new people.

"I think you've got to have communications as one of the priorities all the time. It's like everything else: You just have to take the time. You have to accept that it's worth the time it takes to do it."

> **VOICES FROM THE FRONT LINES**
>
> ### Managing the Long-Term To-Do List[16]
>
> "My to-do's are generally long projects that can almost never be completed in less than one week—or one month, for that matter."
>
> "My list runs like a background program in my brain. Downtime always kicks off the next task or sets the agenda for thinking through the next several tasks, also in background. Amazingly, when forward tasks come up, solid directional proposals are there so strategies can be formulated to either delegate for further action or accomplish the task quickly."
>
> "As the CEO, my 'to-do' list is made up of primarily long-term strategic items, and therefore one would not expect many to be completed on a single day; some take weeks, some months, and a few take years to complete."

FLOAT TIME

It is essential that "float time" be built into any list to allow for unanticipated events that can throw any prearranged schedule into disarray. There are various ways to do this, ranging from creating smaller lists to actually scheduling an hour or two of planned free time.

Mike Indursky, Senior Vice President of Strategic Planning and Marketing at Unilever, creates his lists with a Palm Pilot but always sets aside specific time for unanticipated events. "You have to make choices on what you're going to do. I set aside two hours on my calendar to create flexibility in my day. My best work is at 11 at night."[17]

> **VOICES FROM THE FRONT LINES**
>
> ### Allowing for the Unexpected[18]
>
> "Any list that I start the day off with usually changes by around 75 percent through the day, with the other items moving out to later dates or being made redundant by the new items. Usually the list is a combination of my Outlook calendar and notes in a day-per-page diary, and I limit it to critical tasks only. Of all the tasks completed during a day, only around 20 percent appear on any sort of list."

Some managers find that having a lot of work even has an upside. By forcing them to concentrate on things that must happen immediately, it ensures that there is action rather than inaction. However, a tight time frame also increases the pressure to make sure that the actions being taken truly advance the organization.

BALANCING TASKS WITH TIME

No matter what techniques you use to decide which tasks will get how much of your time, the tasks chosen need to be related clearly to the overall organizational direction. While accomplishing items on a list might seem somewhat tactical, those items will eventually create incremental forward motion for the individual, the department, and, ultimately, the organization—that is, if the tasks are connected to the overall company direction. Managing for the short term requires that managers be more productive, and executing items on a list is one way to measure that productivity. At the same time, simply creating the list, when done thoughtfully, can help focus attention on what really matters to a manager and an organization.

VOICES FROM THE FRONT LINES

When Are Managers Productive?[19]

"I'm most productive at home when managing projects that demand involved thinking and minimal interruption. At work, I'm productive when managing tasks—things that must be reviewed and processed fairly quickly."

"Most effective when there are few meetings, and I can close the door."

"Actually, I find I am most productive under tight time commitments, especially getting ready for a specific event or deadline. However, I am also at my greatest efficiency when no one is around to either distract or bother me. Because of the social nature and information exchange of my responsibilities, it is difficult to cut short tasks that have opportunity for social interaction, including telephone conversations. The Internet has both added to the efficiency and also taken away from it."

14

Successful Meetings for the Short Term

Most executives and managers spend a considerable amount of time in meetings, and managing for the short term requires strict rules if those meetings are to be productive. These rules deal with what happens at meetings, how they should be run, when they should be held, and who should attend them. Many organizations even have created their own guidelines for how to run and attend internal meetings, hoping to increase efficiency and effectiveness.

One of the reasons there is so much corporate focus on meetings is the amount of time they take. Internal scheduled meetings take up at least one-fifth of the workweek of a majority of executives and managers, and in many cases, they take up much more[1] (see Figure 14.1).

However, the view of whether those meetings are productive is mixed[2] (see Figure 14.2). Overall, about 40 percent of executives and managers feel that more than 60 percent of their meetings are productive; about 34 percent feel that less than 40 percent of their meetings are productive. The rest feel that roughly half—somewhere between 40 and 60 percent—of their meetings are productive.

As might be expected, senior executives are slightly more likely than managers to feel that a greater percentage of their meeting time is productive. Only 4.4 percent of managers feel all their meetings paid off, compared to 9.7 percent of executives (see Figure 14.3). The percentage who consider 81–99 percent of their meetings productive also is higher for senior executives. Conversely, managers are much more likely than executives to feel that 20 percent or fewer of their meetings were productive.

Regardless of one's level in the organization, the fact is that in difficult economic times, with downsizing, hiring freezes, and increased workload, no one has the time to waste in an unproductive meeting. The challenge is to increase the percentage that are truly needed and eliminate those that aren't.

FIGURE 14.1

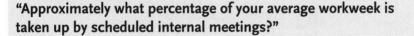

"Approximately what percentage of your average workweek is taken up by scheduled internal meetings?"

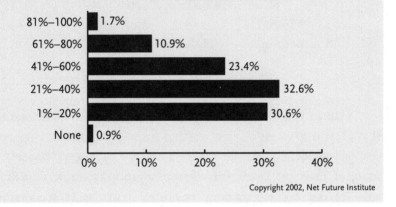

FIGURE 14.2

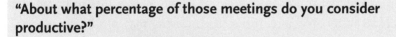

"About what percentage of those meetings do you consider productive?"

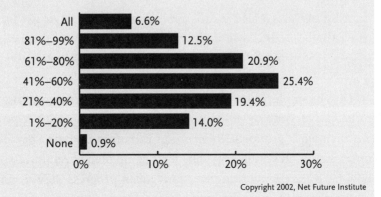

FIGURE 14.3

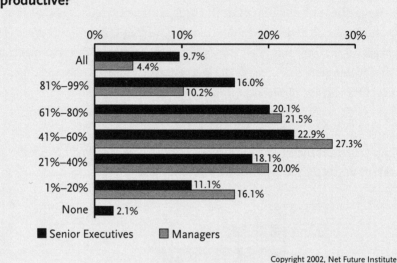

"About what percentage of those meetings do you consider productive?"

"A lot of times a leader calls a meeting because he or she thinks that's leading, when it's just wasting time—and probably upsetting a few people if they had the guts to admit it," says Jerry Sodorff, President of Thought Leadership Group, a group of trainers in Richardson, Texas, who help corporations develop managers' leadership and career-management skills.[3]

Managing a meeting for the short term involves deciding if the meeting will get the company closer to where it wants to be in some concrete, actionable way. If not, the meeting may not be necessary.

> A lot of times a leader calls a meeting because he or she thinks that's leading, when it's just wasting time—and probably upsetting a few people, if they had the guts to admit it.

One example is the regularly scheduled "status meeting," held to keep everyone up-to-date on what is going on with a project or within a work group. Such meetings can often become a game of one-upsmanship, in which everyone feels compelled to remind their peers how hard they're working and how much progress they're making.

If a project is generally on track, there are other ways to keep everyone current. Options include electronic bulletin boards on internal company Web sites, and circulation of brief status reports. Meetings should be reserved for when problems need to be addressed or when things begin to get off track. "Having a meeting just because we've always had it is the best reason not to have a meeting," says Sodorff. "If we take action at a meeting, the next meeting should be if we get off track. If we're on track, maybe we don't have to have a meeting."

Managing for the short term can help managers adopt the "don't meet to fix it if it isn't broken" approach. If managers are making incremental forward progress, that progress should be measured in small steps so that feedback can lead to quick correction of problems before they become large. A manager who is paying attention to that ongoing stream of feedback can use it to correct course more quickly. Those ongoing corrections can help keep a project or department on track and reduce the number of meetings required to figure out what went wrong and how to fix it once a project has been derailed.

Eliminating unnecessary meetings is important for another reason: morale. "Especially after September 11, people began to get more involved in asking, 'What's my individual contribution? How can I feel good about myself as I go about my daily work?' I think those feelings have been there all along; we're just talking about them more," Sodorff says.

QUANTIFYING THE VALUE OF MEETINGS

Unnecessary or unproductive meetings not only contribute little to the company's progress, but they also leave participants without a sense of accomplishment that helps them feel good about their work. And at a time when it is more important than ever that workers and managers be true contributors to their employers, the feeling that work hours are well spent is critical to motivating a workforce.

When managing for the short term, the quantification of everything, as discussed earlier, applies to meetings as well. One way to gauge how effective meetings are for you personally is to create a system to measure meeting results against your division's progress in an ongoing fashion.

For example, at Delta Air Lines, where 80,000 employees work to move more than 100 million passengers a year, time is of the essence. Responsibility for determining how well those passengers are treated while onboard falls to Cheryl Scales, Director, Customer Satisfaction, In-Flight Services, at Delta. On a light day, Scales attends a half-dozen internal meetings, and she caps the amount of time that she spends in meetings at 50 percent of her week.[4] However, Scales has created a simple system to ensure that meeting results match her group's activities and performance. On an ongoing basis, all activities are rated as a red, yellow, or green light. The objective is to move reds to yellow and yellows to green. Says Scales:

> When we're running on all cylinders, we're all around green. We ask, from a management process, "Did you green-light them or leave them on yellow?" My group regularly gives me a summary of reds to yellow, so either I or the team can identify a process breakdown if there are a lot of reds. Before a meeting, we typically post on our internal Web site so we can go and see the reds, yellows, and greens at the beginning of a team meeting. I manage my own reds, greens, and yellows at other people's meetings and create my own to-do list.
>
> There are certain meetings I don't control, and I will tell them in advance that I have one hour and a hard stop. I try to set a time constraint of a half hour to an hour at most for meetings. If you allow a lot more time, you don't get much more than more anecdotal information. We deal with one to three issues per meeting; it's too difficult to manage more than that in one meeting. People can only process so much! At the beginning of the meeting, we ask, "What are the key questions we have to ask or answer by the end of the meeting?" For meetings not under my control, it is important for me to clearly understand what's expected of me. I try to understand in advance. You can see your milestones along the way with the stoplight chart.

MANAGING FOR THE SHORT TERM AT MEETINGS

Before the Meeting

Everyone is familiar with the concept of "You get out of it what you put into it." When managing for the short term, where measurable

Voices from the Front Lines

What Makes a Problem Meeting?[5]

"I would characterize the nonproductive meetings I attend as either (a) encounter groups, (b) repetitive brainstorming sessions, (c) punishment for past sins, (d) lacking agendas and published minutes (see b), (e) opportunities to improve posturing skills, or (f) required to prevent backstabbing."

"I don't know if it is because I work in Latin America, but I feel that we are not sufficiently focused on objectives when we come to meetings. It seems hard to get to the point—and especially hard to stick to it!"

"Not only do I spend a great deal of time in these meetings, but they normally have to be rescheduled at least once or twice. For some reason, people refuse to use the simple e-mail and scheduling tools our company provides to make this easier, or they are time-zone ignorant."

"The 'teleconference' often [is] the worst offender, because it lacks the visual clues that subtly stimulate people to do better! I also observe that online chat allows—indeed, encourages—a host of side meetings during teleconferences."

"If I go to a meeting with 20 issues, I come back with 10 resolved. In the process, however, I return with 25 open issues, as there are 15 new ones added to replace the 10 that were resolved. Meetings and e-mail seem to be like bad chain letters that are self-perpetuating."

"The art of meeting preparation is lost. So much time is wasted because folks come (1) without agendas; (2) without issues clearly identified; and (3) no concept of the outcome desired. E-mail doesn't help, as some people think it replaces meetings/discussions, which actually take longer to resolve electronically than simply getting together face to face in a well-structured/run meeting!!!! HELP!!!"

"Meetings scheduled by higher-level managers do not have as much value added in terms of strategic and tactical results and movement. The higher-level meetings' main purpose seems to focus on informing execs, with little value moving downward."

results are everything, investing time and resources before a meeting is critical. Otherwise, topic drift, circular debates that lead nowhere, and confusion can eat up time and prevent anything definitive from resulting. Coming to a meeting totally prepared can have a ripple effect on other attendees in the future; also, less collective time is wasted getting everyone up to speed on the scheduled issues. At times and at certain management levels, more time should be spent planning for the meeting than in the meeting itself. And when executives become comfortable with managing meetings for the short term, they often end up with enhanced long-term results.

> **Think of it as a marketing tool you can use to sell people on the idea that your meeting will be worth their time.**

Create and Master the Agenda

An agenda may be the single most important tool for making a meeting productive. For any meeting you run, make creating one a habit. Specify whether this is an information-gathering session or a decision-making session. Also, spell out what participants can expect to leave with that helps them do their job, whether that is a decision, greater clarity about an issue, or an action plan. Think of it as a marketing tool you can use to sell people on the idea that your meeting will be worth their time. Yes, it takes more effort, but remember: You're asking people to spend time at your meeting. Letting them know what's in it for them makes them more likely to contribute actively instead of feeling forced to sit through one more meeting.

The agenda should include approximate times for discussion of

---

Voices from the Front Lines

Agenda Is Key[6]

"We are fairly rigorous in our expectations that internal meetings are given the same kind of planning and focus that we would also do for any external meeting. Therefore, 90 percent of the time there will be an agenda and desired outcomes of the meeting. This not only helps participants to prepare appropriately (making the meeting more productive in itself) but also [ensures] that the right people can attend to increase the likelihood of reaching the desired outcome."

"The keys to a good meeting are: (1) show up on time; (2) have an agenda; (3) be prepared; (4) be prepared; (5) be prepared."

each issue, based on its relative importance. Setting expectations up front can prevent someone from feeling that they are being cut off.

If an agenda is not supplied for a meeting you'll be attending, ask the person who requested the meeting what items will be discussed and what outcomes are expected. If the person requesting the meeting doesn't supply an agenda, you might put one together based on the meeting leader's responses to your questions. Or you might recruit other attendees to join in the request for an agenda. And if you can't get anyone to provide an agenda, it might be a meeting worth skipping.

Be Prepared

Meetings can be more effective if participants have used e-mail properly to prepare for the meeting. E-mail can help organize the meeting in advance and supply the information that is likely to be needed. Collected in advance or during the meeting itself, it can be disseminated and acted on immediately instead of everyone having to wait until the next meeting for it to be retrieved and discussed.

If, as the meeting leader, you know that certain information is likely to be needed for the group to take action, suggest in advance that the person responsible for it collect and distribute it for review before the meeting, or bring it with them. This step alone could save another meeting that might otherwise be needed later. Even if you're only a participant, an e-mail that asks whether the information will be available in advance will be welcomed by your colleagues.

During his years at Audio Centre in Montreal, President and owner John Banks found himself getting less and less out of internal meetings than he wanted. With 75 employees and stores in Montreal and Ottawa, Banks made an abrupt change.[7] After more than 20 years of leading meetings one way—not as prepared as he would have liked—Banks took a totally different tack. "I had a revelation. I was spending hours accomplishing zero at meetings." Banks continues:

> I now do an elaborate preparation in advance of any meeting. What is my objective? How do I want to feel at the end of the meeting? Instead of going in with a simple agenda, I go in with much more thinking done on my part. I look at it from the perspective of "Do I have a real understanding of the theory of the subject? What is the essential thing I want?"

I'm often setting direction, so I really try to understand and look at it from the perspective of the individuals sitting there. Are there things that will put them in conflict? I'm now spending two hours to plan a one-hour meeting, but as the chief executive, the more time I spend, the more effective they are.

Banks attends about 10 meetings a week, most of which he runs. The amount and quality of preparation by executive management are not lost on other managers in those meetings; many quickly realize they also had better be prepared in advance to keep up with the boss. Better preparation also leads to better meeting follow-up, since the desired outcome is identified in advance.

People got used to having mediocre meetings, but now it's totally different. I take minutes during the meeting, and they're more objective-oriented. I want results, and they take time and contemplation before the meeting. I don't leave home in the morning if I'm not ready for the meeting. This means really understanding the issue and determining "What is it I really want?"

For example, I have a guy in charge of purchasing for the company, and I'll sit and say, "Am I really clear what I want out of the purchasing department?" What is the ideal situation? What is the relationship I want between vendors and purchasing? Then, I'll come down and say, "What behavior would I like to have in terms of his attitude to the vendors and the employees? How should he be spending his time?"

VOICES FROM THE FRONT LINES

Finding the Upside to Meetings[8]

"Meetings are a necessary evil. Our organization is small and dynamic, and it would be impossible to have everything written out and thought through in an effort to avoid some of the time spent in the meetings."

"If we are committed to a consensus type of management style, then meetings become an essential element [in] building consensus."

"Ever since the business climate/economy turned downwards, the meetings I attend seem to be much more productive. Perhaps it's because everyone is a little more focused given the current business environment."

Then, in the meeting, I give the overall and say, "This is what John Banks wants," and he knows I'm very serious about the aspects of management and his attitude toward suppliers.

An understanding of the attitudes of the meeting attendees is critical, because you have to see how it can get in the way of an objective. The key is the time in preparation; it's really everything.

Granted, not everyone has the advantage of being the top executive as well as the owner of the company. However, as in most service businesses, the managers and employees at Audio Centre are highly skilled and trained to be very customer-focused. Premeeting time invested in focusing on measurable objectives can save having to take yet another meeting to address issues that remained unresolved because of inadequate preparation.

Be Focused

In some cases, being focused means saying no to meetings that don't absolutely require your presence, or that are not concerned with your core contribution to the company. Ask yourself these questions:

- Will I primarily gather information or give information?

- What is the worst that can happen if I don't attend this meeting?

- How will attending this meeting improve my ability to help the company achieve its goals? Is that potential for improvement greater than whatever might be produced by the other ways I might spend that time?

- Are there alternative ways to get or give the information?

Agree on Desired Outcomes

One of the best ways to keep a meeting on track is to get agreement up front on what the meeting should accomplish. Again, this could be a decision and the next steps necessary to execute it. It could be getting feedback on a proposal. Whatever the purpose, having everyone agree early on—even before the meeting—what the participants want to gain from the meeting can be a useful tool in keeping the meeting on track. Having that agreement makes it easier for the

---

VOICES FROM THE FRONT LINES

Don't Go[9]

"Our present CEO has achieved dramatic success in this area. Before he came on board, I spent 80 percent of my workday in unproductive meetings. By empowering the function heads to just get on with it, we now meet for coordination purposes biweekly, and with our teams as needed. I suspect, however, that my reply will be an exception in an over-meetinged world."

"At this point in time, I can select the meetings I am involved in and, therefore, avoid the ones that I do not think are worth the time. That is why I have a low percentage of meeting time and a high rating for value of meetings attended."

"It took me three years to train my staff not to drag me into meetings that were unproductive for me as they didn't require my involvement. I have also taught them to manage their attendance at internal meetings similarly. Also, not to attend every meeting in person but by phone so that it only takes up an hour instead of three hours (getting to and from meetings). This also applies to e-mail and not getting dragged into 'e-mail meetings' where the e-mail system starts getting used as a chat line."

---

person running the meeting to cut off discussion that seems to be leading away from the intended goal.

During the Meeting

Stay Focused

One of the most common complaints of managers is about meetings that drift off the subject or are hijacked by someone with a different agenda.

That's not to say that sometimes drifting off track doesn't raise interesting or important side issues. However, someone needs to be responsible for noting those issues and getting agreement to set them aside temporarily so the group can pursue whatever the meeting was intended to deal with. It doesn't matter who keeps the meeting on track, as long as it stays on track.

For example, when Andrew Scott, Vice President of IT at

Aerosoles, the New Jersey–based shoe manufacturer with more than 500 employees in 85 retail stores throughout North America, began implementing an ERP (Enterprise Resource Planning) system, a multi-year process, he found himself frequently having to report to management on the progress of the implementation, as well as manage his own staff of 14. "I have to provide information to my management as well as retrieve information from them on a regular basis," says Scott.[10]

"I make sure to have an agenda and stay on target with that agenda. I have to manage the side conversations, and I try to do it respectfully. Otherwise, they'll be sitting in the meeting forever on one topic for days. You can talk for days and not get the main objective accomplished," says Scott. "At the end of meetings, I've had to say we have to meet again, because although we got something accomplished, we didn't accomplish our objectives. I don't have a lot of time, so I have to say in meetings 'Is this what we really want to talk about right now?'"

Another reason to stay focused is to show respect for other people's time. They came with assumptions that items on the agenda were worth spending precious minutes or hours on. If the meeting drifts away from the agenda, that time may be wasted if the nonagenda discussion is less relevant to all the participants.

If you're at the meeting, contribute what you can. If you have no contribution to make, try to get information from the meeting in some other way. Some people take laptop computers to meetings, not to use in connection with the meeting, but to do a little e-mail management when they feel they have nothing to offer. It might be viewed as an efficient use of time, but it also raises the question of whether the manager needs to be at the meeting in the first place. It also can be perceived as disrespectful of the other meeting participants. In effect, the person is saying to both the meeting owner and others attending, "My time is more valuable than yours; maybe you have the time to devote to this, but I don't."

However, bear in mind that cultural differences may affect how people behave at meetings. For example, Western executives are often surprised to discover that Japanese meetings are run by rules different from those in North America.

"Coming from a Canadian background, where I would run meetings crisply with an agenda, specific objectives, and expected outcomes, and assuming that participants have prepared their materials first, it is quite a culture shock to experience meetings in the Japanese milieu," says Michael Monette, Vice President for Strategic Planning and Development, St. Joseph Development at St. Joseph Corporation, the largest privately owned print and digital production and communications company in Canada.[11] Monette currently consults for a client in Japan, and he has learned that meetings there tend to have a completely different pace from those he has been used to attending: "Many meetings here seem to revolve around consensus building and tend to go on for many hours. As a result, the pace is slow and laborious.

"Any new idea or concept, if raised during a meeting, must be discussed fully, debated, and hashed out until all participants reach some kind of common understanding before moving on. If the new concept tabled was secondary to the primary objective of the meeting, the primary objective is effectively derailed during this time, sometimes resulting in the expiration of the meeting time allotment (which is often many hours).

"Another interesting behavior, which I think can only be truly understood after living through many multi-hour meetings, is to watch certain members seemingly fall asleep. One might think that this is a terrible thing to do, but most often it is recognized as a sign of 'comfort.' If a manager closes his or her eyes (mostly his, given the current work demographics), most people consider that the manager is comfortable with what his people are saying, so he does not need to worry [and] stay alert. This behavior is not rampant, but it does cause one to wonder sometimes. As the Japanese tend to put in very long days, it seems likely that some people are just simply tired, or run out of the stamina to withstand the long meetings without some physical manifestation.

"Overall, I would estimate that perhaps 25 percent of any meeting is truly on task, from a North American perspective. The remainder is related to consensus building, posturing, power brokering, sidetrack discussions, and just spending time together as a group because this is the cultural norm."

Clearly, astute managers will need to understand the difference between meetings that run according to cultural norms and ones that are simply badly managed.

Flow Information Both Ways

Make sure the agenda includes some way to ensure that feedback occurs. Even if focusing on incremental steps and keeping the meeting short means that feedback does not occur at that meeting, one of the next steps should make clear what the mechanism is for getting that feedback.

Run on Time

Start promptly, even if someone isn't there. If the topic is important—and to take up people's time, it should be—the point about timeliness will be made. You can't afford to waste the time of six people for one person who isn't there.

For example, at Osprey, the 10-year-old North Carolina–based consulting firm that specializes in e-business and enterprise systems for the manufacturing industry, meetings had gradually begun starting later and later.

President and COO Tom Wilson found that meetings began five to seven minutes late, which doesn't sound like much until you add it all up.[12] "Once people started coming seven minutes late, then others figured the meeting would not start on time, so they started coming late," says Wilson.

Somewhat ironically, Wilson and his team conducted a series of meetings to set up rules for all future meetings. The first rule that everyone agreed was critical was that meetings must start on time.

VOICES FROM THE FRONT LINES

Keep 'Em Short[13]

"The longer-duration meetings tend to be less effective than more [frequent], shorter meetings."

"Meeting management is a dying skill. Meetings that last longer than two hours have diminishing returns."

"We have an unwritten rule: No meeting goes beyond one hour unless absolutely necessary, or it is driven by a project team leader. This helps us focus on the subject matter and move on once [it is] completed."

"It created an environment of peer pressure and it made meetings faster," Wilson says. "We created an awareness that if you schedule a 30-minute meeting, it needs to end within 30 minutes." This focus on the details of how meetings should be conducted improves calendar integrity and allows managers to accurately schedule their time— essential when managing for the short term.

With rules in place, companies such as Osprey find themselves running better. "We've gotten pretty good at laying out the issues, saying we're going to make a decision at this meeting and bringing something to closure," says Wilson.

Even if no decision is required during the meeting, have someone keep time. If the session is designed to gather input from everyone, set a time limit on each person's discussion. And encourage them to pass if they don't need to contribute.

Provide a Sense of Resolution

Take a few minutes at the end of the meeting to summarize what has been accomplished. This not only helps reinforce the outcome, but it is a subtle reminder that the participants' time has not been wasted. And knowing that responsibility for a summary waits at the end of the meeting is an incentive for whoever is running the session to make sure that something has been accomplished to summarize.

After the Meeting

Hold People Accountable

One of the least rewarding business experiences can be attending a one- to two-hour meeting where agreement ultimately is reached on a pressing issue but nothing gets done. With managers attending so many meetings, sometimes it is difficult even to remember who was

---

VOICES FROM THE FRONT LINES

Little Things Can Make a Difference[14]

"Showing measurable results from a meeting is critical. Good pastries also help."

supposed to do what after a particular meeting. Everyone leaves feeling that an issue is resolved, only to find out at a meeting a few weeks later that something fell through the cracks. A question about follow-up might bring the answer, "Oh, I thought you were going to do that." It is important that at the outset of the meeting the "next steps" are determined and that a person is clearly responsible for execution of each of those steps.

When managing for the short term, accountability is key, even at meetings. Who is responsible to do what when the meeting is over? "You must document meetings," says Colleen Doty, Systems Manager at Tricon Global Restaurants, the $7 billion Kentucky-based restaurant company with 190,000 employees around the world.[15] The former PepsiCo subsidiary controls KFC, Pizza Hut, and Taco Bell, with more than 30,000 locations in 100 countries. With several direct reports, Doty attends 10 to 20 meetings per week, half of which she takes the lead on. "We're informal, but you have to be on time, especially if you're the host. You have to monitor conversations. It's important to have an agenda," says Doty. "The key is to have a productive meeting where everyone benefits. It's also helpful to document action items. This information refreshes everyone's memory and communicates next steps."

Limit the Frequency of Meetings

The reality is that despite the pace of the market and the pace of work, things generally do not change that much in a day, or at least not every day. Therefore, for most organizations, the number of meetings that occur very frequently, such as daily, should be reduced. E-mail can be used to keep most managers informed, and meetings can be reserved for creating results that move the business forward.

The problem is that once regular meetings become institutionalized—sometimes after many, many years of them—the pattern can be difficult to change. However, that is precisely what must be done. Managing for the short term requires that executives and managers justify to themselves everything they do. As has been discussed, the yardstick is measurable results. Does the meeting move the organization forward? Is it productive? What value do I add to the meeting?

When Garth Howard took over as President and COO of Ikano Communications, a data network service provider headquartered in

Salt Lake City, he found that the management team was meeting every day, which was too often.[16] As a former senior executive at Key Bank, Fidelity Investments, American Express, and Convergys, Howard had decades of meetings experience. At Ikano, he immediately limited his staff meetings to one per week.

However, simply reducing the number of meetings without improving the effectiveness of those that remain does not improve the situation. At Ikano, the number of meetings was cut but the efficiency was increased.

"Originally, I put all eight people who reported to me on each agenda, so everybody on the agenda felt they had to contribute," says Howard. "As it worked out, if one person took 20 minutes, the next would take 21 minutes. I decided to change it so that now the agenda starts blank. Staff members then come to me and bring a topic if they feel it should be on the agenda. This way they no longer had to bring something to staff meetings just to be on the agenda. Initially people didn't trust it. In reality, if it's not a key issue I didn't want people just regurgitating that they were getting their job done. Now they keep it short and they keep it concise."

In terms of reconciling the short and the long term, it also is important to connect meetings to the organization's goals. "Every meeting we have has to be against the core values and what we are hoping to accomplish," says Howard. An effective way to create this linkage between core values and results is to go back to the concept of incremental forward motion.

Focus on Incremental Forward Motion

Meeting agendas tend to expand, especially if everyone is given an opportunity in advance to review the items to be discussed. Someone adds an issue, someone else adds another, and before long the agenda is impossible to complete in the time allotted. When the meeting is over, there can be a sense that the issue targeted for the meeting ultimately did not get resolved, requiring yet another meeting.

Managing an agenda for the short term involves working with the kind of immediate, focused steps discussed earlier. The more specific the items on the agenda, the more concrete the results are likely to be. Rather than trying to solve all the problems of the company at one meeting, the focus should be on moving the organization forward at least a little. When every meeting moves the business in a forward direction—and does not get hung up in reviewing all major current and ongoing issues—the meeting attendees will consistently take more out of the meeting.

This is where e-mail—and even the telephone—comes in. E-mail is one of the best tools for creating incremental forward motion, both internally and externally. As most managers know, e-mail has altered the need for many internal meetings. It has not totally eliminated them, but it does redefine what can be accomplished at a meeting versus through electronic communications. Before e-mail, getting everyone together to discuss something was often done because it was actually more efficient than sending a memo around for everyone's feedback. Now, however, each meeting must be scrutinized to see whether it deserves to occur, or whether it's simply a habit left over from the days before e-mail.

E-mail also affects the frequency of external meetings, in addition to cutting travel costs. Once a relationship exists between, say, a buyer and a seller, there is less need for as many face-to-face meetings. "The less I deal with meetings, the more I get done," says Caryn Tanis, President of Media Network International, Inc., a Miami-based advertising sales firm for publishers worldwide.[17] "They don't serve a lot of purpose. Most of the time, it only takes a short phone conversation or a quick e-mail. E-mail is the simplest thing in the world. You can do a little at a time with e-mail, because you can do one thing at a time."

It is that ability that makes e-mail such a good example of incremental forward motion—the kind of action that, as we have seen, can take an organization into its long-range future, one step at a time. The trick is to know when to use a meeting and when to use e-mail or telephone.

Taming the E-Mail Monster

Nowadays, e-mail management is a must skill for any executive or manager; questions about it drew one of the highest response rates in our research history. Because e-mails are so easy to send, managers

get more of them and are expected to respond more promptly—
because everyone knows how easy it is to reply. Consider:

- Seventy-one percent of executives and managers spend one hour
  or more of each day sending, receiving, reading, or writing
  e-mail[18] (see Figure 14.4).

- A little more than one-fourth—27 percent—of executives and
  managers spend three hours or more a day using e-mail.[19]

- Fewer than 10 percent of executives and managers are spending
  less than 30 minutes a day on e-mail.[20]

Running on E-Mail

E-mail both enhances productivity and makes its own demands.
"Two years ago, we processed 25,000 e-mails a day," says Leo Crawford, CIO for Orange County, California, and its 16,000 employees."[21]
"Now we process 800,000 a day. We don't know why there was such
an increase; it just happened."

Only 25,000 of those 800,000 e-mails come from outside the
organization; most are either completely internal or sent outside. "I
don't have many staff meetings anymore," says Crawford. "I can keep
in contact with my staff. You can't hide anymore, and there are

FIGURE 14.4

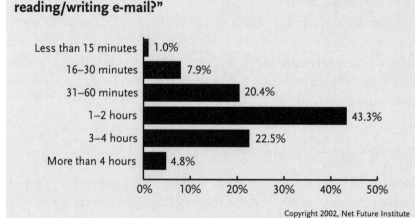

"How much time daily do you spend sending/receiving/
reading/writing e-mail?"

Less than 15 minutes 1.0%
16–30 minutes 7.9%
31–60 minutes 20.4%
1–2 hours 43.3%
3–4 hours 22.5%
More than 4 hours 4.8%

records of decisions. Information is like fish: It's better fresh. E-mail keeps that information fresh."

With a daily e-mail volume about the same as that of Orange County, Westchester County, New York, executives found that e-mail dramatically increased efficiency. "We run on e-mail," says Norman Jacknis, CIO of Westchester County.[22] "We now have a lot more focus at meetings. I get 20,000 e-mails a year."

Jacknis spends six to seven hours a day reading, filing, and writing e-mails, often at midnight or one o'clock in the morning. "Periodically I go hide and go through my e-mail," he says.

Managing E-Mail

As these two examples illustrate, e-mail used thoughtfully can be used to streamline processes. Though many managers and workers feel buried in a daily blitz of e-mails, the flow and selective storage of e-mails can not only reduce the number of unnecessary meetings but also can help manage daily, weekly, and monthly activities.

Robin Ellerthorpe, Senior Associate and Director of Consultants at OWP/P, leverages his e-mails by using them in place of a traditional to-do list.

"You spend all your time making up lists and never get to them. Many times a tough issue gets on the front burner and there's no immediate resolution, so it goes to the back burner," says Ellerthorpe, who manages a 12-person business unit in the Chicago-based, fully integrated architecture firm.[23]

Ellerthorpe organizes his tasks in contextual groups, such as a leadership context or a project context, and filters routine tasks, such as doing employee reviews or writing proposals, into time previously used to read newspapers to and from work. He uses e-mails to order tasks within those contexts.

"I don't do lists for my day, but I have sets of issues in the back of my mind," he says. "I keep things around me that remind me. I use my daily e-mails to order the context of what I'm working on. I file them and reread them. I keep the ones I'm on task for in my in-box. Others are essentially writing my lists for me. Once an e-mail gets filed, it's really off my list."

Managers also use e-mails as a fail-safe, so that important tasks do not leave the radar screen. E-mails that don't matter are eliminated.

"I have an old Franklin Planner, so I use it to work off an outline," says Tom Lupo, Senior Vice President of Luxelle International, the $6-million-a-year cosmetics business.[24] Lupo outlines six to eight points daily. "I work hard, coming in at 6:30 A.M. and banging away until around until six at night. What I don't get done I shift to the next day, but I stay with my list."

Lupo tries not to be heavily involved in "office stuff," staying focused on his own priorities for the day. He deals with 80 to 100 e-mails a day. "It can be a distraction. However, it leaves a trail, so I can go back and use it as a backstop in my networking."

"E-mail is yet another means to avoid personal interaction with people," says Phil Merdinger, Principal and Worldwide Partner in Business Development at William M. Mercer, the operational and strategic human resource consulting firm.[25] "But e-mail can be a marvelous productivity enhancer when used the right way."

Merdinger receives 40 to 50 e-mails a day, and he tends to look at most of them. He uses e-mail in conjunction with his Palm Pilot as his filing system and as a way of managing his to-do list. "It helps me manage the sending of information to people as an FYI, and I use it a lot instead of regular mail." The reality is that with 12,500 employees scattered throughout offices in 125 cities and 34 countries, e-mail is the most effective way for Merdinger and other Mercer managers to keep everyone tied in on a real-time basis to what is going on.

E-Mail That Matters

Though the overall view of e-mail is positive, its misuse is frustrating; 68 percent of executives and managers say that 25 percent or more of the e-mail they receive is unnecessary[26] (see Figure 14.5). Twenty-one percent say that more than half is unnecessary.

And it isn't just spam cluttering up the inbox; 68 percent of senior executives and managers say that the majority of the e-mail they receive is internal[27] (see Figure 14.6). Some of those e-mails are directives and details for projects that keep organizations moving; others are merely FYIs.

FIGURE 14.5

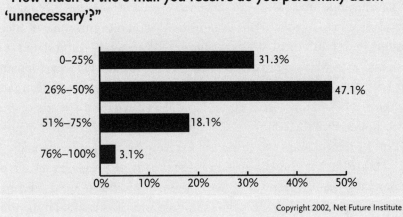

"How much of the e-mail you receive do you personally deem 'unnecessary'?"

Dealing with an overflowing inbox requires discipline. Pete McGinn, CEO of United Health Services in Binghamton, New York, which serves hospitals, nursing homes, physician practices, and HMOs in a four-county area, tries to limit his e-mail checks.[28] "When I'm disciplined, I don't check it more than two to three times a day; if I'm not, I might check it 12 times a day," says McGinn, who receives 50 to 60 e-mails a day. He clusters the time he spends responding to e-mail to a couple of half-hour sessions a day. Otherwise, the more often he checks it, the more time he spends working on it.

The worst category of e-mail is the one that just doesn't matter, contributing little or nothing to a dialog. What it does contribute is more

FIGURE 14.6

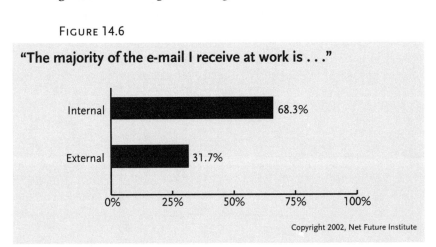

"The majority of the e-mail I receive at work is . . ."

inbox clutter. I call such messages "e-mail multipliers," because they do little other than expand exponentially the number of e-mails sent.

Automated messages are another problem. Michael Manahan receives e-mail messages throughout the day and night, some of them automated equipment-status reports.[29] "I'm totally inundated by e-mail," says Manahan, who, as Manager of Application Development at Kraft Food Service, supports computer users throughout the organization. Manahan receives 60 to 70 e-mails a day and spends one to two hours over the course of the day dealing with those that matter. "The senders all expect a response. I try my best to get to them all."

Managing for the short term means using the various means of communication appropriately. Meetings can provide a lot of information about internal alliances of employees and the personal dynamics that shape relationships among colleagues. In fact, that information can be as useful as the content of the meeting itself. They can also be good for resolving many small issues simultaneously. And if managed properly, they can still be the most efficient way to get resolution on issues and define the steps to be executed once a decision is made and the meeting is over. E-mails can improve meeting efficiency by helping to organize premeeting tasks; it can also keep people current and be managed around other tasks and meetings.

The key to meeting and e-mail productivity is to use the same techniques that are used to connect various levels of management to one another, and to juggle the various tasks and interruptions that come up day to day. Managing for the short term is just as important when working in a group as it is in improving individual performance.

15

The Law of Expanding Immediacy

Business opportunities appear and disappear in the blink of an eye, and companies must move quickly if they want to take advantage of these short-term opportunities while they are available. Sales campaigns that used to run for six months to a year may now last for 30 days—even less if companies use new technology and real-time information to adjust them on the fly, as we saw in the chapter about the role of information in decision making.

> Even organizations that do not subscribe to the concept of managing for the short term will nevertheless have to learn to operate that way precisely because everyone else is.

As a company begins to manage for the short term, making incremental forward progress, it forces the network of businesses that surround it to operate in the same way. This has created what I call Martin's Law of Expanding Immediacy, which is the following: *The more any business manages for the short term to take advantage of short-term opportunities, the more it forces other businesses to do the same.*

Martin's Law of Expanding Immediacy means that even organizations that do not subscribe to the concept of managing for the short term will nevertheless have to learn to operate that way precisely because everyone else is. When a company's customers, its business partners, and its suppliers are focused on making incremental progress through short-term successes, it will soon find that the shifts and changes that those companies are able to make will inevitably affect its own needs and methods of operation.

For example, if a computer retailer keeps less inventory on hand to allow itself the ability to adjust orders based on real-time information about customer demand, computer makers will be forced in turn to gear their manufacturing operations toward a more demand-driven system. The retailer's advertising agency must find quicker ways to drive demand for products in that rapidly changing inventory. And the retailer's competitors will find themselves under pressure to match the up-to-the-minute availability of new products.

The same is true on an individual level. The more people there are within an organization who manage for the short term, the more their colleagues are forced to do the same. Others will be held to the same standards for performance as managers who produce demonstrable results by managing for the short term.

The Law of Expanding Immediacy means that the need for shorter time frames generally is spreading throughout the business world, and when they become standard in one area, the more they are required in other, related areas.

The Law of Expanding Immediacy also has implications for the kind of attitude adjustment we have discussed. As we have seen, many managers are not accustomed to thinking about managing for the short term as a positive. They are frustrated because they feel they spend too much of their time doing things that take them away from their "real" work. They feel that managing for the short term is something they are forced to do rather than something over which they have control. And too often, they see their plight as unique, or as the result of bad management at their organization.

The Law of Expanding Immediacy underlines a great truth of modern business life: Everybody is in the same situation, facing the same kinds of pressures for immediate action, demonstrable short-term results, and more work to do than can be done. The more successful businesses and individuals are at managing for the short term, the more they reinforce and expand the need for it everywhere else.

It also means that the situation is unlikely to change. Just as the networking of everything and everyone has become part of the fabric of business, so too will its effects. And one of those is the need to manage for the short term. As we have pointed out repeatedly throughout this book, this is neither good nor bad. It just *is*. And it means that, like it or not, everyone is going to need to find new ways not just to get through the long days but also to feel better about how they spend that time.

IMMEDIACY AS COMPETITIVE ADVANTAGE

We have pointed out previously that close customer connections can help executives make sure that strategy is attuned to the short-term needs of the marketplace. The Law of Expanding Immediacy applies to customers and the information that can be derived from them as well. The more other companies raise consumer expectations by making it easy and fast to do business with them, the more immediacy those same consumers will demand of you—even if your company is in an entirely different industry. Satisfying those demands can provide at least a temporary competitive advantage; more important, failing to do so can result in a serious disadvantage.

At some level, executives and managers realize that both information and relationships with customers are key to long-term success; both are cited almost equally as the areas that will provide an organization with the greatest strategic competitive advantage in the future[1] (see Figure 15.1). Interestingly, information technology was considered slightly more important to the future than customer service, seen as the current source of competitive advantage. In the survey about current competitive advantage, IT was roughly tied with research and development, and both are substantially behind customer service.

Both areas point to the importance of understanding customer needs as a source of strategic competitive advantage. And since customer needs are usually focused on the immediate, immediacy becomes a key weapon in the battle for competitive advantage.

Whatever departments are most critical for competitive advantage at your company, their actions must be linked to overall vision and

FIGURE 15.1

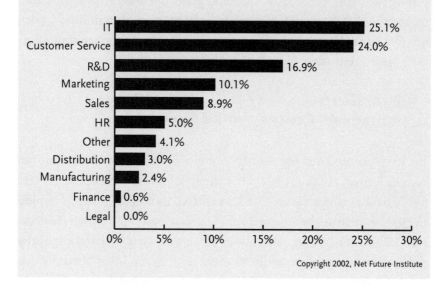

"What department do you believe will provide your organization with the most strategic competitive advantage two years from now?"

Department	Percentage
IT	25.1%
Customer Service	24.0%
R&D	16.9%
Marketing	10.1%
Sales	8.9%
HR	5.0%
Other	4.1%
Distribution	3.0%
Manufacturing	2.4%
Finance	0.6%
Legal	0.0%

Copyright 2002, Net Future Institute

strategy, which managing for the short term will not eliminate. In addition to setting overall corporate goals, strategy will help determine corporate culture and create the environment in which managing for the short term can flourish.

WHEN 1 + 1 + 1 EQUALS 4

As managers become more accustomed to and comfortable with managing for the short term, strategy will include preparation for the downside of any strategic goals, and accommodate shifts in how a vision is executed day to day. It will acknowledge up front the challenges of implementation. And it will look to interim short-term results to help assess when and how strategy may need to be altered.

Massive projects with a big payoff at the end are being replaced by an approach that favors incremental forward progress, with demonstrable interim results. The two approaches may arrive at the same destination. However, the second will have permitted adjust-

ment and fine tuning along the way, to ensure that the original destination is still the appropriate one.

More important, it will have provided incremental benefits as the
project progressed. For example, constant pulse-taking may have
produced additional market information. It may have produced
information that prevents planned spending on something that was
proved unnecessary. It may have led to the creation of spin-off products discovered while pursuing the original plan.

> Sometimes those incremental benefits can even prove to be
> more valuable than the original goal itself.

Those along-the-way benefits produced by the "incremental forward progress" approach required to manage successfully for the
short term must be added to the sum total of the value of the project
itself. Doing so demonstrates that incremental forward progress is not
just a necessity but can actually increase the value of the overall project, even if the goal remains the same.

VOICES FROM THE FRONT LINES

What Provides Competitive Advantage?[2]

"While we couldn't be successful without a strong technology infrastructure, it is our emphasis on service from the front line that our customers really value."

"Service is the most significant thing that differentiates this company
from its competitors. Today customer service provides the most strategic competitive advantage."

"Expect supply-chain management, integrated with design, to be the
future."

"I don't really think any one department is 'the key' department to
form the long-term competitive advantage. It is a team effort to produce
a well-oiled machine."

"Although IT is very important, as is adequate competitive pricing, we
are a people business and we win new business on customer service
every time."

By managing for the short term, managers can maximize the value of the original project. They will not only accomplish the ultimate goal but also will realize and maximize the added value created by individual steps taken to get there. And sometimes those incremental benefits can even prove to be more valuable than the original goal itself. Who remembers what glue 3M was trying to produce when it came up with the reusable adhesive that led to Post-it Notes?

Implementing Change

In some cases, individual managers and parts of organizations already are managing for the short term (though they may not feel good about it). In others, as we have noted, a certain amount of attitude adjustment may be needed. Either way, anyone who attempts to change the negative mind-set associated with managing for the short term may face a certain amount of internal skepticism. It will come as no surprise to anyone who has ever tried to implement change that managers and executives feel the biggest impediments to change come from inside the organization, not outside[3] (see Figure 15.2).

Figure 15.2

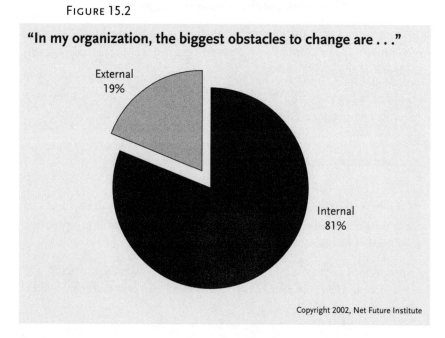

"In my organization, the biggest obstacles to change are . . ."

External 19%

Internal 81%

Copyright 2002, Net Future Institute

However, getting long term and short term in sync by creating a better understanding of how short-term moves can produce long-term success can improve that negative mind-set. The immediate positive results that managing for the short term focuses on can help persuade others in the organization of its value.

The Law of Expanding Immediacy can help here, too. It's useful to remember that you're not the only one having to focus on a shorter time frame than you might like. Looking around you at how your suppliers, distributors, and customers are behaving can be instructive; what you'll see is that everyone is facing the same challenges. And the fact that they are doing so means that whether or not they prefer it, your colleagues are probably going to have to manage for the short term themselves.

When thinking about how to change the organization, the concept of incremental forward progress also comes into play. Beginning to manage yourself for the short term and getting those positive, demonstrable results is the first step in demonstrating to others how managing for the short term can benefit the organization. If you can implement it for yourself, your action will encourage others to try for the same results. At some point, as we saw above, the Law of Expanding Immediacy will begin to come into play, and other departments will be forced to live up to the results it has produced for you.

REMEMBERING TO LOOK IN THE REARVIEW MIRROR

Incremental forward progress also has another benefit. It can help provide regular doses of success that can help managers feel better about what they do day to day.

When there is so much to do, it's easy to focus on everything that remains to be done. There is always more work to do than there is time to do it; an ever-increasing number of incoming tasks will arrive before you have found a way to complete the existing ones.

Managers also have to remember not to focus only on the road ahead. They must also look in the rearview mirror occasionally—not just to see whether other cars are coming up behind them, but to look at how far they have come.

> Managers may need to make an extra effort to look in the rearview mirror regularly and tally up just what they *have* accomplished.

It's easy to celebrate success at the end of a megaproject. That's when champagne and bonuses tend to appear, and when senior executives may suddenly learn previously obscure managers' names. However, with the disappearance of the megaproject, it's also increasingly easy to forget to celebrate the progress that has been made. Incremental successes don't tend to make a big splash. However, as we have seen, they are not only the wave of the future but may even add up to greater value than a megaproject.

With to-do lists as daunting as they are today and tasks being broken into smaller segments, managers may need to make an extra effort to look in the rearview mirror regularly and tally up just what they *have* accomplished. Being able to look back at where you were when you started and compare it to where you are now can remind you that you haven't been simply spinning your wheels.

GETTING LONG TERM AND SHORT TERM IN SYNC

When an organization and its individuals are working at cross-purposes, it leaves the organization out of sync with itself. An executive with an understanding of the business as a whole, as well as the corporate strategy and vision, tends to make decisions and pronouncements based on that knowledge. However, a middle manager who knows his workforce well might interpret or translate the strategy based on the context in which he operates. And a longtime employee with that same organization—one who has seen various executives come and go—might make decisions based on what he or she knows will work with the company's customers.

Everyone may be trying their best, but the disconnect that we have cited throughout this book means that the full potential of a company's strategy and employee knowledge is rarely realized. Workers are not sufficiently informed about how they can support the strategy, and the strategy is not as informed by the changing information of the marketplace as it should be. This leaves the organization unable to take advantage of information for greatest competitive advantage. It also leaves both senior executives and individual managers frustrated because they and the organization are not as effective as they could be.

Techniques for managing for the short term will have increasing influence on how a corporation views itself and its mission. Vision and strategy will provide the necessary discipline required in managing for the short term, which, in turn, will make individuals, departments, and entire business entities more successful quarter to quarter.

By enabling managers to match their customer-derived knowledge with the company's overall strategy, and helping them understand their day-to-day role in achieving it, organizations can achieve the sort of incremental successes that can drive a company forward toward its goals. And that ability represents managing for the short term at its best.

Notes

CHAPTER 1: The New World of the Short Term

1. Commissioner's Statement on the Employment Situation, Bureau of Labor Statistics, December 2001.

2. "2001 Staffing Study" survey published by the American Management Association (October 2001). Survey conducted with 1,631 member companies, most of which employ more than 100 people and gross more than $10 million.

3. U.S. Department of Labor Reports, "Mass Layoffs," November 2000 and November 2001, Bureau of Labor Statistics.

4. Based on NASDAQ, NYSE, and AmEx data for March 2000 through October 2001 as supplied on www.marketdata.nasdaq.com.

5. From a Net Future Institute global survey of 391 business executives on the subject of Perceptions of Timelines, conducted in May 2001.

6. "Strategic Planning—Forward in Reverse?" by Robert H. Hayes, published in the *Harvard Business Review,* November–December 1985.

7. All verbatim comments from respondents to a May 2001 Net Future Institute survey of its members about how they as managers and executives define "short term" and "long term."

8. From a Net Future Institute global survey of 391 business executives on the subject of Perceptions of Timelines, conducted in May 2001.

9. All verbatim comments from respondents to a May 2001 Net Future Institute survey of its members about how they as managers and executives define "short term" and "long term."

10. All verbatim comments from respondents to a March 2001 Net Future Institute survey of its members about whether managers and/or

their organizations are primarily focused on the short or long term in their decision making.

11. First coined by the author in *Net Future* (McGraw-Hill, New York, 1999).

12. "U.S. International Transactions," Second Quarter 2001, U.S. Bureau of Economic Analysis.

13. U.S. Bureau of Economic Analysis, survey of current business, preliminary estimates for 2000, issued June 2001.

14. U.S. Bureau of Economic Analysis, survey of current business, preliminary estimates for 2000, issued June 2001.

15. "Measuring Globalization," A.T. Kearney, Inc., and the Carnegie Endowment for International Peace, published in the January–February 2001 issue of *Foreign Policy*.

16. "Measuring Globalization," A.T. Kearney, Inc., and the Carnegie Endowment for International Peace, published in the January–February 2001 issue of *Foreign Policy*.

17. "Best Practices in Corporate Communications (Executive Summary "Best Practices in Global Communications 2000"), conducted by CARMA International with 50 leading companies.

18. "Procter & Gamble Says Fiscal 2nd Half to Be Hurt by Turkey," Bloomberg News Archive, February 26, 2001.

19. Based on the author's interviews with Gerald Stahl, data networking account executive with AT&T.

20. From a Net Future Institute global survey of 412 business executives on the subject of Management Decisions, conducted in March 2001.

CHAPTER 2: The Manager and the Business Blur

1. Based on the author's interviews with Paty Wright, Senior Director of Corporate Business Development, Metro Orlando Economic Development Commission (EDC).

2. Based on the author's interviews with Greg Carroll, Manager, Southeast Region, Aetna, Inc.

3. Based on the author's interviews with Liz Carbon, Pharmacy Director for Distribution at Premier, Inc.

4. *The Digital Planet 2000: The Global Information Economy.* Information published by the World Information Technology and Services Alliance, based on research by International Data Corporation, November 2000.

5. From a Net Future Institute global survey of 399 business executives on the subject of the Impact of the Networked World, conducted in January 2001.

6. All verbatim comments from respondents to a September 2001 Net Future Institute survey of its members about e-mail usage and management.

7. All verbatim comments from respondents to a July 2001 Net Future Institute survey of its members about whether managers spend most of their time on tasks they or others deem relevant to the business.

8. All verbatim comments from respondents to a July 2001 Net Future Institute survey of its members about whether managers spend most of their time on tasks they or others deem relevant to the business.

9. From a Net Future Institute global survey of 324 business executives on the subject of Departmental Impediments to Change, conducted in March 2001.

10. All verbatim comments from respondents to an August 2001 Net Future Institute survey of its members about how many items managers have on their to-do list or lists, and how many they accomplish in a day.

11. From a Net Future Institute global survey of 399 business executives on the subject of the Impact of the Networked World, conducted in January 2001.

12. From a Net Future Institute global survey of 399 business executives on the subject of the Impact of the Networked World, conducted in January 2001.

13. Based on the author's interviews with Joe Puglisi, CIO of EMCOR Group.

14. All verbatim comments from respondents to an August 2001 Net Future Institute survey of its members about how many items managers have on their to-do list or lists, and how many they accomplish in a day.

15. From a Net Future Institute global survey of 410 business executives on the subject of Executive Productivity, conducted in August 2001.

16. From a Net Future Institute global survey of 410 business executives on the subject of Executive Productivity, conducted in August 2001.

17. Based on the author's interviews with Nancy Weil, Senior Vice President, Marketing, at a subsidiary of a $3 billion financial services corporation.

18. All verbatim comments from respondents to an August 2001 Net Future Institute survey of its members about when and where managers feel they are most productive.

19. From a Net Future Institute global survey of 543 business executives on the subject of Employee Retention, conducted in October 2000. Number derived from weighted survey responses.

20. From a Net Future Institute global survey of 419 business executives on the subject of Relevance of Everyday Work, conducted in July 2001.

21. "Realities of the Executive Job Search," conducted by Drake Beam Morin (2000), which tracked the career-transition experiences of 3,652 executives in the United States.

22. "CEO Turnover and Job Security," Drake Beam Morin (2000). Study covered 476 private and public companies from 25 countries representing 50 industries, with workforces ranging from 660 to more than 900,000 employees.

23. "CEO Turnover and Job Security," Drake Beam Morin (2000). Study covered 476 private and public companies from 25 countries representing 50 industries, with workforces ranging from 660 to more than 900,000 employees.

24. "CEO Turnover and Job Security," Drake Beam Morin (2000). Study covered 476 private and public companies from 25 countries representing 50 industries, with workforces ranging from 660 to more than 900,000 employees.

25. "CEO Turnover Reports," 1997–2001 by Pearl Meyer & Partners.

26. Christian & Timbers Index of Fortune 1000 CEO Replacements (June 30, 2001).

27. Challenger, Gray & Christmas, Inc., Chief Executive Monthly Report, Chief Executive Departures.

28. Based on the author's interviews with John Challenger, CEO of Challenger, Gray & Christmas.

29. Based on the author's interviews with Harry Somerdyk, Managing Director of the Publishing Practice of Spencer Stuart.

30. Based on the author's interviews with B. George Saloom, President of Zions Data Services Company.

31. Based on the author's interviews with Moe El-Gamal, President and CEO, Global Systems, Inc.

32. Based on the author's interviews with John Thomas Flynn, CEO of TechEd Strategies.

33. From a Net Future Institute global survey of 419 business executives on the subject of Organizational Communication, conducted in August 2001.

34. From a Net Future Institute global survey of 419 business executives on the subject of Organizational Communication, conducted in August 2001.

CHAPTER 3: The Disconnect and Its Impact on the Organization

1. All verbatim comments from respondents to a March 2001 Net Future Institute survey of its members on the subject of Management Decisions.

2. Based on "Self-Interest, Altruism, Incentives & Agency Theory" by Michael C. Jensen, Harvard Business School, and published in *Journal of Applied Corporate Finance* (Summer 1994) and "Foundations of Organizational Strategy," Harvard University Press, 1998. Professor Jensen coauthored an article on Agency Theory with William Meckling in the early 1970s.

3. The definition of agency relationship from Harvard Business School professor Michael C. Jensen and William Meckling, University of Rochester, from "Theory of the Firm: Managerial Behavior, Agency Cost and Ownership Structure," Volume 3, *Journal of Financial Economics,* page 5, October 1976, with permission from Elsevier Science.

4. Based on the author's interviews with Laurence Bunin, CEO of Handshake Dynamics, on whose board the author sits.

5. All verbatim comments from respondents to a March 2001 Net Future Institute survey of its members on the subject of Management Decisions.

CHAPTER 4: Managing for the Short Term vs. Planning for the Long Term

1. Based on the author's interviews with Randall King, President and CEO of Redix International, Inc.

2. From a Net Future Institute global survey of 412 business executives on the subject of Management Decisions, conducted in March 2001.

3. From a Net Future Institute global survey of 412 business executives on the subject of Management Decisions, conducted in March 2001.

4. All verbatim comments from respondents to a May 2001 Net Future Institute survey of its members about how they as managers and executives define "short term" and "long term."

5. Based on the author's interviews with Vickie Tillman, Executive Vice President, Credit Market Services, Standard & Poor's.

6. Based on the author's interviews with Michael Franks, Director of Strategic Planning for O'Sullivan Furniture.

7. Based on the author's interviews with Robert W. Selander, President and CEO of MasterCard International.

8. Based on the author's interviews with Mike Indursky, Senior Vice President, Strategic Planning and Marketing, Unilever Cosmetics International.

9. Based on many personal interviews and verbatim comments from many of the 3,000 Net Future Institute members in 58 countries.

10. Based on the author's interviews with Tyler C. Tingley, Principal and Chief Executive Officer of Phillips Exeter Academy

11. Verbatim comment from a respondent to a May 2001 Net Future Institute survey of its members about how they as managers and executives define "short term" and "long term."

12. From a Net Future Institute global survey of 324 business executives on the subject of Departmental Impediments to Change, conducted in March 2001.

CHAPTER 5: It's All About the Numbers

1. Based on the author's interviews with Art Cohen, Senior Vice President of Advertising, ACTV, Inc.

2. Based on the author's interviews with Joseph Hovancak, Sales Center Vice President at AT&T.

3. Sixth Annual "Route to the Top" Survey of Fortune 700 executives, published by executive search consultants Spencer Stuart in February 2000.

4. "CEO Turnover and Job Security," Drake, Beam Morin (2000). Study covered 476 private and public companies from 25 countries representing 50 industries, with workforces ranging from 660 to more than 900,000 employees.

5. Based on the author's interviews with Fred Marshall, Chief Technology Officer, Berendsen Fluid Power

6. Based on the author's interviews with Jan Hoffmeister, Vice President of Intellectual Capital Management, Skandia Insurance Company, Ltd.

7. Based on the author's interviews with Bob Sircy, Vice President and Corporate Controller of Southwestern/Great American, Inc.

8. Based on the author's interviews with James Guest, President of Consumers Union.

9. Based on the author's interviews with Margo Souza, CEO of Harry Souza and Daughters.

CHAPTER 6: Incremental Forward Motion

1. Based on the author's interviews with Carl Wilson, CIO of Marriott International.

2. Based on the author's interviews with Ralph Menzano, CIO of South Eastern Pennsylvania Transportation Authority.

3. Based on the author's interviews with Edward Cypert, Vice President and Deputy General Manager of TRW Systems.

4. Based on the author's interviews with Bruce Petro, CIO of AmericanGreetings.com.

5. Based on the author's interviews with Bruce Johnson, Vice President, Human Resources, at Timberland.

6. All verbatim comments from respondents to a May 2001 Net Future Institute survey of its members about how they as managers and executives define "short term" and "long term."

7. Based on *Fortune* magazine's list of Best Companies to Work For.

8. Based on the author's interviews with Karl Schoen-Rene, Second Vice President, Information Systems Organization at a U.S. insurance company that preferred not to be named.

9. Based on the author's interviews with the service manager at a resort area Mercedes-Benz dealership.

10. Based on the author's interviews with Rich Engelage, President of Auto Dealer Direction.

11. From a Net Future Institute global survey of 328 business executives on the subject of the Dynamics of Change, conducted in February 2001.

12. Based on the author's interviews with Guy Gray, Senior Vice President, Contact Center Operations and Telecommunications, Cendant Corporation.

CHAPTER 7: Are We Communicating?

1. From a Net Future Institute global survey of 419 business executives on the subject of Organizational Communication, conducted in August 2001.

2. All verbatim comments from respondents to a September 2001 Net Future Institute global survey of its members about Effective Communication by Executive Management.

3. Based on the author's interviews with Tom Murach, Senior Manager at PricewaterhouseCoopers.

4. Based on the author's interviews with Terry Ransford, Senior Vice President, Northern Trust.

5. All verbatim comments from respondents to a September 2001 Net Future Institute global survey of its members about Effective Communication by Executive Management.

6. Reprinted by permission of *Harvard Business Review*. From "What Is Strategy?" by Michael E. Porter, November–December 1996. Copyright © 1996 by the Harvard Business School Publishing Corporation; all rights reserved.

7. Based on the author's interviews with Sharafat Khan, Partner and Practice Leader, Human Capital Advisory Services, Deloitte & Touche.

8. All verbatim comments from respondents to a September 2001 Net Future Institute global survey of its members about Effective Communication by Executive Management.

9. Based on the author's interviews with Steven Rudnitsky, President of Kraft Food Service and Executive Vice President of Kraft Foods.

10. All verbatim comments from respondents to a September 2001 Net Future Institute global survey of its members about Effective Communication by Executive Management.

11. All verbatim comments from respondents to a September 2001 Net Future Institute global survey of its members about Effective Communication by Executive Management.

12. "Measuring Organizational Trust: A Diagnostic Survey and International Indicator" (June 2000) by International Association of Business Communicators Research Foundation.

13. All verbatim comments from respondents to a September 2001 Net Future Institute global survey of its members about Effective Communication by Executive Management.

CHAPTER 8: Communicating Down the Line

1. Based on the author's interviews with Jill Bemis, Finance Director, Metropolitan State University, St. Paul, Minnesota.

2. All verbatim comments from respondents to a September 2001 Net Future Institute global survey of its members about Effective Communication by Executive Management.

3. Based on the author's interviews with Guy Gray, Senior Vice President, Contact Center Operations and Telecommunications, Cendant Corporation.

4. From a Net Future Institute global survey of 291 business executives on the subject of Contact Integration, conducted in July 2000.

5. From a Net Future Institute global survey of 291 business executives on the subject of Contact Integration, conducted in July 2000.

6. All verbatim comments from respondents to a September 2001 Net Future Institute global survey of its members about Effective Communication by Executive Management.

7. Based on the author's interviews with Christine Parren, Phoenix Site Manager, Cendant.

8. All verbatim comments from respondents to a September 2001 Net Future Institute global survey of its members about Effective Communication by Executive Management.

9. Based on the author's interviews with Kevin Callahan, President and CEO of Exeter Health Resources.

10. All verbatim comments from respondents to a September 2001 Net Future Institute global survey of its members about Effective Communication by Executive Management.

CHAPTER 9: Leading for the Short Term

1. Based on the author's interviews with Michael D. Parker, President and CEO of The Dow Chemical Company.

2. All verbatim comments from respondents to a Net Future Institute global survey of its members about Effective Communication with Management, conducted in October 2001.

3. Based on the author's interviews with Diana Dykstra, President and CEO of Vandenberg Federal Credit Union.

4. Based on the author's interviews with Leo Mullin, Chairman and CEO of Delta Air Lines.

5. From "The IT Alignment Index," an online survey by *CIO* magazine and the consulting firm ICEX. Survey included 420 respondents surveyed in January 2001. Reprinted through the courtesy of CIO/Darwin.

6. From a Net Future Institute global survey of 394 business executives on the subject of Leadership in the Net Future, conducted in January 2001.

7. "Linking Communication Competence to Business Success: A Challenge for Communicators" (June 2001) by International Association of Business Communicators Research Foundation.

8. From a Net Future Institute global survey of 394 business executives on the subject of Leadership in the Net Future, conducted in January 2001.

9. Results of a Wirthlin Worldwide telephone survey conducted by National Quorum in January 2000 with a representative random sample of 1,012 adults 18 years or older, 581 of which were employed full- or part-time. Reported in the Wirthlin Report, March 2001.

10. Based on the author's interviews with Antonio Monteiro, CIO of Internet Securities.

11. All verbatim comments from respondents to a Net Future Institute global survey of its members about Effective Communication with Management, conducted in October 2001.

12. All verbatim comments from respondents to a Net Future Institute global survey of its members about Effective Communication with Management, conducted in October 2001.

13. Based on a global Net Future Institute survey of 318 business executives and managers on the subject of Effective Communication with Management, conducted in October 2001.

14. Based on a global Net Future Institute survey of 318 business executives and managers on the subject of Effective Communication with Management, conducted in October 2001.

15. Based on a global Net Future Institute survey of 318 business executives and managers on the subject of Effective Communication with Management, conducted in October 2001.

16. Based on the author's interview with Dave Carlson, Programming and Internet Development Manager for the Antioch Company and Creative Memories.

17. All verbatim comments from respondents to a Net Future Institute global survey of its members about Effective Global Communication with Management, conducted in October 2001.

18. Based on the author's interviews with Pat Traynor, Vice President, Web Hosting Services, AT&T.

19. Based on the author's interviews with Terry Ransford, Senior Vice President, Northern Trust.

CHAPTER 10: Managing People for the Short Term

1. Employee Turnover Study conducted by Sibson & Company, a subsidiary of Nextera, in August 2000.

2. 2000 Employer Benchmark Survey, National Association of Colleges and Employers.

3. "The War for Talent 2000" (revised 2001), based on a survey of 6,900 executives and managers conducted by McKinsey & Company, Inc.

4. Results of an online survey on turnover and knowledge management conducted by Primix Solutions, Inc., in 2000.

5. Results of an online survey on turnover and knowledge management conducted by Primix Solutions, Inc., in 2000.

6. Report on job satisfaction issued by the Conference Board, October 2000.

7. "What Impacts Job Satisfaction?" conducted by Wirthlin Worldwide, September 2000, for Xylo Report. Based on telephone interviews with 1,002 respondents.

8. Report on job satisfaction issued by the Conference Board, October 2000.

9. In the report "What Impacts Job Satisfaction?" conducted by Wirthlin Worldwide in September 2000 with 1,002 respondents, the following reasons were cited as why they felt their company was employee-focused: perks, benefits, and employee discounts, 29 percent; salary and bonuses, 25 percent; enjoyable work environment, 23 percent; recognition of work performance, 22 percent.

10. From a Net Future Institute global survey of 304 business executives on the subject of Employee Retention and Recruitment, conducted in November 2001.

11. All verbatim comments from respondents to a November 2001 Net Future Institute survey of its members about the challenges of recruiting versus employee retention.

12. Study analyzing data from 107 companies conducted by Getzler & Company, 2000.

13. From a Net Future Institute global survey of 304 business executives on the subject of Employee Retention and Recruitment, conducted in November 2001.

14. Based on author's discussion with Diane Berry, Vice President of Research for people[3], a Gartner Company, which researches IT compensation.

15. These three verbatim comments are from respondents to a November 2001 Net Future Institute survey of its members about the challenges of recruiting versus employee retention.

16. Verbatim comments are from three different respondents to a November 2001 Net Future Institute survey of its members about the challenges of recruiting versus employee retention.

17. All verbatim comments from respondents to an April 2001 Net Future Institute survey of its members about the impact of short-term versus long-term incentives.

18. Based on the author's interviews with Larry Kleinman, Senior Vice President, HR, at SAP America.

19. Based on the author's interviews with Raj Singh, CEO of Brainhunter.com.

20. IT Market Compensation Study (2001) conducted by people[3], a Gartner Company.

21. Report on job satisfaction issued by the Conference Board, October 2000.

22. Findings reported by Linda Pittenger, President and CEO of people[3], at the Gartner Executive Program Roundtable in February 2001.

23. Verbatim comment from a respondent to a November 2001 Net Future Institute survey of its members about the challenges of recruiting versus employee retention.

24. Based on the author's interviews with Carol Rohm, Vice President of PrideStaff, Inc.

25. Online survey conducted by Primix Solutions, Inc., of more than 500 managers in North America, which included senior executives in 2000.

26. All verbatim comments from respondents to an April 2001 Net Future Institute survey of its members about the impact of short-term versus long-term incentives.

27. Findings reported by Linda M. Pittenger, President and CEO of people[3], at the Gartner Executive Program Roundtable.

28. IT Market Compensation Study (2001) conducted by people[3], a Gartner Company.

29. From a Net Future Institute global survey of 405 business executives on the subject of Employee Productivity, conducted in April 2001.

30. All verbatim comments from respondents to an April 2001 Net Future Institute survey of its members about the impact of short-term versus long-term incentives.

31. From a Net Future Institute global survey of 405 business executives on the subject of Employee Productivity, conducted in April 2001.

32. Based on a Net Future Institute global survey of 304 business executives on the subject of Employee Recruitment and Retention, conducted in November 2001.

33. Verbatim comments from three different respondents to an April 2001 Net Future Institute survey of its members about the impact of short-term versus long-term incentives.

CHAPTER 11: Using Information to Navigate Through Decisions

1. All verbatim comments from respondents to a June 2001 Net Future Institute survey of its members about their organizations' budgetary and planning cycles.

2. Based on the author's interviews with Brett Strouss, Director of Channel Marketing, SAP.

3. From a Net Future Institute global survey of 365 business executives on the subject of the Value of Customer Information, conducted in April 2001. Numbers derived from weighted survey responses.

4. Based on the author's interviews with Laurence Bunin, CEO of Handshake Dynamics. The author is on Handshake Dynamics' board of directors.

5. From a Net Future Institute global survey of 393 business executives on the subject of Customer Expectations, conducted in December 2000. Numbers derived from weighted survey responses.

6. From a Net Future Institute global survey of 393 business executives on the subject of Customer Expectations, conducted in December 2000. Numbers derived from weighted survey responses.

7. Case study on www.siebel.com.

8. Based on the author's interviews with Tim Stanley, Vice President of Information Technology Development at Harrah's.

9. Based on author's interviews with Bill Bass, Senior Vice President for E-commerce and International Catalog Operations for Lands' End.

10. Based on author's interviews with Scott Bauhofer, Senior Vice President and General Manager of BestBuy.com.

11. Based on the author's interviews with Mitzi Thomas, Assistant Vice President of Corporate Communications, Brotherhood Mutual Insurance Company.

12. From a Net Future Institute global survey of 363 business executives on the subject of Budget Revision, conducted in June 2001.

13. From a Net Future Institute global survey of 338 business executives on the subject of Departmental Competitive Advantage, conducted in February 2001.

14. All verbatim comments from respondents to a June 2001 Net Future Institute survey of its members about their organizations' budgetary and planning cycles.

Chapter 12: Getting to What Matters

1. Based on the author's interviews with Barry Herstein, Chief Marketing Officer of the Financial Times Group.

2. Based on the authors interviews with Kathy Ball-Toncic, Vice President, Capital Markets, Financial Fusion, Inc.

3. All verbatim comments from respondents to an August 2001 Net Future Institute survey of its members about how many items managers have on their to-do list or lists, and how many they accomplish in a day.

4. Based on the author's interviews with Carolyn Dickson, Municipal Marketing Manager at BFI.

5. Based on the author's interviews with a senior manager at a U.S.-based steel manufacturing company who preferred not to be identified.

Chapter 13: The More You Do, the More You Do

1. All verbatim comments from respondents to an August 2001 Net Future Institute survey of its members about when and where managers feel they are most productive.

2. Based on the author's interview with Janice Hayes, Executive Director of the Bibliocentre, Toronto, Ontario, Canada.

3. All verbatim comments from respondents to an August 2001 Net Future Institute survey of its members about when and where managers feel they are most productive.

4. From a Net Future Institute global survey of 353 business executives on the subject of Styles of Task Management, conducted in August 2001.

5. From a Net Future Institute global survey of 353 business executives on the subject of Styles of Task Management, conducted in August 2001.

6. From a Net Future Institute global survey of 353 business executives on the subject of Styles of Task Management, conducted in August 2001.

7. Based on the author's interviews with John O'Brien, independent consultant.

8. All verbatim comments from respondents to an August 2001 Net Future Institute survey of its members about how many items managers have on their to-do list or lists, and how many they accomplish in a day.

9. All verbatim comments from respondents to an August 2001 Net Future Institute survey of its members about how many items managers have on their to-do list or lists, and how many they accomplish in a day.

10. Based on the author's interviews with Robert Copple, Senior Counsel, Motorola Law Department.

11. Based on the author's interviews with John Madden, owner of Contemporary Audio.

12. All verbatim comments from respondents to an August 2001 Net Future Institute survey of its members about how many items managers have on their to-do list or lists, and how many they accomplish in a day.

13. Based on the author's interview with Michael Hayes, Integrated Marketing Communications Lead at IBM.

14. All verbatim comments from respondents to an August 2001 Net Future Institute survey of its members about how many items managers have on their to-do list or lists, and how many they accomplish in a day.

15. Based on the author's interviews with John Ogrizovich, Vice President of Waste Management, Inc.

16. All verbatim comments from respondents to an August 2001 Net Future Institute survey of its members about how many items managers have on their to-do list or lists, and how many they accomplish in a day.

17. Based on the author's interviews with Mike Indursky, Senior Vice President, Strategic Planning and Marketing, Unilever Cosmetics International.

18. All verbatim comments from respondents to an August 2001 Net Future Institute survey of its members about how many items managers have on their to-do list or lists, and how many they accomplish in a day.

19. All verbatim comments from respondents to an August 2001 Net Future Institute survey of its members about when and where managers feel they are most productive.

CHAPTER 14: Successful Meetings for the Short Term

1. From a Net Future Institute global survey of 350 business executives on the subject of Meetings and Productivity, conducted in November 2001.

2. From a Net Future Institute global survey of 350 business executives on the subject of Meetings and Productivity, conducted in November 2001.

3. Based on the author's interviews with Jerry Sodorff, President of Thought Leadership Group.

4. Based on the author's interviews with Cheryl Scales, Director, Customer Satisfaction, In-Flight Services, at Delta Air Lines.

5. All verbatim comments from respondents to a November 2001 Net Future Institute survey of its members about meetings and productivity.

6. All verbatim comments from respondents to a November 2001 Net Future Institute survey of its members about meetings and productivity.

7. Based on the author's interviews with John Banks, President and owner of Audio Centre.

8. All verbatim comments from respondents to a November 2001 Net Future Institute survey of its members about meetings and productivity.

9. All verbatim comments from respondents to a November 2001 Net Future Institute survey of its members about meetings and productivity.

10. Based on the author's interviews with Andrew Scott, Vice President, Information Technology, Aerosoles.

11. Based on the author's interviews with Michael Monette, Vice President for Strategic Planning and Development, St. Joseph Development at St. Joseph Corporation.

12. Based on the author's interviews with Tom Wilson, President and COO of Osprey.

13. All verbatim comments from respondents to a November 2001 Net Future Institute survey of its members about meetings and productivity.

14. All verbatim comments from respondents to a November 2001 Net Future Institute survey of its members about meetings and productivity.

15. Based on the author's interviews with Colleen Doty, Systems Manager, Tricon Global Restaurants.

16. Based on the author's interviews with Garth Howard, President and COO of Ikano Communications.

17. Based on the author's interviews with Caryn Tanis, President of Media Network International.

18. From a Net Future Institute global survey of 480 business executives on the subject of e-mail, conducted in September 2001.

19. From a Net Future Institute global survey of 480 business executives on the subject of e-mail, conducted in September 2001.

20. From a Net Future Institute global survey of 480 business executives on the subject of e-mail, conducted in September 2001.

21. Based on the author's interviews with Leo Crawford, CIO of Orange County, California.

22. Based on the author's interviews with Norman Jacknis, CIO of Westchester County, New York.

23. Based on the author's interview with Robin Ellerthorpe, Senior Associate of Facilities Consulting, OWP&P Architects, Inc.

24. Based on the author's interviews with Tom Lupo, Senior Vice President of Luxelle International.

25. Based on the author's interviews with Phil Merdinger, Principal and Worldwide Partner in Business Development, at William M. Mercer.

26. From a Net Future Institute global survey of 480 business executives on the subject of e-mail, conducted in September 2001.

27. From a Net Future Institute global survey of 480 business executives on the subject of e-mail, conducted in September 2001.

28. Based on the author's interviews with Peter McGinn, CEO of United Health Services in Binghamton, New York.

29. Based on the author's interviews with Michael Manahan, Manager of Application Development, Kraft Food Service.

CHAPTER 15: The Law of Expanding Immediacy

1. From a Net Future Institute global survey of 338 business executives on the subject of Strategic Competitive Advantage, conducted in February 2001.

2. All verbatim comments from respondents to a February 2001 Net Future Institute survey of its members about strategic competitive advantage.

3. From a Net Future Institute global survey of 328 business executives on the subject of the Dynamics of Change, conducted in February 2001.

Index